Society and the Language Classroom

edited by

Hywel Coleman

CAMBRIDGE
UNIVERSITY PRESS

Published by the Press Syndicate of the University of Cambridge
The Pitt Building, Trumpington Street, Cambridge CB2 1RP
40 West 20th Street, New York, NY 10011–4211, USA
10 Stamford Road, Oakleigh, Melbourne 3166, Australia

First published 1996
First printing 1996

Printed in Great Britain at the University Press, Cambridge

A catalogue record for this book is available from the British Library.

Library of Congress cataloguing in publication data applied for.

ISBN 0 521 49616 0 Hardback
ISBN 0 521 49949 6 Paperback

CE

Contents

Contents

Buat teman-temanku,
para pengajar Bahasa Inggeris di UNHAS, UGM,
ITB dan LAN

Acknowledgements

I would like to thank the following:

- the contributors to this volume, not just for their insights (which are clear for all to see) but also for their patience
- my colleagues in the TESOL team in the School of Education at the University of Leeds, for giving me time to complete the editing of this book
- Jill Carroll, for her work on the wordprocessing of the text
- colleagues at CUP, particularly Alison Sharpe
- Katharine Mendelsohn, for her unobtrusive editing
- an anonymous reader, who provided detailed feedback on a draft of this book.

I would also like to thank David Hayes, Adrian Holliday and Fauzia Shamim, with whom I have discussed the ideas expressed here on many occasions.

I am particularly grateful to all the teachers and their learners – in many different parts of Asia and Africa – who have allowed me into their classrooms over the last fifteen years. Above all, I must thank my English-teaching colleagues and friends in Indonesia for, without them, my 'autonomous' assumptions would never have been questioned. It is to them that this book is dedicated.

Contributors

Dick Allwright, Department of Linguistics, Lancaster University, Lancaster, UK

Brigid Ballard, Study Skills Centre, Australian National University, Canberra, Australia

J. Keith Chick, Department of Linguistics, University of Natal, Durban, South Africa

Hywel Coleman, School of Education, University of Leeds, Leeds, UK

Martin Cortazzi, School of Education, University of Leicester, Leicester, UK

Adrian Holliday, Language Studies Department, Canterbury Christ Church College, Canterbury, UK

Lixian Jin, Department of Human Communication, De Montfort University, Leicester, UK

Virginia LoCastro, Division of Languages, International Christian University, Tokyo, Japan

Mary Muchiri, Communication Skills Department, Kenyatta University, Nairobi, Kenya

Fauzia Shamim, Department of Linguistics, University of Karachi, Karachi, Pakistan

1 Autonomy and ideology in the English language classroom[1]

Hywel Coleman

Autonomy and ideology

For the purposes of this book, *society* is interpreted as all of those wider (and overlapping) contexts in which are situated the institutions in which language teaching takes place. These include – but are not limited to – the international, national, community, ethnic, bureaucratic, professional, political, religious, linguistic, economic and family contexts in which schools and other educational institutions are located and with which they interact.

Brian Street (1984) identifies 'autonomous' and 'ideological' attitudes to the role of literacy in society. An autonomous approach assumes that literacy has an identical function in every society; in other words, all literate cultures ought to employ literacy for the same purposes. However, if in a particular situation this is patently not the case, then – from an autonomous perspective – literacy in that context is seen to be 'deviant' or 'inadequate'. An ideological approach, on the other hand, is culturally embedded and recognises the significance of the socialisation process in the construction of the meaning of literacy for members of society. Literacy is allowed to mean whatever the culture in which it is found wants it to mean. Adopting an ideological approach does not permit evaluative judgements to be made about the role of literacy in any particular society.[2]

What happens if we borrow Street's distinction and apply it to education? In order to explore this, let us take higher education as a case study.

Autonomy and ideology in higher education: a case study

An autonomous approach would presumably insist that higher education can have only one function (or one set of functions), that there is only one possible set of behaviours which is appropriate in a higher education system, and that the same criteria can legitimately be employed for judging success and failure in all higher education systems. Any evidence that a particular system or an individual institution or even an individual academic is deviating from the norms would, we must assume, indicate that the system or the institution or the individual is in some sense inadequate.

Alternatively, an ideological approach allows us to consider the possibility that every society creates its own meaning for higher education. In turn, this requires us – particularly if we are outside observers – to exercise great care in examining and commenting on systems and on the institutions and individuals within those systems. We must be prepared to find that each society has its own requirements of higher education, and the possibility of universities having universally relevant roles therefore becomes remote.

Let us examine this issue in more detail by looking at a number of opinions about higher education in two different parts of the world – Indonesia and Great Britain – as expressed by members of those two societies. These opinions were all published at one point in historical time (the mid 1980s), and most of them were found in well-regarded and influential newspapers.

PASSAGE A

In 1975, the Department of Education introduced a policy for the development of higher education. The thinking underlying this policy was that the development of higher education should be aimed at the creation of a 'national higher education system'. Higher education must be able to play a dynamic role as a prime mover in the process of modernising the population.

This passage is taken from Nurjamal (1984, my translation). The point of view which is put forward in this description of the role of higher education is clearly that of a national government (in this case, that of Indonesia), as mediated by a journalist. Higher education is seen as having a very clear function in the development process: that is, to 'modernise the population.'

PASSAGE B

The culture and prosperity of a country depend on its knowledge base, comprising both education and research. Universities are the keystone without which the whole structure collapses. Each level of education takes the knowledge it receives from the one above, but this chain has to end somewhere. This is with the universities, which fulfil their true and peculiar service to the community by their duty to preserve knowledge by scholarship and learning, to add to knowledge by original research, and to disseminate knowledge by teaching. This inseparable triad is the proper business of a university, and all that is not conducive or incidental to these ends is a squandering of a precious resource.

This passage represents the attitude of a senior university administrator in Britain expressing himself at some length in *The Times Higher Education Supplement* (Fellgett 1986). For the author, higher education has three functions: to preserve knowledge, to add to knowledge, and to disseminate knowledge. These functions in turn give the university a unique and indeed crucial role in society. Without universities, according to Fellgett, the whole fabric of society disintegrates.

PASSAGE C

One of the factors which motivates someone to become a university lecturer is that by doing so one expects that one's children will be accepted as students in the institution where one is working. This acts as a powerful moral force which makes people continue to work as university lecturers, even though they are aware that if they worked outside the field of higher education they would be able to obtain greater material rewards than they receive from state universities. However, at the present time there are indications that this motivation is no longer binding people to their institutions in the way that it used to. Several changes have taken place in our higher education system. One of these is that there is no longer a guarantee that lecturers will be able to get their children places in the university where they are working. In reaction, one is beginning to hear complaints from lecturers to the effect that they see little point in working hard in order to educate other people's children when their own children cannot be found places in the institution to which they have devoted the whole of their working lives. This is an understandable reaction from people who are experiencing disappointment.... We cannot now avoid being concerned about what will happen when the 'desire to serve' of the lecturers and administrators whose children have not been accepted evaporates completely.

Passage C (Soetrisno 1986, my translation) claims to represent the perceptions of lecturers in the Indonesian higher education system, although of course this may be a purely idiosyncratic viewpoint. Nevertheless, the passage is taken from a lengthy article which was originally published in *Kompas*, one of the most respected Indonesian daily newspapers, and we can therefore assume that, in its context and at that particular point in history, it does not express a particularly extreme point of view. The author argues that the motivation of university lecturers for their work may be threatened by recent changes which make it increasingly difficult for them to ensure that their own children are able to be educated in the institutions where they themselves teach.

Behind this statement lie several assumptions. First of all, it must be the case that the author considers that it will be useful for the children of these lecturers to study at university. If this were not true, then being denied the opportunity to do so would not provide a cause for complaint. At the same time, there would seem to be an implication that personal relationships have played a role in determining whether or not applicants are selected for study. If this is true, then of course the function of the university becomes extremely complicated, and the criteria for judging the success of students may also be rather difficult to unravel.

It may be that I am making too much of this passage. However, its very peculiarity (from my own point of view, that is), combined with its appearance in a respectable publication, serve to indicate that higher education systems in different cultures may have roles which are quite different from those with which outside observers are familiar.

PASSAGE D
A study at Lancaster University sought to examine educational objectives in higher education by interviewing lecturers. ... Most lecturers saw university education as having general effects on the quality of students' learning and thinking, and their own specialism as making a distinctive contribution to this educational process. ... The unifying theme of lecturers' views about the main purpose of university education can be summarised by the term *critical thinking*. ... In the interviews with lecturers there was substantial consensus about the importance of critical thinking.

The passage is taken from Entwistle (1984: 2–4), who looked at the assumptions which British university lecturers *claimed* were underlying their work. It appears that the development of critical thinking in students is perceived as being of supreme importance. It is interesting to note that this differs from the viewpoint put forward in Passage B. In the earlier extract, it appeared that the senior administrator in a British university saw the function of the university in terms of its contribution to the creation, preservation and dissemination of knowledge, and the role which this process has in the maintenance of society. For university lecturers, however, the role of the university is to encourage students to develop as individuals. One wonders whether these two points of view are easily compatible. Incidentally, Entwistle observes that there was little evidence that what the interviewed lecturers did in their teaching actually contributed to the development of critical thinking in their students.

PASSAGE E

The implementation of the credit semester system in private universities requires greater attention. ... In an interview with *Kompas* earlier this month, [Michael Utama] mentioned several negative side effects of the credit semester system. One of these is that students are encouraged to become extremely individualistic. ... According to Michael Utama, the system still has weaknesses which demand attention. These include the problem that the credit semester system creates a competitive spirit which in turn leads to students developing an individualistic character. ... If this system is to be introduced throughout the country, then the government will have to stipulate how many credits a student can take each semester. At the moment the number of credits which a student can take is constrained only by the student's academic record in the preceding semester. By restricting the number of credits which students can take, it will be possible to maintain their spirit of co-operation.

This passage is taken from an article in the same respected Indonesian newspaper (Anonymous 1984, my translation). The interesting argument put forward by Michael Utama, who is an academic at Satya Wacana Christian University, one of Indonesia's most prestigious private institutes of higher education, is that the credit semester system allows students the freedom to work hard and accumulate any number of credits within their capability. He believes that this is counterproductive, as it breeds individualism. For the interviewee, it is clearly important that universities should encourage the development of a co-operative spirit among their students. Academic achievement alone is insufficient.

PASSAGE F

If a decision taken recently at Exeter University were reflected in the world of sport, the World Cup might have concluded with all participating teams, in order of size of the countries represented, receiving a small trophy. ... The outcome of matches need not have been reported, although interested parties might have been free to make discreet inquiries. That way, invidious comparisons between winners and losers could be avoided. Next week, Exeter University will, within departments, graduate its students in alphabetical order, and at the graduation ceremony their class of degree will not be indicated. ... Individual results will be known within departments or among friends. But from the point of view of parents, and the wider community represented at the ceremony, such distinctions are apparently to be deliberately obscured. ... Who will value academic excellence if the universities do not?

The final passage is by Penney (1986), and probably represents the viewpoint of a taxpaying member of the British public. From this point of view, university education is equivalent to a massive competitive sports event. The purpose of the process is to determine winners and losers, and to certify the winners in a public manner. The contrast with the attitude expressed in Passage E above is striking.

These six extracts – five of which are taken from newspaper articles – provide differing perspectives on higher education in two societies, Britain and Indonesia. Three important points emerge from this comparison of expectations.

- First, it is clear that there may be several different parties who have an interest in what a higher education system is doing. These parties include the national government, senior academic administrators, university lecturers, students, parents, taxpayers, and prospective employers. (Not all of these parties are represented in my survey above.)
- Second, the different parties concerned may have very different expectations of the same higher education system. In Indonesia, for example, the government apparently sees the universities as instruments for modernisation and social change, whilst some lecturers consider that universities provide a mechanism for the advancement of their own families. Yet others see universities as places to foster co-operation among members of society.
- Third, very different patterns or constellations of expectations may emerge in different cultures. These expectations which different parties have of one particular system may or may not coincide or overlap with each other. The expectations may or may not be realised. And realisation of expectations may be partial or complete. In other words, every system of higher education is likely to be under pressure from several different sources. The way in which those influences interact with each other will differ from one society to another, possibly even from one institution to another.

What are the consequences of the interplay of these various influences? One conclusion to be drawn is that, if the principles on which academic systems function differ from each other, then there is a strong possibility that the criteria which need to be satisfied in order to be certified as 'successful' also differ from one system to another. This is not to suggest that the criteria of success which apply in some systems are necessarily more 'lax' than those in others, but, rather, that the criteria are simply different.

Moreover, it seems reasonable to conclude that what actually happens within universities will differ just as the particular constellation of influences, pressures and expectations differs. In other words, what universities actually do, and the behaviour which is appropriate in universities, may differ from one institution to another, and is even more likely to differ from one society to another. In every case, the functions which a university actually performs will be the result of compromise between the various influences which bear upon it. And in every case, the behaviour which may be observed within any particular university will, in sociological terms, be functional. In other words, that behaviour will be appropriate to and interpretable in terms of what it is that the institution is doing.

Taking the argument one step further, we can see that the concept of the universality of the academic enterprise must be a myth. The strength of the myth of academic universality can be illustrated by the following anecdote.

For the most part, as educated and mature members of society, we are prepared to be tolerant if individuals who are clearly alien to our own culture exhibit exotic behaviour. We are willing to interpret their eating habits, their way of dressing, their interactional style and so on as being consistent with the mores, principles and customs which are current in the culture from which these individuals originate, even if these features of behaviour are not consistent with the mores, principles and customs valid in our own society. Quite rightly, we do not assume that human behaviour should be universally uniform. Consequently, we are generally able to avoid the danger of judging the behaviour of others in terms of the principles which happen to be current in our own society. We may even pride ourselves on our cross-cultural awareness and toleration.

However, when it comes to behaviour in the academic context, we are often much less tolerant. Indeed, there is a very strong tendency for us to interpret exotic behaviour in the academic context as being not merely peculiar but actually inadequate. An example, from an Australian university, is provided by Ballard and Clanchy (1984: 14)

> ... an Indonesian postgraduate student ... was writing her thesis
> on Indonesian literature. ... Her supervisor complained: 'This
> work is not up to the level of senior high school students. It is

7

disastrous for a student at postgraduate level.' Yet, as the student explained, her approach to literary criticism was exactly the style used in her own country and the tradition in which she had been trained. Apparently, academics tend to assume that there are universals of academic behaviour. Behaviour which deviates from these norms must necessarily be inferior.

A universalist assumption underlay some early thinking regarding the teaching of study skills or English for Academic Purposes. The assumption was made explicit by Candlin, Kirkwood and Moore (1975: 2-3, 8–9)

> ... reasoning processes are common to the scientific and technical stock-in-trade of speakers of a variety of languages [and therefore] it may be the case in teaching EST that one is indeed involving specialist learners in performing in the target language those mental processes and intellectual operations already familiar to them from their 'doing science' in their mother tongue. ... here we lay claim on the student's professional competence and in language teaching involve him [*sic*] in procedures with which he may be already familiar. Once again it is clear that the task is ... designing a course to develop recognition and production abilities in verbal and non-verbal modes for well-known techniques.

But Candlin and his colleagues found that the participants in their study skills course which was based on this 'universalist' principle then failed to behave in a predictable way (1975: 25):

> ... often students produce 'stylistic infelicities' which reflect a lack of precision in their modes of thought – i.e. they produce written and/or spoken utterances which are either illogical or else vague and unclear.

This frustration is an excellent example of an 'autonomous' approach and of the dangers which the adoption of such an approach may lead to. From the point of view of Candlin *et al.*, the study skills course was adequate because it was based on an assumption about the ubiquity of certain 'procedures' and 'techniques'. When course participants – academics from other parts of the world – were found not to share these procedures and techniques then the fault lay not in the course needs analysis and design but in the tendency of the foreign academics to think in 'illogical', 'vague' and 'unclear' ways.

Much progress in EAP needs analysis and course design has been made in the last twenty years, of course, but I suspect that autonomous views still lurk not very far below the surface (see 'The persistence of the autonomous approach' later in this chapter). And indeed, as Ballard in Chapter 8 shows, autonomous attitudes are not difficult to find in Australian academia even now. (Phillipson argues that much ELT activity emanating from Britain has been 'politically disconnected' (1992: 250) from the educational contexts in which it takes place. Whilst we may not necessarily share his belief that this constitutes evidence of 'linguistic imperialism' (1992: 15), it is clear, nevertheless, that such 'disconnection' inevitably gives rise to an autonomous view of the sort of behaviour which is appropriate for the language classroom.)

An ideological approach

The preceding section has argued that there is little justification for adopting an autonomous approach when we look at behaviour in higher education – and particularly when we consider English language teaching in universities. But this focus on higher education has been meant simply as a case study. In fact the central argument of this book is that an alternative – ideological – approach is required when we look at what is going on in language classrooms at *any* level, in any type of educational institution. The purpose of this book, then, is to explore the proposition that behaviour in the classroom can be explained or interpreted with reference to the society outside the classroom. Ballard, in Chapter 8, illustrates this proposition in the following way:

> In a society that emphasises respect for the past and for the authority of the teacher, the behaviour of both teachers and students will mirror these values. A society that rewards independence and individuality will produce a very different classroom etiquette.

The contributions to this argument are organised in four parts. Part 1, *Society and the school classroom*, examines social explanations for the behaviour of learners and teachers in school classrooms. It does this through two contrasting studies: firstly through Keith Chick's detailed investigation of one episode from a mathematics lesson in a senior primary class in a South African school, and then through Virginia LoCastro's wide-ranging critique of English language syllabus reform in Japan.

Part 2, *Society and the university classroom*, consists of four chapters, by Coleman, Holliday, Shamim and Muchiri. Their discussions look at universities in Indonesia, Egypt, Pakistan and Kenya, respectively. Coleman is concerned to find parallels between 'performances' in university classrooms and those observed in other cultural contexts, whilst Holliday focuses on the contrast between expatriate and Egyptian lecturers' teaching styles. Shamim describes and explains student resistance to innovation in one postgraduate class at the University of Karachi. Muchiri, meanwhile, looks in detail at the examination behaviours of undergraduate students in Kenya.

In Part 3, *Changing places and the language classroom*, our attention is directed not so much on the internal workings of universities but, rather, at the difficulties which arise when individuals move between academic cultures. Thus Ballard presents us with a study of what happens when Asian academics become students in an Australian institution, and Cortazzi and Jin examine the clash of 'learning cultures' which occurs when students in universities in China are taught by Western teachers.

The final part of this book, *Socialisation and the language classroom*, consists of just one chapter. This is Dick Allwright's argument that we do not always need to look outside the classroom for explanations of 'non-pedagogical' behaviour found inside the classroom. Allwright's contribution acts as a counterbalance to the approach which is adopted by the other investigations in the collection.

Among the issues which emerge from the various contributions, the following are particularly significant.

The effort to understand   In a very honest account, Chick reports the 'often tortuous paths' which he pursued in his attempt to interpret classroom behaviour and teacher resistance to change. This *effort to interpret* is a feature of several contributions to this volume: Coleman records his own 'astonishment' at an early stage in his discussion of university classrooms in Indonesia, for example, whilst Shamim reports her 'frustration and anger' at her initial inability to understand student behaviour in her classroom in Pakistan. Holliday at first found the parameters of his curriculum development task in an Egyptian university to be problematic, although an ethnographic approach eventually helped him to understand this problem. In each case, the observer describes a process in which an autonomous perspective is abandoned – sometimes with difficulty – for a more ideological interpretation of the observed phenomena.

The learning of 'other things'   In some situations, the language classroom may be the context for the learning of other things in addition to – or even in place of – language. The contributions of Chick, LoCastro, Muchiri, Coleman, and Cortazzi and Jin argue particularly strongly in this way. These 'other things' may include an understanding of the respective roles and responsibilities of teachers and students, the maintenance of face, and the development of student solidarity. If this hypothesis is confirmed, then, of course, innovation in classroom methodology may have unexpected repercussions for the teaching/learning of these 'other things'.

Alternatively, if these issues are not taken into consideration, then innovations in classroom practice may be taking on some unexpected functions even when they do apparently take root.

The student socialisation of teachers   Allwright suggests that learners 'could sometimes perhaps be said to socialise their teachers into being the sorts of teachers they themselves want.' Shamim illustrates this in her description of the way in which her attempts to introduce methodologically inappropriate innovations failed in the face of student hostility. Eventually, and reluctantly, she found herself adapting to the students' expectations. Cortazzi and Jin argue that Western teachers teaching in Chinese institutions *ought* to 'move towards the Chinese culture of learning', although as yet there is little evidence that this is taking place.

The counterproductiveness of pedagogical effort   The contributions of Allwright, Ballard, Chick, Holliday and Shamim all recognise – and in many cases illustrate – the fact that so much of the pedagogical effort which we find in classrooms is actually counterproductive. There are two aspects to this issue. In some cases, innovations which are intended to facilitate learning may be so disturbing for those affected by them – so threatening to their belief systems – that hostility is aroused and learning becomes impossible. In other cases, teaching which is aimed at enabling the transition to other academic contexts may simply confirm the participants' indigenous behaviour.

The persistence of the autonomous approach

In the late 1980s, three major international conferences were organised to explore the issue of the relationship between culture and language learning. These were the 1986 RELC Conference in Singapore on 'Patterns of Classroom Interaction in Southeast Asia', the 1988 Hong Kong Institute of Education conference on 'Teaching and Learning Styles Within and Across Cultures: Implications for Language Pedagogy', and the 1989 SELMOUS/BALEAP Conference in Leeds on 'Socio-Cultural Issues in English for Academic Purposes'. Publications emerged from each of these events (Das 1987, Bickley 1989 and Adams, Heaton and Howarth 1991 respectively).

What is striking about these studies of the influence of culture on the language classroom is how reluctant many researchers have been to concede that there is in fact any such influence. The collection edited by Das, for example, carries the title *Patterns of Classroom Interaction in Southeast Asia*. Even where contributors to this volume make use of classroom data (e.g. Coulthard 1987) they frequently forget to tell us anything about the context in which the data was found. Indeed seven of the ten contributors to the Das volume say nothing at all about classroom interaction in Southeast Asia.

Bickley (1989) appears to adopt an ideological standpoint himself, and yet many of the contributors to his collection argue against it. Maley (1989: 20), for example, takes up what he terms – somewhat oddly – a 'relativist' position and argues that 'we are in danger of exaggerating the significance of cross-cultural factors.' And Gilbert's contribution to the same volume takes a briskly dismissive line (1989: 230):

> ... learning styles are often culture and language specific. ... [Nevertheless] the lessons for the second language teacher are obvious. ... Students going abroad to study will do what they have always done to adapt to the style of the classroom and get on with the learning. Teachers in the United States where students in one class may represent all the varieties of learning style preferences that are possible are wasting their time if they try to write lesson plans for their learners' preferred cognitive style.

Adams *et al.* (1991) seem to hold an 'ideological' perspective and they are supported in this by some of their contributors (e.g. Bloor and Bloor 1991; Coleman 1991). But even here some researchers take a broadly autonomous line. Furneaux *et al.* (1991: 79), for example, group all overseas students in their study into one 'non-native speaker' category, and then conclude that '[British] lecturers and NNS students at the beginning of their studies at Reading ... have similar views on seminars. ... Thus lecturers and NNS students seem to be thinking broadly along the same lines.'

What the Singapore, Hong Kong and Leeds conferences reveal, then, is the continuing strength of the autonomous approach to the study of classroom behaviour. Even when researchers are willing to explore the significance of culture in the English language classroom, this interest is often restricted either to discussion of the cultural inappropriacy of textbooks and the content of lessons (see, for example, many of the contributions in the volumes edited by Harrison 1990 and by Brock and Walters 1993) or to the 'teaching' of culture (e.g. Valdes 1986, Barro *et al.* 1993 and Kramsch 1993).

The essentially autonomous interpretation of classroom behaviour, as we have seen, is still extremely powerful. Pennycook makes the observation that teacher education for TESOL has been curiously reluctant to ask questions 'about the social, cultural and political contexts of education in any critical fashion' (1994: 142). Nevertheless, there are signs of a gradual questioning of the autonomous hegemony: Bailey and Nunan, for example, acknowledge the importance of the 'sociocultural context in which language learning and teaching take place' (1996: 359).

The implications of an ideological view

It is important to emphasise that a non-universalist – an ideological – approach to the study of behaviour in the English language classroom does *not* imply cultural stereotyping or simplistic labelling. On the contrary, it recognises the extraordinary diversity of human behaviour and human achievement. It argues that we are all, as unique individuals, nevertheless at the same time members of interlocking and overlapping communities and social systems, from the family to the nation state and beyond. In our different ways and to different degrees we influence the other members of each of those communities, just as we in turn are influenced by them. What we *do* is the product of the interaction between ourselves and this cobweb of influences. Returning to the definition provided by Street (1984), we can see that the construction of the *meaning* of the English language classroom must be culturally embedded.

What are the implications of such a view? Many of the implications emanating from this perspective are explored by the individual contributors to this volume. Among them are the following:

1 We should be aware that every manifestation of classroom practice *may* have meaning and value in its own context.
2 Before seeking to sweep away traditional modes of behaviour, therefore, we must examine them with care and seek to understand them.
3 When making recommendations for innovation in English language methodology, we must carry out the equivalent of an environmental audit of the impact of our proposed changes. In other words, we must seek to predict what the knock-on effect of methodological change is likely to be.
4 When making recommendations for innovation, we must explore the possibility – at least – of exploiting current patterns of behaviour as a way of achieving the desired change.
5 In particular, we must be alert to the possibility that learners are making effective use of learning opportunites in non-classroom contexts.
6 We must be very cautious in making evaluative judgements of current classroom practice, particularly if as observers we do not share the same ideology as the principal participants in the classroom event.
7 We must question whether there are universally appropriate ways of evaluating the success or otherwise of English language teaching projects.
8 We must learn to question the ideological origins of our own assumptions about all aspects of English language teaching in institutional contexts.

Above all, what the chapters in this book indicate is that we must learn to look at our own work with a greater sense of humility and at the work of others with increased openness.

Notes

1 Some of the ideas in this introductory chapter were discussed in a paper with the title 'The Appropriacy of Teaching Study Skills', which I presented during the Conference on 'Studying with English', held at the University of Bristol on 5th and 6th January 1988. An even earlier version was presented at the British Council English Language Centre, Jakarta, Indonesia, on 10th April 1987.
2 There is, of course, a parallel between Street's autonomous/ideological distinction and the distinction between prescriptive and descriptive approaches in linguistics.

References

Adams, P., B. Heaton and P. Howarth (Eds.') 1991. *Socio-Cultural Issues in English for Academic Purposes.* (Review of ELT vol. 1 no. 2.) London: Modern English Publications/Macmillan.

Anonymous. 1984. Sistem kredit semester di PTS perlu digalakkan. *Kompas* 26 Mei 1983. In Ngadijono Miharjo (Ed.) 1984 *Bunga Rampai Pendidikan Harian Kompas 1981–1984.* Ujung Pandang: mimeo, 93.

Bailey, K. M. and D. Nunan (Eds.) 1996. *Voices from the Language Classroom.* Cambridge: Cambridge University Press.

Ballard, B. and J. Clanchy. 1984. *Study Abroad: A Manual for Asian Students.* Kuala Lumpur: Longman Malaysia.

Barro, A., M. Byram, H. Grimm, C. Morgan and C. Roberts. 1993. Cultural studies for advanced language learners. In D. Graddol, L. Thompson and M. Byram (Eds.) *Language and Culture,* 55–70. Clevedon, Avon: Multilingual Matters.

Bickley, V. (Ed.) 1989. *Language Teaching and Learning Styles within and across Cultures.* Hong Kong: Institute of Language in Education.

Bloor, M. and T. Bloor. 1991. Cultural expectations and socio-pragmatic failure in academic writing. In Adams, Heaton and Howarth, 1–12.

Brock, M. N. and L. Walters (Eds.) 1993. *Teaching Composition Around the Pacific Rim: Politics and Pedagogy.* Clevedon, Avon: Multilingual Matters.

Candlin, C. N., J. M. Kirkwood and H. M. Moore. 1975. Developing study skills in English. In K. Jones and P. Roe (Eds.) *English for Academic Study with Special Reference to Science and Technology: Problems and Perspectives,* 1–30. (ETIC Occasional Paper.) London: The British Council.

Coleman, H. 1991. The testing of 'appropriate behaviour' in an academic context. In Adams, Heaton and Howarth, 13–23.

Coulthard, M. 1987. Feedback in language teaching and language learning. In Das, 51–58.

Das, B. K. (Ed.) 1987. *Patterns of Classroom Interaction in Southeast Asia.* (Anthology Series 17.) Singapore: SEAMEO Regional Language Centre.

Entwistle, N. 1984. Contrasting perspectives on learning. In F. Marton, D. Hounsell and N. Entwistle (Eds.) *The Experience of Learning,* 1–18. Edinburgh: Scottish Academic Press.

Fellgett, P. B. 1986. A latter-day dissolution? *The Times Higher Education Supplement* 15 August 1986.

Furneaux, C., C. Locke, P. Robinson and A. Tonkyn. 1991. Talking heads and shifting bottoms: The ethnography of academic seminars. In Adams, Heaton and Howarth, 74–87.

Gilbert, R. A. 1989. The dangers of learning styles in the Mandarin/English classroom. In Bickley, 227–35.

Harrison, B. (Ed.) 1990. *Culture and the Language Classroom.* (ELT Documents 132.) London: Modern English Publications.

Kramsch, C. 1993. *Context and Culture in Language Teaching.* Oxford: Oxford University Press.

Maley, A. 1989. Divided worlds: divided minds. In Bickley, 20–33.

Nurjamal, D. 1984. Pelaksanaan SKS di perguruan tinggi: memerlukan kejelasan dan ketegasan. *Kompas* 26 Juli 1983. In Ngadijono Miharjo (Ed.) 1984, *Bunga Rampai Pendidikan Harian Kompas 1981–1984.* Ujung Pandang: mimeo, 95.

Penney, G. 1986. Wrong equal rights. *The Times* 11 July 1986.

Pennycook, A. 1994. *The Cultural Politics of English as an International Language.* Harlow: Longman.

Phillipson, R. 1992. *Linguistic Imperialism.* Oxford: Oxford University Press.

Soetrisno, L. 1986. Sipenmaru dan pengabdian dosen/pegawai universitas negeri. *Kompas* 24 Agustus 1984. In Ngadijono Miharjo (Ed.) 1986, *Bunga Rampai Pendidikan Harian Kompas 1984–1985.* Ujung Pandang: mimeo, 91.

Street, B. V. 1984. *Literacy in Theory and Practice.* (Cambridge Studies in Oral and Literate Culture 9.) Cambridge: Cambridge University Press.

Valdes, J. M. (Ed.) 1986. *Culture Bound: Bridging the Cultural Gap in Language Teaching.* Cambridge: Cambridge University Press.

Part 1 Society and the school classroom

The relationship between society at large and events in school classrooms is investigated in Part 1 of this volume. Keith Chick's focus of attention is mathematics teaching carried out through the medium of English in schools in KwaZulu, South Africa, whilst Virginia LoCastro examines the teaching of English as a foreign language in schools in Japan.

Chick begins his discussion by highlighting the widely recognised phenomenon that, in schools for black people in the former apartheid South Africa, classroom interaction was characterised by teachers playing highly authoritarian roles and with students initiating very little. Most student contributions to classroom events were in the form of chorus responses to teacher prompts.

Chick argues that the features of 'teacher volubility' and 'student taciturnity' which he found in the South African middle school (or 'senior primary') classroom may also characterise classrooms in other parts of the world. On the other hand, the very high frequency of chorusing, in Chick's view, is 'not found ... in classroom discourse throughout the world.' (In fact, LoCastro, in her contribution to this volume, also identifies 'choral reading aloud sentence by sentence' of English texts to be a common feature in Japanese language classrooms. Coleman 1988 has observed what he calls 'the completion chorus phenomenon' in secondary school English language lessons in Sénégal, and Ikranegara 1981 has found a very similar mode of interaction, which she calls 'echoic responses', in rural primary schools in West Java, Indonesia. Nevertheless, we need to be extremely cautious in assuming that there are any structural or functional similarities between phenomena which are superficially similar. That is to say, there may be many different types of classroom chorusing and each may play a different role in its own context.)

Chick was prompted to investigate chorus responses because so many classroom teachers and students appeared to be reluctant to give up this mode of interaction and because they were resistant to what he considered to be 'more egalitarian' forms of interaction associated with the communicative approach. He describes the 'tortuous paths' which he followed trying to make sense of classroom behaviour. Chick's original hypothesis was that trying to impose a communicative approach was 'possibly a sort of naive ethnocentrism.' His interim analysis of the data indicated that the characteristics of the classroom behaviour of both students and teachers reflected culturally specific Zulu patterns of interaction; concurrently he felt that these patterns of behaviour had unfortunate pedagogic consequences for the learners.

Later, however, Chick was obliged to revise his interpretation of the observed classroom behaviour. He placed this behaviour in its wider social context – a society founded on strict segregation between people of different races where resources for education and other services were allocated differentially (see also Peachey 1989 on teacher-student ratios in black South African primary schools). Eventually, Chick came to the conclusion that the fundamental explanation for what he had found was not, after all, that Zulu interactional styles had simply been transported into the classroom. Rather, he found that teachers and students were jointly creating a pattern of classroom co-existence which enabled them to avoid the 'oppressive and demeaning effects of apartheid ideology.' Whilst this pattern of behaviour – which he terms 'safe-talk' – helped the parties involved to maintain their dignity, the tragic irony is that it also reinforced the social inequalities which lay at the heart of the apartheid system.

The significance of Chick's contribution to this discussion lies in his rejection of a simplistic link between what we find inside the classroom and what occurs in wider society. Instead, he obliges us to consider the possibility that the relationship between what happens in society and what occurs in the classroom is a highly complex one. In this case study, what takes place inside the classroom must be seen as an effort by those involved to maintain some self-respect when society at large grants them no respect at all. Collusion in the classroom, then, masks inequities in society at large.

Chick uses a mathematics lesson as a neutral site for an examination of the context into which he has been trying to introduce communicative language teaching concepts. LoCastro, meanwhile, focuses explicitly on English language teaching. Her scope is very broad, since she looks at classroom behaviour not only in the context of late 20th century Japanese society but also in its historical perspective.

LoCastro succeeds in identifying the external and historical influences on the 'gross' features of classroom behaviour, but also – even – on the central pedagogical concerns of teachers and pupils, including for example punctilious attention to correctness in grammar. She argues, therefore, that in order to make sense of the behaviour found in the Japanese secondary school English lesson, we need to take both a diachronic view of Japanese society since the 1860s and a synchronic view of contemporary Japan. This is an important contribution to the discussion of the relationship between society and classroom events.

LoCastro's discussion (like the study of education in China by Cortazzi and Jin in Chapter 9) takes a national perspective, rather than concentrating on a particular classroom or institution in detail. Essentially, LoCastro is concerned to demonstrate that the new English language curriculum issued by the Japanese Ministry of Education in 1989 and 1990 – although at first sight appearing to be well founded in that it takes into account the most recent thinking on curriculum design – actually shows 'a gross mismatch between the supposed aims and the socio-cultural context.' The aims of the new syllabus appear to have been determined not on the basis of an analysis of the needs of Japanese students but, rather, on an assumption that applied linguistic concepts developed in the Anglo-American applied linguistic context can be adopted uncritically into a very different situation. If LoCastro's analysis is correct, then her case is a perfect illustration of what Holliday (in Chapter 5 below and 1994) describes as the hegemony of the 'BANA' (British, Australasian and North American) model. And, as Holliday (1991) has warned us, if curriculum innovation is not sensitive to its socio-cultural context, then 'tissue rejection' – the failure of transplanted ideas and procedures to flourish in a new environment – is likely to occur.

LoCastro suggests that one of the dangers of deriving a new syllabus from Western models is that it is deceptively easy to translate terminology without successfully transferring meaning. She goes so far as to propose that there is a 'possibility that "communication" itself may not be a universally shared concept'; if this is the case, what, then, does 'the communicative approach' mean? LoCastro's warning about the risks involved in borrowing terms from one sociocultural context for mapping onto indigenous concepts in another context, resulting in semantic mismatches, is also taken up by Coleman in Chapter 4.

The very important conclusion to LoCastro's chapter – which in fact mirrors one of the central arguments of this volume – is that 'language classrooms, as part of the overall educational system, may be the context for the learning of other things.' Even more starkly, it appears that English language teaching is 'subordinate to the learning of culturally valued, normative behaviour.'

References

Coleman, H. 1988. Teaching large classes of mixed ability groups: Report on a National Seminar for In-Service Pedagogic Advisers, Sénégal, 30 November–2 December 1988. Leeds: Unpublished report prepared for the British Council.

Holliday, A. 1991. Dealing with tissue rejection in EFL projects: The role of an ethnographic means analysis. Lancaster University: Unpublished Ph.D. thesis.

Holliday, A. 1994. *Appropriate Methodology and Social Context*. Cambridge: Cambridge University Press.

Ikranegara, K. 1981. Two schools: On functions of language in the classroom in Indonesia. Paper presented at the Third International Conference on Austronesian Linguistics, Denpasar, Indonesia, 19th–24th January 1981.

Peachey, L. 1989. *Language Learning in Large Classes: A Pilot Study of South African Data*. Project Report 8. Leeds: Language Learning in Large Classes Research Project.

2 Safe-talk: Collusion in apartheid education[1]

J. Keith Chick

Introduction

Background to the study

There is widespread agreement amongst observers about what were the essential characteristics of interactions in schools for black people in South Africa under the former apartheid system: highly centralised, with teachers adopting authoritarian roles and doing most of the talking, with few pupil initiations, and with most of the pupil responses taking the form of group chorusing. Schlemmer and Bot (1986: 80) report a senior African school inspector as stating that black pupils were discouraged from asking questions or participating actively in learning and explain that it was regarded as impolite and even insubordinate to ask questions or make suggestions in class. Thembela (1986: 41) refers to classroom practice being characterised by rote learning and teacher-centred instruction.

Most observers, moreover, agree that the educational consequences of such interaction styles were unfortunate. Schlemmer and Bot (1986) and Thembela (1986), for example, argue that the use of such styles oppressed creativity, initiative and assertiveness. MacDonald (1988) claims that there are aspects of metacognition and disembedded thinking crucial to advanced learning and to effective functioning in a technological society which these styles of interacting and learning did not promote.

I became very aware of the possible negative educational consequences of the overwhelming preference for such styles of interaction in schools for black people in South Africa, through my involvement with in-service teacher education projects which had, as one of their primary objectives, the fostering of communicative approaches to the teaching of English in KwaZulu schools. (KwaZulu was a patchwork of geographical areas on the eastern seaboard of South Africa which, in terms of apartheid policy, was designated a 'homeland' for Zulu people. At the time of the study reported here, the total population of native speakers of Zulu was almost seven million; they thus constituted the largest language group in South Africa. Zulu speakers live in many parts of South Africa, but at that time approximately five million of them lived in KwaZulu.)

A number of the implementors of the in-service teacher education projects complained about the reluctance of many of the teachers, and even some of the students, to adopt the more egalitarian, de-centralised ways of interacting associated with these approaches to language teaching. This reluctance was pervasive enough to make at least some of those involved with the in-service projects, including myself, question whether the choice of communicative language teaching as a goal was an appropriate one. Given that communicative language teaching approaches had their origins chiefly in Europe and the USA, contexts very different from those which obtained in KwaZulu, I began to wonder whether our choice of communicative language teaching as a goal was possibly a sort of naive ethnocentricism prompted by the thought that what is good for Europe or the USA had to be good for KwaZulu. I reasoned that, in order to discover whether the goal of communicative language teaching was appropriate or not, it would be necessary to discover why students and teachers in KwaZulu schools found it so difficult to transfer to styles compatible with communicative language teaching. With this goal in mind, I encouraged Marianne Claude – who, under my supervision, was engaged in action research/in-service education with teachers in a peri-urban area of KwaZulu – to collect, by means of participant observation, interviews and discussions with the teachers, relevant ethnographic data, including classroom interactional data. I supplemented this with my own participant observation and discussions with teachers during visits to classrooms elsewhere in KwaZulu. In this chapter, I report on my analysis and interpretation of some of this data.

My thinking at this stage was heavily influenced by the findings of research I had completed earlier, working within the interactional sociolinguistic framework developed by scholars such as Gumperz (see, for example, 1982a, 1982b) and Erickson (see, for example, 1975 and 1976). In analysing interethnic encounters between a white South African English-speaking academic and Zulu graduate students at the University of Natal (see Chick 1985) I had identified putative culturally-specific Zulu-English interactional styles. These styles are characterised, amongst other things, by the preference by higher status speakers in asymmetrical encounters (i.e. those in which there are marked differences in the relative status of the participants) for what Scollon and Scollon (1983) term solidarity politeness, including the politeness or face-preserving strategy of volubility (much talking), and by lower status speakers for what they term deference politeness, including the strategy of taciturnity (avoidance of talking). I hypothesised that KwaZulu teachers and students found it difficult to transfer to styles compatible with communicative language teaching because these styles, which call on students to be voluble, differ markedly from those which predominate in a wide range of domains within the Zulu-speaking community, and which are transferred to their use of English in academic and other settings.

Incidentally, to avoid misinterpretation, I need to clarify that I am using 'preference' not in its lay sense of speaker's or hearer's individual preferences. Rather, I am borrowing a technical term from ethnomethodology, a branch of sociology concerned with investigating how people organise and make sense of social activities. As Levinson (1983: 307) explains, 'preference' is not a psychological notion but a structural notion that corresponds closely to the linguistic concept of markedness, according to which certain linguistic features are more basic and conventional and occur more frequently ('unmarked') than other features (referred to as 'marked'). Thus, when Zulus who have relatively low status choose deferential politeness, it is not because they like behaving deferentially, or that they 'feel' deferential, but rather because such behaviour is conventional, or as Lakoff expresses it, 'targeted'. She explains (1979: 69) that each culture has implicitly in its collective mind a concept of how a good human being should behave: 'a target for its members to aim at and judge themselves and others by'.

Organisation of the study

Most research reports imply that the research which they are reporting on proceeded in very orderly and logical ways, and that the researchers, from the outset, were more knowledgeable and insightful than they actually were. The false starts, the partial understandings and the dead ends do not feature. In this chapter I will be departing from this tradition, and sharing with my readers the often tortuous paths I followed in exploring the significance of interactional styles widely employed in schools for black people in South Africa.

To begin with, I report on my micro-ethnographic analysis of an episode in a lesson in a KwaZulu classroom. The general goal of micro-ethnographic analysis is to provide a description of how interlocutors set up or constitute contexts that allow them to make sense of one another's messages. My specific purpose was to try to establish why teachers and students in such classrooms found it difficult to transfer to styles compatible with communicative language teaching. The analysis reveals interactional behaviour consistent with the putative Zulu-English inter-actional styles identified in the interethnic encounters referred to above. More significantly, it reveals that such styles served valuable social functions for students and teachers alike. This could account for why teachers and students were reluctant to abandon such styles, despite the fact that the academic consequences of such preference were probably unfortunate.

I then explain how my growing awareness of the limitations of micro-ethnographic research in general, and explanations of pervasive school failure amongst dominated groups in terms of culturally-specific interactional styles in particular, prompted me to re-examine my classroom interactional data. Critics have pointed out that micro-ethnographic studies often take insufficient account of how pervasive values, ideologies and structures in the wider society (macro context) constrain what takes place at a micro level. Accordingly, I give an account of the historical, structural circumstances which contributed to making primary school education for most teachers and students in so-called black education in apartheid South Africa such a traumatic experience. Finally I offer a reinterpretation of the analysed data. I suggest that what is most significantly displayed in this episode is not culturally-specific Zulu interactional styles, but styles consistent with interactional norms which teachers and students interactionally con-stituted as a means of avoiding the oppressive and demeaning effects of apartheid ideology and structures. Following McDermott and Tylbor (1987) I see the teacher and her students as *colluding* in preserving their dignity by hiding the fact that little or no learning is taking place. While serving the short-term interests of teachers and students, such strategies, I suggest, contributed to the widely documented high failure rate in black education in apartheid South Africa, and made teachers and students resistant to educational innovation. The strategies thus served to reinforce and reproduce the inequalities between the various population groups which characterised apartheid society.

Culturally-specific interactional styles as barriers to innovation and learning

With the goal, then, of trying to establish why many teachers and students in KwaZulu schools resisted the adoption of egalitarian, de-centralised ways of interacting, I carried out a fine-grained micro-ethnographic analysis of an episode in a video-recorded mathematics lesson, initially with the help of Marianne Claude (who had observed the lesson while it was taking place) and, later, independently. I selected this episode from the corpus collected by Marianne Claude because it contains features that I had observed in many lessons taught by teachers who were highly regarded either by students or by school authorities in the KwaZulu educational system. In other words, I chose part of a 'good' lesson. I did this to ensure that I would be analysing conventional 'targeted' behaviour in Lakoff's sense. I chose a content subject rather than an English lesson so as to lessen the chance that the teacher's style might have been influenced by Marianne Claude's intervention.

I based the analysis on methods developed by interactional socio-linguists (see, for example, Gumperz 1982a) who, rather than impose their own categories, attempt to access the interpretative or inferential processes of the participants by repeatedly playing the video or sound recordings to the participants and/or informants who share their cultural backgrounds, and by eliciting interpretations from them about progress-ively finer details of the discourse. I make use of transcription conven-tions which highlight the nature of turn exchange and which provide information about the supra-segmental phonology of the episode. Latch marks (⌊) are used to show smooth exchange of turns without overlap, while square brackets are used to signify simultaneous speech ([ ). Underlining is used to signify phonological prominence such as stress or marked pitch movement. The 'shape' of the pitch movement is indicated above the part of the utterance where this occurs, and so (') signifies rising tone.

Relevant contextual information is that the class consisted of 38 students of both sexes who were native speakers of Zulu, whose average age at the time was fourteen years, and who were in their seventh year of schooling (the fourth year of the Senior Primary phase). The teacher, whom I shall refer to as Mrs Gumbi, also a native Zulu speaker, was 32 years of age and had completed ten years of schooling and two years of teacher training. Mrs Gumbi conducted the entire lesson from the front of the classroom, making considerable use of the board. The students were crowded into multiple-seat wooden desks arranged in rows facing the board. The lesson took place through the medium of English. (In KwaZulu schools English served as the medium of instruction across the curriculum after the first four years of schooling through the medium of Zulu.)

As the video-recording shows, the focus of the lesson was 'elements which form the union set'. At the start of the lesson Mrs Gumbi introduced the notion of elements of a union set with the aid of the board. Elements were written on the board, and common elements pointed to. She individually nominated one student to answer a question but, significantly, only after the information to be provided had been written on the board. The few other student responses took the form of teacher-initiated group chorusing.

The lesson continued:

1 Mrs Gumbi: but I know that these two elements are common
2 because they are found in set B as well as in set C do you get
3 that
4   Students: |yes

5 Mrs Gumbi: |now now a let us <u>form</u> the universal set the
6 univers I mean sorry union set is the <u>set</u> which
7 has the <u>elements</u> of <u>both</u> sets get it B ánd [C
8   Students: [C
9   Mrs Gumbi: |<u>collect</u>
10 the elements of those two sets and write them to<u>gether</u>
11 all them they will form u<u>ni</u>on [set
12   Students: [set
13   Mrs Gumbi: |<u>can</u> you try to tȯ list
14 the elements of the union set
15   Student A: |<u>two</u> [three
16   Mrs Gumbi: [that is tẃo
17   Student A: |<u>three</u>
18 Mrs Gumbi: |thrée
19   Student A: |<u>four</u>
20   Mrs Gumbi: |foúr
21   Student A: |<u>five</u>
22   Mrs Gumbi: |fíve
23   Student A: |<u>six</u>
24   Mrs Gumbi: |síx
25 Student A: |<u>seven</u>
26 Mrs Gumbi: |séven
27   Student A: |<u>eight</u>
28   Mrs Gumbi: |eíght and eight . . .
29 what type of set is this now . . . it is á [union set
30   Students: [union set
31   Mrs Gumbi: |<u>it is</u> a
32 union set because we have been <u>list</u>ing now at the elements
33 of set B to<u>gether</u> with the elements of sét [C
34   Students: [C
35   Mrs Gumbi: |<u>to form</u> one
36 set which called what . . . a u<u>ni</u>on [set
37   Students: [set
38   Mrs Gumbi: |<u>but</u> re<u>member</u>
39 when you <u>list</u> the union set the elements for for the union set
40 do not repeat those elements which are written twice do you get that
41   Students: |yes

42	Mrs Gumbi:	do not repeat them list them once OK
43	Students:	yes
44	Mrs Gumbi:	do you understand this
45	Students:	yes
46	Mrs Gumbi:	do you understand this
47	Students:	yes

What is immediately striking about this episode (as also the lesson as a whole) is the coincidence of teacher volubility and student (particularly individual student) taciturnity, characteristics of interactions in the formerly segregated schools for black people in South Africa, which, as I noted above, have been commented upon by many observers. Mrs Gumbi in this extract, as elsewhere in the lesson, does most of the talking. Indeed, of the total 19 minutes duration of the lesson as a whole, five seconds short of 16 minutes consists of teacher talk. Also the students' opportunities to talk (with one or two exceptions) are reduced to group chorusing.

Volubility on the part of the teacher, which Scollon and Scollon (1983) regard as a solidarity strategy, and taciturnity on the part of the students, which they regard as a deference strategy, is consistent with the culturally-specific interactional styles I had found evidence for in my analysis of interethnic encounters between Zulu-English speakers and South African (white) English speakers (Chick 1985). This finding might, therefore, be seen as lending credence to the notion that the interactional styles employed in KwaZulu classrooms were similar to those used in a wide range of domains within the Zulu-speaking community.

A problem for this interpretation is that teacher volubility and student taciturnity have been shown to be characteristic of classroom discourse in many parts of the world including white, middle class European (see, for example, Sinclair and Coulthard 1975) and USA classrooms (see, for example, Mehan 1979). Indeed Ellis (1987: 87) suggests that teacher-centred instruction, which has been so pervasive in black education in South Africa, is derived from classroom practices common in pre-war European schools. An equally, if not more plausible interpretation, is that teacher volubility and student taciturnity are features of institution-specific rather than culturally-specific discourse. According to this interpretation, the source of teacher volubility and student taciturnity is the asymmetrical distribution of social power and knowledge between teachers and students evident in educational institutions throughout the world.

What is not found, however, in classroom discourse throughout the world is the chorusing behaviour evident in this episode, which is why I chose to focus on it in my analysis. Closer examination revealed that two kinds of cues to chorusing are provided by Mrs Gumbi. The one kind of cue involves the use of a set of yes/no questions: 'do you understand this?' (lines 44 and 46); 'do you get that?' (lines 2–3 and 40); 'OK' (line 42); 'isn't it?' and 'do you see that?'; 'can I go on?' (elsewhere in the lesson). The second kind of cue involves the use of rising tone on accented syllables (e.g. lines 7, 11, 29, 33, 36). This cue is also used as a prompt to individual student responses in a sequence (lines 16, 18, 20, 22, 24, 26 etc.). What this suggests is the operation of a relatively simple prosodic system in which a restricted set of prosodic cues is used for a wide range of prosodic functions. Interestingly, this observation is consistent with my finding in a study of interethnic encounters (see Chick 1985) that Zulu-English speakers rely less than do white South African English speakers on prosodic cues to signal (together with kinesic, paralinguistic, lexical and syntactic cues) the relationship between different parts of the text, the relative importance of information units, speaker transition points and so on. This may be related to the fact that the prosody of Zulu, a tone language, is very different from that of English.

The closer examination of the chorusing behaviour in this episode points to a possible explanation for the difficulty which teachers and students in KwaZulu schools have in transferring from the putative culturally-specific Zulu-English styles (of which the system of prosodic cues is apparently a distinctive feature) to styles compatible with communicative language teaching. I examined, first, the possibility that the chorusing elicited by the one kind of cue (rising tone), in certain cases, serves the academic function of reinforcing certain key information items and, perhaps, helping the students to become more familiar with (to memorise?) technical terms (e.g. lines 29–30). However, further analysis revealed that it is often not *new* information that students are asked to chorus, but information already available to the students before the lesson (e.g. in lines 12 and 37 the students are required to supply the word SET rather than the name of the set that they have learnt about in the lesson). Elsewhere in the lesson the rising tone prompts them merely to complete words (e.g. intersecTION; we are looking for the unKNOWN). The fact that the information value of items chorused is often low prompted me to investigate the possibility that the primary function of the chorusing elicited by this kind of cue is social rather than academic.

I also examined the possibility that the chorusing elicited by the other kind of cue (the set of questions) serves the academic function of enabling Mrs Gumbi to access the level of her students' understanding so that she can know whether or not to recycle her explanation at a lower level of abstraction. However, I discovered that the chorused responses are without exception 'yes'. This suggests that the questions are not really open questions, and that their function is to signal participation rather than level of understanding, i.e. it is again social rather than academic in purpose.

The social function of chorusing became even more clearly evident when I examined the lesson as a whole. I discovered that the students are required, in response to both kinds of cue, to provide mainly confirmative one- or two-word responses, or responses which repeat information on the board or information which has been recycled again and again by Mrs Gumbi. This suggests that chorusing gives the students opportunities to participate in ways that reduce the possibility of the loss of face associated with providing incorrect responses to teacher elicitations, or not being able to provide responses at all. It is interesting to note that the chorusing is more evident at the beginning of the lesson than later on. Once responses have been well rehearsed, so that the chance of being wrong publicly is reduced, more individual responses are elicited, and at the end students are even invited to leave their desks and carry out the very public act of writing their responses on the board.

There is, of course, nothing unusual about teachers needing to resort to face-saving strategies, since the asymmetrical role relations between teachers and students to be found in most parts of the world ensure that the risk of face-threat is great. As Cazden (1979: 147) explains, 'teachers, by the very nature of their professional role, are continuously threatening both aspects of their students' face constraining their freedom of action; evaluating, often negatively, a high proportion of student acts and utterances; and often interrupting student work and student talk'. To reduce this risk, teachers employ face-saving strategies such as expressing directives indirectly by means of interrogatives, e.g. 'Can you open your books, please?' This strategy reduces the sense of imposition associated with the directive by suggesting that the students are free to decide whether or not to comply. However, the need to resort to face-saving strategies is particularly great in KwaZulu classrooms because the asymmetry in the relative status of teachers and students is marked. This reflects the marked asymmetry in the relative status of adults and children in the wider community. According to Marianne Claude's informants (see Chick and Claude 1985), an adult in that community has the right to ask any child, who may well be a stranger, to do errands for them (i.e. take a message to someone; buy something at the shop) and may even chastise a child not their own.

Another striking feature of this episode is the remarkably rhythmic manner in which teacher and students synchronise their verbal and prosodic behaviours, particularly in accomplishing the chorusing sequences. Context analysts (e.g. Scheflin 1973; Condon 1977; Kendon 1973, 1979; McDermott, Gospodinoff and Aaron 1978) have demonstrated that participants in conversations organise their behaviours in co-operative, reciprocal, rhythmically co-ordinated ways in signalling to one another and negotiating the context of their talk. This enables them to make sense of what it is that they are doing together. In the episode such interactional synchrony is possible, presumably, because the teacher and her students are able to draw on their shared, implicit knowledge of the discourse conventions associated with conventional interactional styles. I suggest that this synchrony contributes to the perception that purposeful activity and learning are taking place.

To sum up, the micro-ethnographic analysis of this episode reveals interactional behaviour consistent with Zulu-English interactional styles identified in a study of interethnic encounters (see Chick 1985). Particularly noteworthy features of the discourse are the chorusing behaviour and the remarkably rhythmic manner in which the participants synchronise their interactional behaviours in accomplishing the chorusing sequences. Analysis revealed that these putative styles serve social rather than academic functions. For example, they help the students to avoid the loss of face associated with being wrong in a public situation, and provide them with a sense of purpose and accomplishment. Something not examined here, but equally important, is that these styles also help teachers avoid the loss of face associated with displays of incompetence. This is because they ensure that the lesson develops along predetermined lines, and that the opportunities for students to raise issues and problems that teachers may not be competent to handle are few. It is for such reasons that I refer to discourse associated with these styles as 'safe-talk'.

What this analysis suggests is that the task of making a transition – from the culturally-preferred interactional styles employed conventionally in KwaZulu classrooms to the styles associated with the more egalitarian relationships required by the communicative language teaching approach – was likely to be fraught with risk for both teachers and students. They all resisted innovation because they had vested interests in the maintenance of 'safe-talk'.

Limitations of explanations of school failure in terms of culturally-specific styles

One of the advantages of doing sociolinguistic research within the context of apartheid South Africa was that one was constantly prompted to reconsider one's interpretations. Many scholars in this context were very suspicious of sociolinguistic research which had an ethnographic orientation, and indeed of ethnography in general. As Kuper, writing during the apartheid era, explained, 'almost by its very nature, ethnographic research may appear to provide some support for the ideological assumptions underpinning apartheid, notably the belief that "traditional" and "tribal" institutions remain viable, and command respect' (1985:1). It was in part the negative reaction of such critics to my analysis and interpretation of the episode referred to above which prompted the reinterpretation outlined below.

Another advantage of researching within the context of apartheid South Africa was that the discriminatory legislation tended to make visible what is normally hidden in democratic societies, namely the mechanisms in the wider (macro) society through which groups and individuals exercise power and deny it to others. It was the visibility of those mechanisms that had prompted me in an earlier study (see Chick 1985) to try to account for how macro-level factors, such as segregation, constrain what takes place at a micro level of interethnic communication. I was, therefore, open to the suggestion that a limitation of my original analysis of the episode was that I had not adequately contextualised my data; that I had not taken sufficient account of the effect on classroom discourse of such factors as the differential funding of the racially segregated school systems, differential teacher-student ratios, levels of teacher training and so on.

I was also familiar with the claim of such critics of micro-ethnography as Singh, Lele and Martohardjono (1988) that, because micro-ethnographers fail to show how the pervasive values, ideologies and structures of the wider society constrain micro-level behaviour, they come perilously close to being apologists for the systems they are investigating. Along similar lines, Karabel and Halsey (1977: 58) are critical of the neglect of macro factors in interactional accounts of the pervasive school failure of minority groups. They point out that:

> Teachers and pupils do not come together in a historical vacuum: the weight of precedent conditions the outcome of 'negotiation' over meaning at every turn. If empirical work is confined to observation of classroom interaction, it may miss the process by which political and economic power set sharp bounds to what is negotiable.

Ogbu (1981), too, while not denying that micro-ethnographic studies have a role in explaining how interaction acts as an immediate cause of a particular child's failure, argues that it is essential also to study how these classroom events are built up by forces emanating from outside these micro settings.

Influenced by such thinking, I concluded that my micro-ethnographic analysis of the episode from the mathematics lesson needed to be informed by a macro-ethnographic account of the schooling provided for black students in KwaZulu. This account, along lines suggested by Ogbu (1981), would be one that showed how the school system was related to social organisation, economy, political organisation, belief system and values, change and so on.

In the section which follows, I provide information about the macro context of schooling for blacks in South Africa during the apartheid era, which I identified as potentially relevant to the reinterpretation of this episode. Since the lesson occurred in a Senior Primary school (fourth to eighth years of schooling) I focus on this phase of the schooling system. I focus also on the role of English as medium of instruction, since research suggests (see, for example, MacDonald 1990) that difficulties associated with the transfer from mother tongue to English in the first year of this phase constrain classroom behaviour in powerful ways.

The macro context of schooling for black people in apartheid South Africa

As most people are aware, *apartheid*, an Afrikaans word meaning literally 'apartness' or separateness, refers to the policy of the Nationalist Party, which, subsequent to its coming to power in 1948, was implemented as a massive programme of social engineering. Racial segregation had been a feature of South African society ever since the arrival of whites in the 17th century. However, after 1948, segregation on racial and even, within racial groups, on ethnic lines, in every sphere of life, was implemented on a scale unprecedented in human history. Not merely were separate institutions such as educational institutions established for different race and ethnic groups, but geographical separation was attempted through the creation of ethnic 'homelands', of which KwaZulu was one.

Exemplifying as it does the classic divide-and-rule strategy, the apartheid policy admirably served the goal of the Nationalist Party of consolidating and increasing the newly-won hegemony of Afrikanerdom. Segregation also served to maintain and increase the privileged status that whites had enjoyed since the 17th century, by facilitating the systematic discrimination against people of colour.

In education, systematic discrimination was evident in the differential per capita expenditure on education for the various population groups. Towards the end of the apartheid era, there were attempts by the government to narrow the gaps between the provision for the various groups. However, as recently as the financial year 1986/7, the per capita expenditure on education for whites was R2508. That for blacks (i.e. Africans rather than Asians or so-called 'coloureds') was only R476, whilst that for blacks in the homelands was still lower; for example, in KwaZulu it was only R359 (South African Institute of Race Relations (SAIRR) Survey 1987/88).

One of the consequences of this differential expenditure, which probably played a role in determining what styles of interaction were possible, was differential teacher-student ratios. In 1987, whereas the student-teacher ratio for whites was 16 to 1, that for blacks in so-called white areas was 41 to 1, and for KwaZulu primary schools 53 to 1 and KwaZulu secondary schools 37 to 1 (SAIRR Survey 1987/88). It is very difficult for teachers, who are responsible for large numbers of students and who usually have to cope with overcrowded classrooms, to facilitate more egalitarian, decentralised ways of interacting.

The more long-term discriminatory effects of segregated education were evident, also, in the differential levels of professional qualification of teachers in schools for the various population groups. According to Du Plessis, Du Pisani and Plekker (1989) whereas, in 1989, 100% of teachers in schools for whites were professionally qualified in the sense of having at least matriculation or higher academic qualifications, as well as a teachers' certificate or diploma, only 20% of teachers in black primary schools and 10% in black secondary schools were professionally qualified.

Of particular relevance to the constraints of macro factors upon classroom discourse is another factor, namely, how apartheid ideology was translated into language medium policy in black education. Hartshorne (1987) reports that, until the Nationalists came to power, the position of English as sole medium of instruction after the first few years of schooling was unchallenged. He reports, further, that the Nationalists:

> made of Afrikaans a symbol of exclusiveness and separateness, and the struggle for Afrikaans became part of the 'mission' to control and rule South Africa. In education this expressed itself in a commitment to separate schools and rigid mother-tongue education policy. (Hartshorne 1987: 88)

This commitment eventually translated into mother-tongue instruction in primary education with English and Afrikaans as compulsory subjects from the first year of schooling, and with both Afrikaans and English as media of instruction in secondary education (half the subjects through English and half through Afrikaans). It was the inflexible and doctrinaire implementation of this policy, and the deafness to the protests of the black community, that sparked the Soweto uprising of 1976. This spread to the rest of the country, almost assuming the proportions of a full-scale civil war. As a consequence of the conflict, the government was forced to concede to the black community the right to choose *either* English *or* Afrikaans as medium in the high schools. In response to further pressure from the community, this right to choose was extended to the higher primary phase. English became overwhelmingly the chosen medium in black education after the first three years of schooling. In 1988, for example, only 20 primary schools (including some very small farm schools) and no high schools used Afrikaans as medium (SAIRR 1988/89).

Though the choice of English as medium represented the will of the people, as MacDonald (1990) explains, in primary education at least, it added to the burdens of teachers and students. She points out (1990: 39) that the apartheid system ensured that most of the teachers in so-called black education did not speak English with confidence or fluency, used outmoded materials, and had almost no contact with English speakers. Also, following the major shift to English as medium in primary education from 1979 onwards, no changes were made to the syllabus for English to prepare the ground linguistically and conceptually for its use across the curriculum. As a consequence, black primary school students were not adequately prepared for the sudden transition to English in the fourth year of schooling concurrently with the curriculum broadening into ten subjects. Nor were most of the teachers equipped to explain effectively in English the new concepts in the various content subjects such as mathematics.

MacDonald and her fellow researchers found that there was a considerable gap between the English competence required for the reading of content subject textbooks in the fourth year of schooling, and the English competence that might have been expected if a student had benefited optimally from English as a second language teaching materials then used in junior primary schools. They also found that there was also a very large gap between this hypothesised optimal competence and the level of competence students actually reached. They estimated, for example, that the vocabulary requirements in English increased by 1000% in the fourth year of schooling. They calculated that a student who had learnt optimally from the ESL materials in the junior primary phase might have encountered not more than half the vocabulary, and might have been unfamiliar with syntactic elements in up to 60% of sentences in science textbooks used in the fourth year of schooling. Moreover they might have been so ignorant of the conventions of expository writing as to experience what is referred to as 'register shock' when reading those texts.

As a consequence, the fourth year of schooling was a time of trauma for both teachers and students; a trauma reflected in the high drop-out rate in black schools at the end of that year (64,100 or 8.9% of the total outflow in 1987 according to the SAIRR Report 1988/89). The researchers found that the effect of those conditions was what they termed 'the loss of meaning'. 'The children are likely to be alienated by what they have to learn, and only dimly perceive the implications and linkages between the concepts they are presented with' (MacDonald 1990: 141). Faced with these odds, teachers tended to resort to providing notes that the students were required to memorise. This gave the impression of real learning taking place, but as MacDonald (1990: 143) points out, the students often learnt what they did not understand, and were usually unable to use what they had learnt because this mode of education did not allow the integration of new information with what had been learnt before.

A reinterpretation: safe-talk as the outcome of collusion between teachers and students

Reexamining my micro-ethnographic analysis of the episode in a mathematics lesson in a KwaZulu classroom, I was struck by the similarity between MacDonald's account of the teachers' response to the trauma experienced in the early years of senior primary schooling and my interpretation of the interactional behaviour in the episode as 'safe-talk'.

My thinking was also strongly influenced by two studies that attempt to trace the relationship between the structure of classroom discourse and the macro context in which it occurs, including the ideologies that are promoted in them. In the first of these studies, Collins (1987) argues that the ideology of ability grouping promoted in school systems in the United States leads students in low ability groups and their teachers to socialise one another into systematic departures from the norms of classroom discourse. Behaviour consistent with these 'emergent' norms (see Mehan 1979: 90) interferes with the reading practice which members of these groups so badly need. Collins argues, further, that the ideology of prescriptivism also promoted in the United States school system results in evaluation being made on the basis of cultural background rather than on academic aptitude. This leads to the systematic exclusion of minority students from opportunities to learn and practise forms of literary discourse.

In the second of these studies, McDermott and Tylbor (1987) analyse an episode in which teachers and students do interactional work to make the illiteracy of one of the students, Rosa, not noticeable. In the process Rosa does not get a turn to practise her reading. They show that while evaluation is constantly taking place, teachers and students *collude* in evaluating overtly only when the evaluation is positive, while, at the same time, making covert, unspoken, negative evaluations. Such collusion hides the unpleasant fact that schooling is structured in such a way as to provide access to opportunities for learning for some students and to deny it to others.

These two studies show how features of the macro context, namely the institutional ideologies and bureaucratic structures, constrain what takes place at a micro level. They also show the participants working together to reshape the structure of their discourse and to socialise one another into a set of sociolinguistic norms that enable them to meet their immediate needs. As Collins (1987: 313) explains:

> Institutional ideologies and bureaucratic organisation forms do not entirely constrain participants; people still strive to make sense of their situation, to avoid or resist that which is demeaning or oppressive.

It was these insights that enabled me to recognise that the 'safe-talk' which I had identified in my analysis of the episode of the mathematics lesson does not represent the inappropriate use of culturally-specific Zulu-English interactional styles. Rather, it represents styles which the participants interactionally developed and constituted as a means of coping with the overwhelming odds they faced in their segregated schools. I suggest that these styles enabled them to collude in hiding unpleasant realities. Thus, for example, the rhythmically co-ordinated chorusing prompts and responses enabled the teacher and students in the episode to hide their poor command of English; to obscure their inadequate understanding of academic content; and to maintain a façade of effective learning taking place. In this way they were able to preserve their dignity to some extent. In terms of this interpretation, commonalities between 'safe-talk' and the putative Zulu-English styles identified in an earlier study (Chick 1985) are features of conventional Zulu interactional styles that survived the process of constituting a new set of norms of interaction. In doing the interactional work involved in constituting these norms, the participants inevitably started by making use of interactional styles most familiar to them.

Unfortunately, as Collins (1987: 313) notes, 'solutions achieved to local problems may have unforeseen consequences which are quite damaging'. 'Safe-talk' has proved to be a barrier both to learning and to educational innovation in South Africa. As such it served to reinforce the inequalities that gave rise to it in the first place.

Conclusion

To sum up, in this chapter I have explored the significance of interactional styles that were widely employed in schools for black people in South Africa. The fine-grained analysis of an episode from a lesson which exemplifies such styles revealed that they served important social functions for teachers, but probably did not promote efficient learning. They also provided support for the hypothesis that teachers and students in KwaZulu classrooms were often reluctant to adopt more egalitarian, decentralised ways of interacting advocated in in-service education because they had vested interests in 'safe-talk'.

A richer contextualisation of the classroom data in terms of the ideology and structures of the wider apartheid society facilitated a reinterpretation of my findings. According to this reinterpretation, 'safe-talk' represents styles consistent with norms of interaction which teachers and students constituted as a means of avoiding the oppressive and demeaning constraints of apartheid educational systems.

One implication of this study is that teaching innovation at the micro level which is not accompanied by appropriate structural change at the macro level is unlikely to succeed. For those like myself who have been engaged in the difficult task of educational innovation within the constraints imposed by the apartheid society, it has been exciting to experience the dismantling of apartheid structures and the assembling of alternative structures. Hopefully, the latter will make it less necessary for teachers and students to engage in 'safe-talk'.

Note

1 I wish to acknowledge the contribution of Marianne Claude, who recorded the interactional data and assisted in the analysis of it, and that of my colleagues Ralph Adendorff and Nicole Geslin for their insightful comments and suggestions.

References

Cazden, C. 1979. Language in education: variation in the teacher-talk register. In J. E. Alatis and G. R. Tucker (Eds.) *Language in Public Life*, 144–62. Washington D.C.: Georgetown University Press.

Chick, J. K. 1985. The interactional accomplishment of discrimination in South Africa. *Language in Society* 14(3): 229–326.

Chick, J. K., and M. Claude, 1985. The Valley Trust English Language Project: research in progress. *Proceedings of the Fourth National Conference of the Southern African Applied Linguistics Association.* Johannesburg: University of the Witwatersrand.

Collins, J. 1987. Conversation and knowledge in bureaucratic settings. *Discourse Processes* 10: 303–19.

Condon, W. 1977. The relation of interactional synchrony to cognitive and emotional processes. In M. Key (Ed.) *The Relationship of Verbal and Nonverbal Communication,* 50–65. The Hague: Mouton.

Du Plessis, A., T. Du Pisani and S. Plekker. 1989. *Education and Manpower Development.* Bloemfontein: Research Institute for Education Planning.

Ellis, R. 1987. Using the English medium in African Schools. In D. Young (Ed.) *Bridging the Gap between Theory and Practice in English Second Language Teaching,* 82–99. Cape Town: Maskew Miller Longman.

Erickson, F. 1975. Gatekeeping and the melting pot: interaction in counselling encounters. *Harvard Educational Review* 45 (1): 44–70.

Erickson, F. 1976. Gatekeeping encounters: A social selection process. In P. R. Sanday (Ed.) *Anthropology and the Public Interest: Fieldwork and Theory,* 111–45. New York: Academic Press.

Gumperz, J. 1982a. *Discourse Strategies* (Studies in interactional sociolinguistics 1). Cambridge: Cambridge University Press.

Gumperz, J. 1982b. *Language and Social Identity* (Studies in interactional sociolinguistics 2). Cambridge: Cambridge University Press.

Hartshorne, K. 1987. Language policy in African education in South Africa 1910–1985, with particular reference to the issue of medium of instruction. In D. Young (Ed.) *Language: Planning and Medium of Education.* Rondebosch: Language Education Unit and SAALA.

Karabel, J. and A. H. Halsey (Eds.) 1977. *Power and Ideology in Education.* New York: Oxford University Press.

Kendon, A. 1973. The role of visible behaviour in the organization of social interaction. In M. Von Cranach and I. Vine (Eds.) *Social Communication and Movement,* 3–74. New York: Academic Press.

Kendon, A. 1979. Some theoretical and methodological aspects of the use of film in the study of social interaction. In G. Ginsberg (Ed.) *Emerging Strategies in Social Psychological Research,* 67–91. New York: John Wiley.

Kuper, A. 1985. *South Africa and the Anthropologist.* London/New York: Routledge and Kegan Paul.

Lakoff, R. 1979. Stylistic strategies with a grammar of style. In J. Oraisainn, M. Slater and L. Loeb Adler (Eds.) *Annals of the New York Academy of Sciences* 327: 53–78.

Levinson, S. C. 1983. *Pragmatics.* Cambridge: Cambridge University Press.

MacDonald, C. 1988. Teaching primary science in a second language: two teaching styles and their cognitive concomitants. In A. Weideman (Ed.) *Styles of Teaching and Styles of Learning.* Bloemfontein: SAALA.

MacDonald, C. 1990. *Crossing the Threshold into Standard Three*. Report of the Threshold Project. Human Sciences Research Council.

McDermott, R., K. Gospodinoff and J. Aaron. 1978. Criteria for an ethnographically adequate description of the concerted activities and their contexts. *Semiotica* 24: 245–75.

McDermott, R. and H. Tylbor. 1987. On the necessity of collusion in conversation. In L. Kedar (Ed.) *Power through Discourse*. Norwood, N.J.: Ablex.

Mehan, H. 1979. *Learning Lessons: Social Organization in the Classroom*. Cambridge, Mass.: Harvard University Press.

Ogbu, J. 1981. School ethnography: a multi-level approach. *Anthropology and Educational Quarterly* pp. 3–29.

Scheflin, A. E. 1973. *Communicating Structures: Analysis of a Psychotherapy Transaction*. Bloomington: Indiana University Press.

Schlemmer, L. and M. Bot. 1986. Education and race relations in South Africa. In G. Kendal (Ed.) *Education and the Diversity of Cultures*. Pietermaritzburg: University of Natal.

Scollon, R. and S. Scollon. 1983. Face in interethnic communication. In J. C. Richards and R. W. Schmidt (Eds.) *Language and Communication*, 156–88. London: Longman.

Sinclair, J. McH. and M. Coulthard. 1975. *Towards an Analysis of Discourse*. London: Oxford University Press.

Singh, R., J. Lele and G. Martohardjono. 1988. Communication in a multilingual society: some missed opportunities. *Language in Society* 17: 43–59.

South African Institute of Race Relations (SAIRR) Reports 87/88; 88/89.

Thembela, A. 1986. Some cultural factors which affect school education for blacks in South Africa. In G. Kendall (Ed.) *Education and the Diversity of Cultures*, 37–43. Pietermaritzburg: University of Natal.

3   English language education in Japan

Virginia LoCastro

Introduction

In 1989 and 1990, the Japanese Ministry of Education, *Mombusho*, released new courses for the study of foreign languages in junior and senior high school respectively (Ministry of Education 1989, 1990). 1993 was set as the implementation date for junior high schools and 1994 for senior high schools. One of the primary aims of the new curriculum[1], a change much discussed in English language teaching circles in Japan, is to require teachers to attend to speaking and listening skills in lessons, thereby placing greater emphasis on the attainment of communicative language ability by the learners. It is hoped that the ubiquitous grammar-translation approach, with its emphasis on reading and, to some extent, writing, will become less common. In addition, to cope with the aims of the new courses of study, teachers are expected to move in the direction of adoption of the communicative language teaching (CLT) approach. In the classical humanist educational tradition (Clark 1987), the innovations have been introduced in a characteristic top-down, power-coercive (White 1988) manner by the Ministry, which presumably anticipates a positive washback effect on Japanese language education. Japanese English language teaching (ELT) has a negative reputation for producing less than competent speakers of foreign languages and the Ministry, along with interested parties in other governmental agencies as well as in the private sector, wishes to improve the current situation in order to promote Japan's increasing role in the international arena.

Since the Meiji Restoration, following Admiral Perry's forced opening of Japan in 1863, English has been the most important foreign language for the majority of Japanese. It continues to hold this position, a direct result of the commercial and strategic role that English plays in the world today. In addition, English has been seen as the language of information and technology transfer, and, more recently, of modern media and culture. English is studied as *the* foreign language, in order to keep pace with the modern world, providing access to the latest scientific, medical and technological developments in the developed countries. It allows Japan to take a stronger role in world affairs.

In addition, English is perceived to be the language of intellectual pursuits. This belief comes from the fact that it was only an élite that pursued secondary and tertiary level education up until World War II and language training was a main part of their formal education. English language ability is perceived as being correlated with intelligence, and study of the language is said to promote intellectual and personal development.

The new courses of study issued by *Mombusho* are being welcomed by some as it is hoped that they will give classroom teachers more freedom within the framework of the mandated curriculum. It is expected that in turn this will lead to more progressive methodologies and practices being adopted. Indeed, sources inside the Ministry itself see the new curriculum as a means to force teachers to change their classroom practices and thereby better help learners to develop the ability to use the language to communicate competently.

Whether one views the new courses of study as a coercive or as a liberating document, there are serious limitations on the extent to which they can be seen as an instrument to achieve change in classroom behaviour. The prognosis for change is compromised once one begins to examine the wider sociocultural context.

The proposals for change

In the discussion which follows, three principal points are made. First of all,[2] the *Mombusho* document ignores the possible implications of the new curriculum for other aspects of the education system. Secondly, as Kennedy (1987) points out, unless the people affected by change (i.e. the teachers and the students) are engaged in the process at all steps along the way, the implemented curriculum is likely to diverge from the planned curriculum to a considerable degree. Thirdly, sociocultural variables need to be taken into account even when the language and terminology used in the Ministry documents are examined.

Let us now consider the extent to which the new courses of study fail to take into consideration features of the sociocultural context. An ethnography of English language education in Japan reveals examples of the context of culture (Halliday 1978: 65)[3] which render the implementation of this new curriculum difficult if not impossible.

Interlocking implications of the new curriculum

Bowers (1983) proposes a model for curriculum development projects through which he attempts to explore reasons for the mismatches which frequently occur between project planning and project implementation. He refers to the interlocking systems, professional and administrative, as being parts of a 'spider's web' (Bowers 1983: 100). This metaphor is useful in that it expresses the fact that change at any point in a curriculum development project can influence or affect other parts of the project, in much the same way that a light touch on one part of a spider's web causes other parts to move.

The spider's web metaphor can be applied to the situation of the new ELT courses of study in Japan. The positive effects of the new curriculum which the Ministry presumably expects are compromised owing to the lack of attention which has been given to other parts of the educational system.

A specific example of an interlocking factor relating to the new curriculum is that of teacher training. The Ministry of Education is promoting the adoption of the CLT approach, yet many of the teachers themselves still do not have a high level of communicative competence in the language. In addition, there is the general lack of teacher education. While the situation is beginning to change, with more and more Japanese language teachers seeking training – particularly overseas – it is still possible for a teacher to become certified to teach English on the basis of having passed a prefectural written examination. (This examination is more likely to test knowledge of concepts related to what is called 'moral education' rather than language teaching.) It is only now that proficiency in the language and knowledge of pedagogy, psychology and methodology are beginning to be considered as important as other aspects of formal education.

The Ministry of Education documents state that, as part of their first degree, university students preparing to become language teachers must undergo teacher training; however, the period of training may be as short as a two-week pre-service assignment in a junior or senior high school. Moreover, individual faculty members exercise their own discretion in drawing up the syllabuses for the courses in the departments where these students major (still often departments of American and British literature). Consequently, it appears that most students are not given the applied linguistics and TEFL courses that would be considered necessary from a Western professional-academic point of view.

It must be acknowledged that, particularly over the last five to ten years, there has been a great increase in the number of 'outside' workshops, short courses and seminars offered in Japan by such organisations as JALT (the Japan Association of Language Teachers), the British Council, and publishers. Individual teachers participate in these to overcome their lack of training. At the time of the writing of this chapter, there are also two American universities offering MA in TEFL pro-grammes which enable individuals to obtain a master's degree without having to go overseas. However, although attitudes are beginning to change, these programmes are not recognised by the Ministry of Education and individuals find resistance at their places of employment to their participating in outside, in-service training activities.

Active involvement as a prerequisite for change

Writers such as Kennedy (1987) and White (1988), who discuss innovation and change in education, and specifically in ELT, frequently draw attention to the need to involve those most affected by the proposed changes in the process of planning. Both Kennedy and White contrast power-coercive with normative–re-educative strategies of change; a normative re-educative approach emphasises the importance of collaboration and a process of deeper involvement and long-term development and openness towards change.

The rationale for Kennedy's (1987) preference for the normative re-educative approach is his contention that, without the involvement of the classroom practitioners who are to implement the proposed changes, there may be covert – and perhaps even overt – resistance to the changes for a number of reasons. One source of resistance may be a general, pervasive hostility towards the Ministry of Education. Another explanation, and one which is more important for the purposes of this discussion, is the fact that classroom practices reflect attitudes and beliefs about language and language learning that are embedded in the sociocultural context. Teaching is a 'cognitive, behavioural activity' (Kennedy 1987: 165) and both aspects – that is, both content and behaviour – reflect 'the society in which the change is to be implemented' (Kennedy 1987: 165).

Questions need to be asked, then, about the extent to which teachers – and perhaps students as well – have been involved in the recent curriculum changes in Japan. Apparently, the new courses of study from *Mombusho* have been written by planners inside the Ministry (possibly with consultants from universities). My informants indicate that there is no evidence of any needs analysis having been conducted or of any consultation with classroom teachers having been carried out.

This is predictable, since the Japanese sociocultural context (which is highly hierarchical and in which there is considerable governmental involvement in many areas of society, including education) would not permit any other approach. In other words, the Ministry's behaviour is within the social norms of Japan. Note that the analysis of students' needs as the major source of input for curriculum change has begun to take place in Anglo-American contexts only fairly recently. Therefore, that student needs analysis is absent from curriculum design in Japan should not surprise us. However, the fact that classroom teachers were also not involved needs to be acknowledged and taken into consideration in evaluating the possible effects of the new curriculum.

Text and interpretation

Resistance to innovation may arise as a result of conflicts between that classroom behaviour which is seen as desirable in the new curriculum and current practices reflecting cultural norms. In addition, the text of the new courses of study may reveal conflicts between the planned changes and the established norms. The *Mombusho*-produced curriculum gives evidence of having been written with the best of intentions, and shows an awareness of current trends in language learning in the Anglo-American context. The overall aims are impressive and incorporate the objective of Japan becoming 'internationalised' through language learning as well as through learning about other cultures in language classes. Throughout the texts, attention is given to the importance of expressing 'one's own personal response' (Ministry of Education 1990: 1). This indicates an awareness of the tendency of Japanese students to avoid oral communication, especially when asked to engage in activities as individuals.

However, despite the laudable intentions, the curriculum remains content-oriented – specifically grammar-oriented – paying only lip service to communicative skills. The underlying attitudes held by the Japanese educational system about language and language learning are reflected in the courses of study. A graded syllabus is viewed as important, the grading based on moving from simple to difficult language structures. Unfortunately, there is little help for teachers in this regard since a clear outline of what the graded syllabus might be for each level is not provided.

In spite of the use of phrases indicating some awareness of communicative language use, one of the aims of the 'language activities' is 'to speak without missing important things, by arranging what one intends to say' (Ministry of Education 1990). One implication here is that successful communication depends on organising elements of sentences in 'correct' order. It is common practice for junior and senior high school teachers of English to provide an English cue or a Japanese phrase or sentence, so as to elicit from learners an English sentence containing the transformed cue or the translation equivalent of the Japanese prompt. This is called *bun o tsukuru*, 'making sentences'[4]. This suggests that Japanese ELT is influenced by a particular culturally-loaded perspective on language behaviour in classrooms. For all the generalised comments made about developing the learners' 'basic ability to understand spoken and written English and to express oneself in English' (Ministry of Education 1990:1), there is no definition of 'communicative ability' articulated in the courses of study.

Thus, it seems that classroom teachers were not consulted during the process of planning and drawing up the new curriculum. Moreover, the document seems to lack specificity in its stated aims, and in fact there appears to be a gross mismatch between the supposed aims and the sociocultural context. Indeed the planners themselves may be unaware of the extent to which the Japanese sociocultural context and all of its interlocking elements make the adoption of notions and concepts from the Anglo-American applied linguistic setting difficult, perhaps impossible. Borrowed terms can be translated, yet the meanings cannot be transferred without extra training, experience and effort, due to the great differences in the sociocultural contexts.

A further example, related to the notion of communicative competence, is the possibility that 'communication' itself may not be a universally shared concept; that is, it may have different meanings in different cultures. In a hierarchical society such as Japan, social variables such as status, age and gender must be taken into consideration when one interacts with others, as those variables require that obligatory lexical and morphological choices be made in utterance production. The same variables may be less salient in the avowedly more egalitarian Anglo-American societies and, moreover, they may be manifested by alternative linguistic and paralinguistic markers. What may appear to be common-sense notions – 'communication' and 'interaction' – thus become problematic with the unexamined adoption of Anglo-American applied linguistic concepts into cultural contexts whose underlying values and belief systems may entail different interpretations. Therefore, the possible misuse of notions from Anglo-American applied linguistics in the Japanese document has to be taken into consideration.[5]

Clearly, neither the lack of involvement of classroom practitioners nor the borrowing of terminology from another sociocultural context for mapping onto indigenous concepts, resulting in semantic mismatches, is without precedent.[6] Nevertheless, these problems do raise questions, both concerning the likely success of the recent innovations and about the extent to which change is genuinely desired.

It is to this latter question that we turn now. An analysis of ELT in its sociocultural context helps to provide an answer.

The sociocultural context

In order to consider the extent of the mismatch between imported terminology and the reality of the situation onto which this terminology is mapped, let us look in detail at three significant aspects of the Japanese sociocultural context. The first of these is the importance of preparation for examinations as a motivating factor in learning English. We turn then to a microanalysis of behaviour in a 'typical' class. This is a composite view, based on evidence collected in a number of English language classes in the Japanese education system. This is followed by a discussion of some macro-level influences on classroom practices and behaviour related to language and language study, in which attention is focused on interactional patterns. The methodology adopted here is qualitative and ethnographic; I base my descriptions and interpretations on evidence from numerous sources, including my own observations as a participant observer for over a decade, as well as from both scholarly and popular press articles, and from informal discussions and unstructured interviews with colleagues and students.[7]

Reasons for studying English

Today, although English is not a requirement for junior or senior high school graduation, virtually all Japanese learners in the public and private education systems study general English throughout their six years of junior and senior high school (for three hours a week in junior high school and five to six hours a week in senior high school). This description is true for all secondary schools, irrespective of the standing of the school. For example, night high schools – for students who are in employment or, more commonly, those who failed to gain admission to a regular high school (see Rohlen 1983) due to low academic ability – still offer general academic English classes rather than more ESP-oriented English classes, or even other subjects, to complement the more vocational nature of the curriculum.

In addition to the importance of English as the language most needed for wider communication (see Dubin and Olshtain 1986), there is another explanation for the popularity of English. That is, English is a *de facto* requirement as almost all entrance examinations for senior high schools and for colleges and universities test achievement in the language. Moreover, many of the large companies examine job applicants' language ability and/or require that applicants sit for some standardised proficiency test, such as the TOEFL or TOEIC tests, or a Japanese-made achievement test, the STEP test. Thus, in addition to the need for English language skills for communication outside Japan and the status attached to such ability (a symbol of an educated, intelligent individual), there are instrumental reasons for the study of English. It may be argued that it is the pressure of having to sit for the English language sections of the university entrance examinations in particular that is the source of motivation for most Japanese learners of English. Indeed informants almost overwhelmingly cite passing exams as the primary motive for studying English, particularly during junior and senior high school.

Composed essentially of grammar, vocabulary, pronunciation and translation questions, the examinations are purposely difficult, based on a view of language as primarily written, literary and sterilised in nature. The spoken language is considered ungrammatical and not worthy of serious study. Given that most if not all of the examinations are written by academics – the same who educate future teachers and who devalue applied linguistics as secondary to linguistics – it is not difficult to understand why a variety of written English significantly different from the contemporary language used for everyday communicative purposes predominates.

The fact that passing examinations is the greatest source of motivation for English language study – in addition to the character of the examinations and the variety of language used in them – results in a situation such that the intended redressing of the imbalance – in favour of an emphasis on all four skills – found in the new *Mombusho* curriculum may be without effect. The entrance examination system can be said to have a deleterious washback effect on methodologies and teacher education; classroom teachers are under pressure to teach 'exam English'. Unless the university examination system is changed, many feel that the new curriculum will be virtually ignored, particularly at the senior high school level.

There are also financial concerns with regard to the entrance examinations. The test writers have something to gain, as well as the publishers who sell numerous test preparation manuals and volumes of copies of old tests. Test preparation academies attract large numbers of students during after-school hours and at weekends. Moreover, the universities themselves also depend for part of their annual income on the fees which aspiring entrants have to pay to sit for the examinations. It might be argued that one way of resolving this problem might be to maintain the examination system itself whilst the types of question could perhaps be changed. Nevertheless, the present system is well entrenched and very resistant to change.

It may be argued that educational systems all over the world exist for the purpose of maintaining the *status quo* and for teaching obedience to and acceptance of the power structures present in a particular society.

The socialisation of learners, with the goal of training them into becoming productive, law-abiding citizens, may be the not-so-hidden agenda of formal education.

The particular manifestations of this hidden curriculum in Japan still show the impact of Confucian influences from China. Formal education is for the general good, with a strong de-emphasis on individualism. The primary schools aim to promote egalitarianism; pupils are not tracked by ability level and emphasis is placed on learning to work with others. Indeed, some people in Japan are in favour of starting formal education at an earlier age for the purpose of teaching children as soon as possible to function in groups. These days, with more one-child families, and the increasing isolation of children due to urbanisation, social planners are concerned about tendencies towards individualism.

In spite of the egalitarian atmosphere present in the primary school system, it is with entry into the junior high schools that the situation changes drastically and the future lives of students are virtually set depending on the junior high school to which they gain admission. According to Rohlen (1983), the gate-keeping function of junior high school admission contributes to the achievement of the essential aim of the Japanese educational system, which is the production of an élite which can run the country by occupying top level positions in the Ministries. The ability to do well in the English language components of the examinations is one of the important elements in this process of selection. This training of an élite has always been the *de facto* purpose of the Japanese educational system and thus it continues to be the means to assure the maintenance of the *status quo*.

Another – related – influence on the education system results from a decision made during the Meiji Era to use the system to promote Japanese nationalism and emperor worship. Van Wolferen (1989: 82) maintains that the Japanese education system today imparts an ideology 'favourable to the System', an ideology of Japaneseness, characterised by submission to the existing socio-political order. This ideology, called *Nihonjinron* (see also Miller 1982), was developed in the nineteenth century and permits the learning of content related to the material achievements of the USA and Europe. However, the 'Japanese "Spirit"' must be maintained 'intact' (van Wolferen 1989: 380) and part of this spirit is the belief that the Japanese cannot learn foreign languages and cannot understand texts in their original versions. Too much access and exposure to other forms of thought are viewed by those in power as dangerous. The folk belief that the Japanese must learn languages through their own language appears in the Japanese-specific approach to the study of Chinese: the written characters are given a Japanese pronunciation and are 'read', by reorganising them to fit Japanese word

48

order (see the comments on the *Yakudoku*[8] method later in this chapter). This is necessary for comprehension to take place, it is believed.

Classroom behaviour

Let us now consider a typical English language class taught by Japanese teachers in the public school system. This ethnographic description is based on some thirty classroom observations over a three-year period and on unstructured interviews with teachers and other colleagues.

In a great majority of cases (80–90% according to some unpublished prefectural board of education surveys), Japanese is the language of instruction in the typically teacher-fronted, teacher-centred classes. There are on average 47 students per class, sitting in six rows with individual desks and chairs, facing the front of the room where the teacher stands or sits on a raised podium. In junior and senior high schools, the teacher may use a microphone, although this practice is more common in the cram schools and universities where the classes may have one hundred or more students.

The strong preference for the use of Japanese to teach English occurs for several reasons. Clearly the grammar-translation approach does not require that the teacher be a proficient speaker of the language; knowledge of content, including linguistic content, is all that is needed. Competence in the spoken language is not necessarily even valued (although this attitude has begun to change with teachers now starting to give positive attention to spoken language proficiency). Yet even Japanese speakers of English who are virtually bilingual opt to use Japanese, according to one informant so as to 'create and maintain good rapport with students.'

In terms of methodology, the grammar-translation approach is by far the most common. A typical lesson consists of the teacher's checking the learners' sentence by sentence translations of a text assigned for homework, the choral reading aloud sentence by sentence of the English version, and the checking of other homework and/or of answers to other exercises from the prescribed textbook or from teacher-made worksheets. There is endless repetition and reading aloud with little evidence that learners understand the texts.

There appears to be little awareness of the discoursal dimensions of language; one finds constant reference to 'sentences' and, indeed, student writing consists of single sentences translated from an original Japanese version. It is common for the teacher to give an explanation with a commentary in Japanese for any newly introduced passage from the textbook or other sources. The sometimes lengthy explanations, translations and commentary are believed to be necessary for the learners to understand the English. Thus the teacher's method is heavily didactic, utilising a deductive approach, with all necessary information conveyed by the teacher to the students, reflecting clearly the classical humanist tradition (Clark 1987). English and other foreign languages are taught as a content subject, as Latin and chemistry often are in the Anglo-American context.

Within the discourse of the teacher, one finds indications of careful attention to formal grammar, word use and pronunciation. Evidence of this can be seen in the stress placed on phonetics and pronunciation exercises, which are reported to take up to 20 minutes of a 50-minute class. Fine points of syntax, based on usage not use, are frequent topics of discussion among teachers and are also the focus of unsolicited student questions. Perfect grammatical accuracy is the objective and, consequently, learners avoid participating in class so as to avoid the chance of making a mistake. Teachers are said to prefer to use Japanese at least partially to avoid the possible loss of face that they might incur should they speak English incorrectly. According to van Wolferen (1989: 379), a tendency towards perfectionism can be said to be a characteristic of Japanese culture in general; this is believed to stem from early Shinto influences which include a belief in the perfectibility of human beings.

The goal of the teacher is to implement the *Mombusho* curriculum as manifested in the prescribed textbooks. Until recently, the mandated curriculum had as its implicit primary aim the development of the ability to read and translate English phrases and sentences, although Ministry of Education officials were reluctant to state so directly. Since the recent introduction of a listening comprehension component in the entrance examination for the University of Tokyo – the most prestigious higher education institution and the yardstick against which almost all Japanese universities measure themselves – teachers have made more effort to use materials to help their students improve their listening skills. The new courses of study from *Mombusho* explicitly require equal attention to all the four skills, thereby proportionately increasing the load on the teachers and learners. The new curriculum, nevertheless, remains predominantly structural and the only reported change with regard to the linguistic aims is a decrease in the number of structures which junior high school students are expected to master. Presumably, the 'displaced' language structures will have to be dealt with at the senior high school level.

Thus, the linguistic content load can be considerable and little attention is paid officially to the fact that not all learners are able to achieve the stated objectives for each grade level. In addition to an unwillingness to track students on the basis of their ability (due to the desire to maintain equality of opportunity), teachers find it difficult to hit the right level, with some students unable to keep up and others having little to challenge them.

This would normally mean a heavy enough burden on the individual teacher; however, the situation is made even more complicated due to the fact that a considerable number of the students may be attending evening and weekend 'catch-up' classes. Parents are willing to spend considerable sums of money to ensure that their children gain admission to prestigious universities, as a diploma from these institutions assures good job and marriage prospects and high social standing. Moreover, these after-hour schools are deemed necessary given that the language classes in all but the best senior high schools do not prepare the learners adequately for university entrance exams. So a situation may arise where a high proportion of the learners in a class in a public school may be present only to meet the legal requirements of attendance, whereas the lessons are seen as irrelevant and deficient.

Emphasis is placed on linguistic content and lexis, in order to provide the foundation for the development of reading comprehension, which has been the actual, unstated goal of English language teaching in the public school system. However, reading has another interpretation within the ELT context in Japan. First of all, it tends to be regarded as synonymous with reading aloud. Experts on reading skills, such as Smith (1982), go so far as to assert that reading aloud is counter-productive, causing the learners to focus on individual sounds and words and so preventing them from activating their knowledge in a way which is essential if global meaning is to be grasped. Yet the notion of reading in Japanese ELT is that it is primarily recitation, i.e. repeated reading aloud chorally or individually. In the new course of study for senior high schools, 'To read aloud in a manner appropriate to the content' (Ministry of Education 1990: 6) is given as one of the five 'Language activities'. In the first year of junior high school, the reading aloud of words, phrases, sentences, and strings of sentences are the only recommended 'Language activities' (Ministry of Education 1989: 2) for that level.

Secondly, in the belief that Japanese learners cannot silently read English sentences 'directly', they are taught a particular technique, the *Yakudoku* method. This is a kind of mental exercise which requires that the words in the English sentence be mentally rearranged and put into Japanese word order for the meaning to be grasped. It is often argued that this has a permanent negative effect on many Japanese learners of English.

Both of these interpretations of 'reading' – reading aloud and

Yakudoku – are deeply rooted in the beliefs that the Japanese process information and messages differently from other peoples and thus that they must learn languages in ways appropriate to their cognitive processing strategies. The aim, as one informant claims, is to make English '100% comprehensible in Japanese'.

Interactional patterns

An ethnographic study of a language classroom would be incomplete if it did not pay some attention to non-verbal aspects of classroom behaviour and interactional patterns. These are both sites of covert or hidden manifestations of values and beliefs current in the wider society. The classroom may be a special environment which differs from other social settings, yet it is a microcosm in which most people in the developed world today spend a considerable amount of time during their formative years; for this reason, it cannot be ignored.

A typical class in Japan will start and end with one student calling the others to order; all stand to bow and formally greet the teacher, who also usually bows, standing. Many classrooms maintain the practice that the student who is responding to a teacher's solicit or is asking a question must stand to do so. In general, however, an overwhelming proportion of class time is composed of teacher talk. During a 50-minute class, just one student may ask the teacher an unsolicited question. The language of the teacher is primarily transactional in that the aim is to convey information to the learners.

In observations, I have noted that at least some teachers adopt what I will call pseudo-interactional language. The teacher asks a question, apparently addressing it to a student, but then answers it, makes an assessment or comment on the answer, and then gives an acknowledgement in the form of a common listener response such as '*Hai, so desu*' (Yes, that is so). Thus, it is possible to find an episode of spoken, interactional language composed of a four-part exchange:

A: SOLICIT
B: RESPONSE
C: ASSESSMENT
D: ACKNOWLEDGEMENT

However, the teacher in effect plays all four roles. This reminds one of the *benshi*, a figure of early Japanese silent movies who would provide a running commentary on the plot and play the characters as well.

Two features of this phenomenon demand comment. Firstly, we find here a conversational or pseudo-conversational pattern that differs from the usual two-part adjacency pair structure which is discussed in the literature on conversational analysis (see, among others, Sacks, Schegloff and Jefferson 1978). In addition, this pattern is adopted by the teacher in a monologue form to engage in pseudo-interactional language behaviour, complete with listener response, reflecting interactional structures which are valued in Japan. The significance of the teacher's use of a pseudo-conversational pattern in teacher talk requires sociocultural, grounded analysis. One interpretation of the teacher's behaviour is that, due to the hierarchical nature of Japanese society, student-teacher interactions are not expected in classrooms. Indeed there is considerable evidence to support this interpretation; for example, Japanese students will commonly wait until after class to talk with the teacher, if they have questions. However, it is also possible that the teacher is playing a socioculturally valued role, not dissimilar to that played by the *benshi* in the silent movies. The teacher, like the *benshi*, is seen as the commentator, as the knower of all information, imparting that knowledge to learners, enlightening them, out of the belief that without that role being performed the learners would be unable to understand.

It is here that another mismatch appears between the overtly stated intentions of the *Mombusho* curricula and actual practice with reference to communicative language teaching. The lack of interaction between teacher and student, and between and among students, as well as the heavy use of Japanese during the lesson, raises questions concerning the implementation of the communicative language teaching approach, now advocated by *Mombusho*. Long and Porter (1985) claim that, in order for the comprehensible input which learners are presumably exposed to in language classrooms to become intake, the learners must be able to use the target language to negotiate meaning with native and non-native speakers of the language. It is clear that CLT – with its emphasis on information-gap activities and role plays, simulations and unstructured tasks – necessarily requires that the learners use the target language to negotiate meaning in order to complete the assigned activities. Yet, it should be obvious that the typical ELT classroom in Japan precludes CLT:

• The target language is not used in general, either by the teacher or the learners, except perhaps for greetings and some fixed expressions. Thus the comprehensible input is inadequate, coming mostly from non-authentic written texts.
• Interactions which would permit or require language use for negotiation of meaning tend not to occur in the classroom, *even in Japanese*, due to expectations of what constitutes permissible behaviour in that environment.

In a culture which views questions of clarification as a means of showing disapproval, and perhaps also of implying that there is confrontation between co-participants (LoCastro 1990), it is understandable that Japanese learners shy away from other than monosyllabic responses to their teacher's display questions. Add to that the strong preference for avoidance of speaking English with each other (Beebe and Takahashi 1989), and one is left with serious questions about the role of formal foreign language instruction in the Japanese educational system.

In discussions, Japanese learners of English will give unsolicited comments to the effect that they do not expect to learn much language in institutional language classrooms. This attitude is reflected in the strong preference for content-oriented English classes in private language schools: adult learners shy away from pure language classes in favour of 'current' English ones where they can study international events through the reading of English language newspapers and magazines. All this leads one to conclude that language classrooms, as part of the overall educational system, may be the context for the learning of other things, and that ELT is subordinate to the learning of culturally valued, normative behaviour.

This ethnographic analysis of ELT classrooms serves to illuminate areas that are problematic with reference to the new curriculum. The teachers' linguistic and pedagogical abilities, current practices reflecting the culture's view of language and language learning, and permissible and valued behavioural patterns all point to areas of tension, conflict, and mismatch with the new curriculum. What then are the prospects for change in ELT in Japan?

Towards change

The multiple, interactive forces influencing the Japanese English language classroom reflect the internal, covert polemic concerning the extent to which Japan in general and the educational system in particular should or should not 'modernise'. It is not surprising that the Ministry of Education's new courses of study should be vaguely written, unclear documents. Some would argue that Japan has already modernised and that it is only a matter of time before the educational system catches up with other sectors of society. Yet, in all societies, the educational system is one of the most conservative sectors and is slow to change. Although some change is occurring, it is taking place only slowly in ELT in Japan. There is a particularly tightly woven web of influences in the Japanese context which makes change problematic, as we have seen above in looking at the mismatches between current practice and the new courses of study.

It is not surprising that today the Ministry of Education remains a powerful conservative means to control the socialisation of Japanese individuals. Some would go so far as to say that it is in fact the Liberal Democratic Party (LDP), the party in power from 1954 to 1993, which has been the real source of power over the education system and that the *Mombusho* has simply responded to pressure from factions within the LDP. Some of the business-oriented interests presumably favour better, more effective language training to facilitate commercial interests, while more conservative elements, which see the Japanese national identity as being threatened by increasing foreign influence, seek the maintenance of the *status quo*.

Thus there appear to be forces within the Japanese government and within Japanese society in general which genuinely seek changes which will lead to competent speakers of foreign languages being produced by the education system. Nonetheless, there are clearly others who fear such changes. Both groups include individuals who are influential at top levels of the government as well as classroom teachers. The fact that the Ministry of Education has produced a document which incorporates some more progressive applied linguistic notions may indicate more favourable attitudes towards change in Japanese ELT. However, my analysis has identified an apparent lack of awareness of the interlocking elements of the context in which the document is to be used, as well as mismatches between the document and the sociocultural context. This gives rise to questions concerning the prognosis for actual change. Clearly change can only occur within the Japanese sociocultural context.

Conclusions

In this chapter, I have presented an analysis of English language teaching in Japan, specifically with reference to the new courses of study for the teaching of foreign languages in junior and senior high schools. In much of the literature on curriculum renewal, there are examples of outside experts being employed to help Ministries of Education engage in innovation of their language curricula. In the case of Japan, the *Mombusho* document can be said to reflect the attitudes and beliefs of that culture, since it has been written by the Ministry itself.

A number of points have been made. The first concerns the interlocking nature of aspects of the education system such that a proposed change in one area of the system necessitates changes in other parts of the system. It has also been observed that planning for curriculum renewal needs to involve those who are to implement the changes, not only because they, the teachers, may otherwise resist the mandated changes, but also because the changes may necessitate the re-education of teachers so that they will change their classroom practices and their attitudes and beliefs about language and language teaching. Thirdly, attention has been drawn to the notion of potential mismatch between the planned curriculum and current practices and classroom behaviour, through an ethnographic microanalysis of ELT classrooms in Japan. Finally, macro-level sociocultural features have been considered with reference to the potential for the proposed changes. Implicitly, throughout, this chapter addresses the conflicts and tensions between the theory, embodied in the new courses of study, and practice.

Ultimately, the basic question concerns the role which English – or other foreign languages – can and should play in the life of the Japanese people. The more active role for English, implied in the new curriculum, seems to raise issues related to culturally valued interactional patterns as well as views of what constitutes language learning, indeed language itself. These are issues which can only be addressed by 'inside' experts, working within their own sociocultural, historical, and economic contexts.

Notes

1 Although one might argue for the use of the plural here – there being junior and senior high school courses of study – the new courses of study are nevertheless commonly referred to as 'the new curriculum.'

2 This listing of the main points to be made in the chapter is artificial in so far as the analytical process is concerned. An ethnographic perspective has been adopted in much of this discussion.

3 'Context of culture' is used here, following Halliday (1978:65ff), to refer to the non-linguistic, 'macro'-level 'situational factors' which influence and constrain language use.

4 *Bun* can be translated as 'composition', 'writings', 'essay' or 'style', as well as 'sentence', leaving its meaning in the Japanese original ambiguous. However, the English version of the document, which uses the term 'sentences', reflects current classroom practice in most junior and senior high schools

5 Note that I am using the English translation.

6 Nor is this the first time that such a 'reinterpretation' of notions and concepts from outside sources has occurred. Nakamura (1964) cites numerous examples of how early Buddhist texts from China were translated into Japanese and, in the process of that act of translation, the text was changed to suit the Japanese context and intentions.

7 Note that, as a relative outsider to the Japanese educational system, I

can take only an etic point of view. Yet I would argue that this is a legitimate point of view, as anthropologists such as Geertz maintain. Both insider (emic) and outsider (etic) perspectives are necessary and useful in order to generate a richer picture of a context; each contributes different kinds of information, one compensating for the lacks in insight of the other.

8 The *Yakudoku* method for reading English is undoubtedly related to the way in which Chinese is 'read'. The main difference is that any time Chinese characters are used in Japan (for example, for Chinese family names) only the Japanese reading or pronunciation is used. With English, when it is read aloud or spoken, the pronunciation that is used follows native-speaker norms.

References

Beebe, L., and T. Takahashi. 1989. Do you have a bag? Social status and patterned variation in second language acquisition. In S. Gass, C. Madden, D. Preston, and L. Selinker (Eds.) *Variation in Second Language Acquisition Volume 1: Discourse and Pragmatics*, 103–25. Clevedon, Avon: Multilingual Matters.

Bowers, R. 1983. Project planning and performance. In C. Brumfit (Ed.) *Language Teaching Projects for the Third World*, 99–120. (ELT Documents 116.) Oxford: Pergamon Press.

Clark, J. J. 1987. *Curriculum Renewal in School Foreign Language Learning*. Oxford: Oxford University Press.

Dubin, F. and E. Olshtain. 1986. *Course Design: Developing Programs and Materials for Language Learning*. Cambridge: Cambridge University Press.

Geertz, C. 1973. Thick description: Toward an interpretative theory of culture. In *The Interpretation of Culture*, 3–32. New York: Basic Books.

Halliday, M. A. K. 1978. *Language as a Social Semiotic: The Social Interpretation of Language and Meaning*. London: Edward Arnold.

Kennedy, C. 1987. Innovating for a change: Teacher development and innovation. *English Language Teaching Journal* 41 (3): 163–70.

LoCastro, V. 1990. Intercultural pragmatics: A Japanese-American case study. Lancaster University: Unpublished Ph.D. thesis.

Long, M. E. and A. P. Porter. 1985. Groupwork, interlanguage talk, and second language acquisition. *TESOL Quarterly* 19 (2): 207–28.

Miller, R. 1982. *Japan's Modern Myth: The Language and Beyond*. New York: Weatherhill.

Ministry of Education. 1989. *Course of Study for Junior High Schools: Foreign Languages – English*. Tokyo: Shoseki.

Ministry of Education. 1990. *Course of Study for Senior High Schools: Foreign Languages – English*. Tokyo: Shoseki.

Nakamura, H. 1964. *Ways of Thinking of Eastern Peoples: India, China, Tibet, Japan*. Honolulu: The University Press of Hawaii.

Rohlen, T. P. 1983. *Japan's High Schools*. Berkeley: University of California Press.

Sacks, H., E. Schegloff and G. Jefferson. 1978. A simplest systematics for the organization of turn-taking in conversation. In J. Schenkein (Ed.) *Studies in the Organization of Conversational Interaction*, 7–55. New York: Academic Press.

Smith, F. 1982. *Understanding Reading: A Psycholinguistic Analysis of Reading and Learning to Read*. New York: Holt, Rinehart and Winston.

van Wolferen, K. 1989. *The Enigma of Japanese Power: People and Politics in a Stateless Nation*. New York: Alfred A. Knopf.

White, R.V. 1988. *The ELT Curriculum: Design, Innovation, and Management*. Oxford: Basil Blackwell.

Part 2 **Society and the university classroom**

The four chapters in Part 2 of the collection consider aspects of behaviour in language classrooms in universities in different parts of the world. In Chapter 4, Coleman examines first year undergraduate classes in a university in Indonesia, while Holliday's study in Chapter 5 is based on data gathered in 70 Egyptian university classes. Shamim, in Chapter 6, looks at the problems of introducing innovation in one postgraduate class at a university in Pakistan. Muchiri adopts a rather different approach in Chapter 7 and looks at examination practices and beliefs in a university in Kenya.

Coleman presents a picture of a number of English language lecturers and their students behaving in a consistent and apparently harmonious way, but doing things which, as an outsider, he at first found difficult to understand. He notes that many other foreign observers have had equal difficulty in making sense of this behaviour. Coleman then describes the process by which he came to an interpretation of the phenomenon; his conclusion is that the English language lesson is contributing to a long and very intensive socialisation process. Finally, he explores the implications of this interpretation, with particular reference to the question of introducing innovation and syllabus reform.

The principal analogy which Coleman employs is with traditional Javanese shadow puppet performances. He argues that there is a striking parallel between the language teacher's performance and that of the deeply revered *dalang* or puppet master. (As we saw in Chapter 3, LoCastro also draws on cultural events as a way of helping her to understand teacher behaviour in Japanese classrooms.)

Coleman suggests that if our purpose in the English language classroom is really to promote learning, then 'tinkering with the ritual' is unlikely to be productive. Instead, only two radical routes are open to us. One is to reject the 'teaching spectacle' altogether and seek to find ways of achieving 'learning festivals' (Coleman 1987) such that teachers and learners alike are prevented from falling back into their original roles. However, this approach carries risks, since – as we have seen – the traditional classroom behaviour apparently has a social function. The alternative, then, is to exploit those informal and unofficial learning procedures which the most successful learners have started to develop independently behind the scenes, as it were, of the public spectacle (see also Coleman 1991, 1993).

Holliday's discussion deals with a relatively unusual situation in which local and expatriate teachers were teaching classes in the same institution at the same time. What Holliday found was that the local Egyptian teachers appeared to achieve a mode of interaction with their students which was more harmonious, more comfortable, more successful, than was that used by their expatriate colleagues. However, this held true only so long as class size remained below approximately 50. In the larger classes, it was the expatriate teachers, using a more 'rational' approach, who appeared to survive more successfully. Holliday explains this in terms of a *Gemeinschaft/Gesellschaft* distinction; that is to say, between a 'small' society in which traditional forms of behaviour are found and a 'large' society which employs rationalisation in determining behaviour.

Holliday hypothesises that, were the Egyptian lecturers to adopt a combined traditional-rational approach in dealing with their very large classes, they would be even more successful than the expatriate lecturers, because the latter can never hope to achieve the same rapport with students, based on shared cultural understanding, which the local teachers enjoy. Moreover, he suggests that 'tissue rejection' (Hoyle 1970; Holliday 1991, 1992, 1994) is likely to occur if the expatriate innovation does not become rooted in traditional forms of behaviour.

In common with the other contributors, then, Holliday sees the importance of tracking the link between beliefs and practices current in wider society and those to be found within the four walls of the classroom. Holliday is ultimately optimistic: he believes that there is scope for achieving a compromise between the traditional and the innovative which will be of value in those contexts where a purely traditional approach has begun to break down.

Shamim's chapter, on the other hand, illustrates in microcosm the danger which several contributors to this collection are warning us of, and that is the imposition on one educational system of ideas taken from another alien system. In Shamim's case, she attempted to introduce a 'communicative' methodology in a small postgraduate Linguistics and Language Teaching class in her university in Karachi, hoping that in this way the students would abandon the silent, non-contributory note-taking role which they normally played. To her dismay, however, she encountered very strong resistance to the change, to the extent that students boycotted lectures. Gradually, as examinations approached,

Shamim found that she was taking on a more authoritarian role. As she gradually compromised her stance and returned to a more traditional mode of behaviour so the students became more relaxed and more satisfied with her teaching.

Shamim describes her attempt to make sense of the student resistance to change. Her conclusion is that this resistance was a consequence of the 'disjunction' between, on the one hand, 'the beliefs and assumptions of the learners derived from the culture of the wider community' and, on the other, the 'culture' of the innovation. She shows very clearly that there are direct links between the norms of Pakistani society (family life, in particular) and the norms of classroom behaviour. In this case study, the disruption of these norms brought about by the teacher's innovation was so great that it outweighed the deference which students normally pay to their lecturers. (As we saw in Chapter 2, Chick's study was itself prompted by his observation that classroom teachers and students appeared to be reluctant to give up their traditional mode of classroom interaction and were resistant to what he considered to be 'more egalitarian' forms of interaction associated with the communicative approach.)

Shamim comments that in most language programmes 'learner acceptance of a proposed change is largely taken for granted.' However, her study disproves the easy assumption that an innovation brought about at the grassroots level, in the classroom, by the teacher who is responsible for that class, will necessarily be successful. Shamim points out, then, that we need also to pay very close attention to the 'dynamics' of change and the institutional and wider cultural contexts in which change is to take place. Ultimately, she argues, we should be looking for indigenous solutions to educational problems which are 'sensitive to the culture of the community'.

There is then some coincidence of views between Shamim's contribution, Holliday's proposal that change must be a compromise between the 'traditional' and the 'modern', and the second of Coleman's two suggestions – i.e. that educational innovation must be founded on what learners are already doing 'behind the scenes'.

Whilst Coleman, Holliday and Shamim focus on university classroom events, Muchiri chooses to look at the effect of national and institutional cultures on university examinations. She begins, like LoCastro in Chapter 3, by providing a historical perspective, and shows that the Kenyan higher education system appears superficially to resemble the British one because of its colonial origins. Over time, however, Kenyan society has changed and so the demands and expectations of that society of its higher education have also changed; what we find, therefore, is a form which still appears to resemble its British model, yet the functions of the British and Kenyan systems have now diverged quite considerably from each other.

The picture which Muchiri presents is a very complicated one. Not only are there conflicts between the values of traditional society and those which are current within universities, but there may also be yet other values, expressed in the National Goals of Education, which do not mesh comfortably either with indigenous beliefs or with international academic conventions.

Muchiri identifies a number of instances in which there is a lack of fit between the values of Kenyan society – values which, not surprisingly, the students bring with them to the university – and the practices that are taken as standard within the institution. One such clash arises from the expectation that those members of a family who happen to be blessed with wealth must share their riches with poorer family members; yet if a particularly bright young person takes a public examination on behalf of a less brilliant relative – so sharing his or her expertise with the less well endowed – that charitable behaviour is interpreted by the system as a criminal act.

Muchiri recognises that Kenyan society is changing rapidly, and that universities in Kenya are also experiencing a period of upheaval. The situation which she describes is, therefore, one in which considerable negotiation over a long period of time will have to take place before a state of equilibrium is reached. One of her conclusions is that the institutions need to look closely at the informal practices which students have developed, to see whether these can be incorporated into the officially sanctioned institutional procedures; this, as we have seen, coincides with one of Coleman's proposals. Muchiri also suggests, in a complementary way, that just as institutions need to find out more about what their students do, so they need to make their values explicit to students, *particularly* if it can be predicted that students come from indigenous societies which do not share those values.

Although Muchiri restricts her discussion to the context of Kenya, she is in effect dealing with the movement of individuals from one socio-cultural environment to another. In Part 3 of this collection, Ballard discusses the same issue, but looks at it in an international dimension, examining the problems which arise when academics transfer from one part of the world to another.

References

Coleman, H. 1987. Teaching spectacles and learning festivals. *English Language Teaching Journal* 41 (2): 97–103.

Coleman, H. 1991. Learners' strategies in the context of tertiary-level large classes. In British Council (Ed.) *Proceedings of the Conference on Academic Communication Skills in African Universities*, 44–57. Nairobi: The British Council.

Coleman, H. 1993. Investigating and exploiting what learners do in large classes. Paper presented at the International Conference on Communication Skills for Nigerian Federal Universities, Nsukka, Nigeria, 29–31 March 1993.

Holliday, A. R. 1991. Dealing with tissue rejection in EFL projects: The role of an ethnographic means analysis. Lancaster University: Unpublished Ph.D. thesis.

Holliday, A. R. 1992. Tissue rejection and informal orders in ELT projects: Collecting the right information. *Applied Linguistics* 13 (4): 404–24.

Holliday, A. R. 1994. *Appropriate Methodology and Social Context*. Cambridge: Cambridge University Press.

Hoyle, E. 1970. Planning organizational change in education. *Research in Education*, May, pp. 1–22.

4 Shadow puppets and language lessons: Interpreting classroom behaviour in its cultural context[1]

Hywel Coleman

Introduction

What is to be done when apparently exotic behaviour is discovered in the language classroom, especially if both the teachers and the learners who are involved perceive their behaviour to be unexceptional? Should we be critical of this behaviour and try to bring about reforms, or should we attempt to make sense of what we find?

This chapter examines the behaviour of a group of non-native speaker teachers of English and their students in an Indonesian university. The question of whether the observed behaviour is restricted to the university in which it was found is considered, and then the attitudes of Indonesian and foreign educationists to this behaviour are discussed. Next, parallels are drawn between this behaviour and the behaviour of performers and audiences in two types of Indonesian cultural event. This leads into an attempt to interpret the meaning of the observed classroom behaviour. The chapter concludes with an exploration of various implications of this analysis. If 'learning' does not normally occur in the classroom, for example, how is it that students do seem to learn the language? Moreover, if we want 'learning' to take place in this context, then it may be that 'teaching' will have to be abandoned. However, questions must be asked about the appropriacy of bringing about such changes.

Behaviour during the English lesson

University English lessons are described here by considering three features: the activities of the teacher, the activities of the students, and the relationship between teacher and students. Before we go any further, however, it is important to note that the picture which follows is one of a situation which existed in the early 1980s. Since then, the university itself has moved to a new campus, most of the teachers who were observed have undergone postgraduate training overseas, and many other changes have taken place.

The following description is based on an intensive programme of classroom observations in one of the major state universities in Indonesia. During the three academic years 1981–1984 I observed 28 different Indonesian lecturers of English teaching something like 500 lessons. In order to illustrate the points which I wish to make I shall be quoting from an observation diary which I kept during the first semester of the 1981–1982 academic year.

Student attendance at the 500 observed lessons totalled approximately 27,000, with 20 to 110 students present at a time; average attendance was 54. The teacher normally stood on a raised platform or behind a lectern, whilst the students sat in a closely packed crowd facing the teacher, usually as near to the front of the lecture hall as possible. In my diary I made the following comment on one visit:

> Arrived at 19.10 and stayed until 19.30. Found a tightly packed group of about 70 students ... just about to begin. (Observation 06)

On another occasion, I noted:

> Arrived at 15.10 ... to find approximately 56 people from a class of 78 present. ... The room is vast ... and only one part of it is used, everybody jammed together as though they were short of space. (Observation 14)

The activities of the teacher

Extracts from the textbook[2] were read aloud to the students by the teacher. From time to time the teacher translated into Indonesian parts of what was being read. Very occasionally some teachers asked the class to repeat in chorus sentences from the original English text. A few teachers also occasionally addressed questions to the whole class or to individuals; answers to these questions were sometimes – but not always – provided by students. The following two observation notes illustrate these teacher activities.

> Arrived at 19.15 and left at 19.30. Found only about 20 of the 63 members of the class present in a huge lecture hall ... As I entered, Teacher C was reading chunks from the passage and asking students to repeat them. (Observation 11)

> Approximately 60 people were present from the 78 on the timetable.... *Kernel Lessons* Episode 1 was being used: 1) Section 1 of the Episode was read very quietly and calmly, once; 2) About four information questions were asked, some to specific individuals, some to the class as a whole ... ; 3) Section 2

was read, twice; 4) About six information questions were asked; 5) Section 3 was read, once; 6) Two information questions were asked. A long silence ensued. Nobody had any idea what was to happen next. Then Teacher B went on to Episode 2 directly: 1) Section 1 was read twice; 2) Students were told to read the same section by themselves ...; 3) Some information questions were asked at one end of the room, but they were inaudible to the rest of us. (Observation 40)

In general, teachers seemed to pay considerable attention to the explanation of grammatical points; these explanations were sometimes given in Indonesian and sometimes in English. There was very little use of the board and no other audio-visual aids were employed. On several occasions, I found that it was difficult to hear what the teacher was saying beyond the second or third row. After one observation I made the following notes:

There are supposed to be 78 people in the class but there seemed to be at least 80 present and dribs and drabs continued to join the group during the time I was present ... Teacher D was addressing a small group of students at the front on the right hand side of the room; he was inaudible to the rest of the class ... The teacher then read the first situation from Unit 1 of *Kernel Lessons*, twice, but this was inaudible. (Observation 03)

The activities of the students

Some students had copies of the textbook and so were able to follow the passages which the teacher was reciting. However, many did not have access to the textbook. My observation diary records :

Teacher C was using Lesson 1 of *Developing Skills* but, he said, only one participant possessed a copy. I lent them mine and, after that, there seemed to be three little knots of students so presumably there were three copies available.... there were still participants without any access to the book. (Observation 11)

Very few students had copies of *Kernel Lessons*; many, indeed, seemed unaware that a set book was actually being used. (Observation 03)

... 23 of the 42 scheduled students present; another one arrived at 19.40. Only 1 in the group had the book being used. (Observation 12)

There was an attendance register which students had to sign, and consequently students were obliged to be present for most of the lesson, or, at least, for the majority of lessons during a semester. But, as we have seen, they were rarely required to do anything more than this. When the teacher asked them to repeat sentences in chorus, some students responded, although there was clearly no obligation for them to do so. Indeed, the fact that the teacher was talking did not mean that students had to listen. There were always several students who spent the lesson reading a novel or writing letters, others who gathered in small groups and chatted quietly among themselves, and still others who moved round the classroom consulting friends or exchanging cigarettes.

Since these aspects of student behaviour surprised me, there are frequent records of them in my notes. Here are some examples:

> By the time I left approximately 75 people were present. ... Throughout the lesson there was a tremendous amount of coming and going, of people changing places, of late comers arriving and searching for seats, and a constant noise of people talking, quite openly and loudly, with each other. (Observation 35)

> Teacher B spends a lot of time talking quietly to a few people in the front row ... and is absolutely inaudible to people at the back. There are some serious conversations going on around me, undisturbed by the fact that an English lesson is happening elsewhere in the room. (Observation 14)

> Approximately 60 students were present from the 68 programmed. ... a group of 3 students – not, presumably, members of this class – were sitting towards the back of the room, chatting together unconcernedly with their feet up on other chairs. (Observation 21)

I later discovered that these three chatting students were indeed members of the class.

Not infrequently, one found students from other classes crowded round the doorway watching a lesson (i.e. watching the lesson as a total event, rather than simply listening to the lecturer). There was even some movement between classrooms, as the next two examples illustrate.

> Arrived at 19.45 ... to find approximately 55 of the 63 students in the class present. ... Some of the students were smoking; other students from other classes came in and noisily removed chairs from the room during the lesson. (Observation 15)

> There were approximately 50 present from the 63 on the programme. Teacher G seemed cool, calm, collected ... tolerates

> a lot of chatter and moving around ... is quite unperturbed when a complete stranger enters, moves a couple of chairs ... and then leaves again. (Observation 22)

It was not unknown for students to bring friends or relatives to sit with them during a lesson. Perhaps the most surprising of all the examples of classroom behaviour which I observed is described in the following extract from my notes:

> Almost 40 people were present, from the 55 on the timetable. The atmosphere was extremely relaxed and informal, with a lot of moving around and discussion. One girl in particular wandered around ... then [went] outside for a couple of minutes, and finally [came] back into the room. Who was she? (Observation 30)

Teacher D called at my house the day after this observation took place and, during our conversation, I asked him who the girl was. He told me that she was the sister of one of the students in the class. On other occasions, I came across female students attending lectures chaperoned by their boyfriends, although the boys were not members of the same class.[3]

However, we must not ignore the fact that, in the middle of all this movement, activity, talking and socialising, there were nevertheless some students who *did* listen to the teacher. Similarly, whilst this description has been based on an extensive corpus of observation notes, there were some teachers who *did* hold students' attention. Some held the attention of all the students for some of the time, or the attention of most of the students for all of the time, as in the following extracts.

> When I entered, Teacher G was using *Kernel Lessons* Unit 1, Situation 6. There is a lot of giggling, smoking, wandering around and general chaos, whenever he asks students to make sentences individually or to answer questions individually. But there is rapt attention when he does the traditional English-teacher act of talking about grammar, but doing it in Bahasa Indonesia. The situation in the class fluctuated dramatically, then, between quiet attention and anarchic chaos. These waves continued throughout the period that I observed him. (Observation 16)

> He was using *Kernel Lessons* Unit 1a, Situations 1 and 2. Teacher H has a very attractive and compelling classroom manner, so long as he keeps speaking Bahasa Indonesia. It is interesting just to sit and watch him as he moves around explaining the purpose of an exercise to the students. He had the

attention of the whole class and there was no coming and going and chatting among the students, though one girl was writing love poetry. (Observation 07)

It may be relevant that both Teacher G and Teacher H were able to command the attention of their audiences *when they were speaking Bahasa Indonesia*. Sutabutr (1986) has observed that, during English lessons in secondary schools in Thailand, interaction between teachers and learners is perceptibly more 'comfortable' and less 'awkward' at those times when Thai rather than English is used.

The relationship between teacher and students

For the outsider, possibly the most astonishing aspect of behaviour during university English lessons was that a harmonious relationship appeared to exist between teachers and students, despite the fact that interaction between the two parties in the classroom was so limited. On the one hand, students did not express any dissatisfaction with the teaching which they were experiencing, though clearly much of what was uttered by the teacher must have been inaudible or incomprehensible to them. On the other hand, teachers did not seem to be perturbed that the students were paying so little overt attention to them. Students, therefore, were not perceived as being disrespectful simply because they were behaving in the way they did. Indeed, at appropriate points, students did not hesitate to demonstrate their respect, for example by addressing their teachers with the honorific terms *Pak* (father) or *Bu* (mother), even though the age differential between students and teachers in some cases was one of only a few years. The identification of teacher as parent is in fact common in Indonesia; consider, for example, the description by Geertz (1976: 332) of the relationship between teacher (*guru*) and student (*murid*) in Javanese mystical sects:

> ... the *guru* is symbolic father to the *murid*. He is often referred to as such; and when a man says 'my parent' he is often talking not about his father but about his *guru*, who, in turn, treats him as a son.

The distribution of the phenomenon

How extensive is the distribution of this phenomenon? The phenomenon was probably not a new one at the time that I observed it. Reading between the lines of a set of recommendations for the improvement of English teaching in Indonesian universities published more than forty years ago (Hill 1954), one can see that even then English teaching possessed many of the features which were found in the early 1980s.

It appears that some other subjects were taught in roughly the same way, at least in the university where most of these classroom observations were carried out. I passed by the open doors and windows of classrooms where other subjects were being taught often enough to be able to notice similarities with behaviour in the English language classroom, even though I made no formal observations of other classes. Writing at the same time, Cummings (1982) also claimed that a very similar technique was used for the teaching of other subjects in other Indonesian universities.[4]

It is possible that some of these features may at one time have been found in schools. The following description by Geertz (1976: 190) of teaching in the more 'modern' Indonesian schools of the early 1950s uses terms which are very similar to those which we have used to describe English teaching in the universities in the early 1980s. The teacher either copied the content of a textbook on the blackboard or dictated the content of the textbook to the students. Thus:

> The few who had textbooks had nothing to do but just sit there, which they did, sometimes chatting quietly with other students; the others just copied and copied and copied.

The report on a nationwide assessment of education in Indonesia in the early 1970s described very similar characteristics in teaching in junior and senior high schools (Beeby 1979: 55, 78). (In recent years, though, there have been massive developments in secondary education, particularly as a consequence of the very successful PKG – 'Strengthening of the Work of Teachers' – Project (see Tomlinson 1990, PKG 1992 and Riyanto and Coleman 1994).)

At least some aspects of this classroom behaviour are not, apparently, confined to Indonesia. Aziz (1981: 140f) and Salleh (1982: 153) identify extreme respect for one's teacher as a prominent characteristic of learners in Malaysia and Singapore respectively, whilst Ballard (1982) believes that respect for the teacher is one common feature of the educational traditions of several parts of Southeast Asia.

In summary, therefore, the detailed picture of classroom behaviour given above is based on data gathered in the English language classes of one university over a three-year period. There are several indications that elements of this behaviour were to be found elsewhere in the same university, in other universities in Indonesia, in other types of educational institution in Indonesia, and possibly in other parts of Southeast Asia.

There is also some diachronic evidence which suggests that this behaviour was not a recent phenomenon. On the other hand, we need to bear in mind the fact that change is taking place very rapidly in Indonesian education at the moment, and that the state of affairs which existed in the early 1980s may now have disappeared.

The Tibetan tea syndrome

If we look at previous descriptions of classroom behaviour in Indonesia, and at attempts to explain why this behaviour should be as it is, we immediately find a sharp difference between Indonesian and foreign commentators. For some Indonesian educationists writing at the time that these observations were carried out, classroom behaviour was relatively unproblematic. Sadtono (1983) concluded that it was the physical environment in which teaching took place and the IQ and motivation of the learner which were of primary importance in ensuring the success of English teaching. Neither the teaching methods as practised nor the teaching materials generally available were considered to be 'real problems' (*tidak begitu menjadi soal*; Sadtono 1983: 41).

This is not to suggest that Indonesian educationists were then or are now complacent about or self-satisfied with the state of education in their country. The collections edited by Miharjo (1984, 1986), for example, show that there is a deep concern among Indonesian educationists about many aspects of education in Indonesia. But, interestingly, teaching methodology and classroom interaction are barely mentioned in these commentaries. Hardjanan (1984), one of the contributors to the earlier of these collections, identified 'eight critical problems' faced by Indonesian universities, but none of these problems was related to methodology or classroom behaviour.[5]

Foreign observers of higher education in Indonesia, on the other hand, have paid considerable attention to the question of teaching methodology, and several of them have found it difficult to avoid making judgemental comments. For example, an early observer, Hill, believed that the teachers were the root of the 'problem' and he argued that teachers who were uncertain of their knowledge and were poorly trained found a teaching method similar to that which we have described to be the least threatening for them (1954: 33). The author of a 1977 Australian report on the English teaching situation at an Indonesian university (Stanfield 1977) made numerous references to 'weaknesses' in teaching and claimed, 'Although in conversations with the teachers I found they "knew their stuff" and expressed unimpeachable opinions, there were some departures from this in practice' (1977: 8). More recently, Cummings concluded that classroom instruction was 'depressingly substandard' (1982: 34) and that it was 'the most distressing facet of Indonesian higher education' (1982: 37). He argued that the problem began in the primary schools but blamed the teachers who 'allowed the search for the rupiah to take precedence over the duty to do their best' (1982: 33).

It has been suggested that one of the reasons that Tibetan tea has such a bad reputation among Westerners is that it is called 'tea', for the name 'tea' arouses certain expectations as to what the beverage will look, smell and taste like. Similarly, most traditional Malay literature has a bad name among European scholars largely because it is called 'literature', since the term 'literature' arouses certain expectations which are then disappointed (Johns 1979: 43).

What expectations does the term 'teaching' arouse for Western educationists? Probably, at the very least, 'teaching' implies two things: firstly, that a particular kind of process involving both teaching participants and taught participants will take place, and, secondly, that as a result of this process the knowledge or ability of the taught participants *with regard to the subject being taught* will in some way be modified. Now, what is particularly striking is that the criticisms of 'Indonesian teaching' have been made by outsiders – just as the criticisms of Tibetan tea and Malay literature have come from outsiders – whereas Indonesian educationists themselves believe that different matters are of immediate and pressing concern. This should alert us to the possibility that English teaching in Indonesian universities has a bad name because it is called 'teaching', since the word 'teaching' arouses certain expectations which are then disappointed. In other words, the discrepancy between the perceptions of Indonesian and foreign educationists must give us pause before we too rush into condemnation of all tertiary level language teaching in Indonesia as 'weak' or 'substandard' and then try to attribute this lack of quality to the teachers' materialism or to overcrowded classrooms in primary schools. Such blanket assertions are extreme and probably not very useful.

Another point which does not permit us to accept the negative evaluative interpretations of Beeby, Cummings, Stanfield and Hill is the harmonious relationship which seems to bind teachers and students together. If students' expectations were that they should be 'learning' about the subject which was the nominal topic of these lessons, and if the students perceived the teaching to be as bad as the commentators suggested, it is difficult to believe that they would not have been extraordinarily frustrated. Now although students may have had grievances about their lecturers' unpredictable attendance or other aspects of university life, there is in fact very little evidence of frustration at the *way* in which teaching was actually performed.

The English lesson as ritual

The arguments of Hill, Cummings, Stanfield and Beeby which we have looked at do not satisfactorily explain why the peculiar conventions of Indonesian university language classes should have been so widespread and so tenacious. However, a remark made by Geertz (1976) with regard to the traditional religious education system in Java may help us to interpret the phenomenon which we have been considering. This is how Geertz describes a lesson involving a *kyai* (religious teacher) and several *santri* (pupils) in a traditional religious school in the late 1950s (1976: 178):

> ... the *kiyayi* [*sic*] chants passages from books of religious commentary ... and the *santris* echo him, line by line. If the *kiyayi* understands Arabic, which is far from always the case, he may comment from time to time on the meaning of certain passages, the *santris* writing his comments in the margins of their books ...

Geertz doubts whether very much is communicated to the *santri* in these lessons, although many of them do learn 'to chant with great skill and artistry a beautiful language of which they have no comprehension' (1976: 186). In any case, as he observes (1976: 178), what is significant is that:

> ... it is not the content but the form which is of primary importance so far as the chanting proper is concerned.

It is clearly true that in the observed university language classes, as well, it was not the content which was of primary importance. Perhaps here we have a clue which will help us to interpret the observed behaviour.

Let us review, briefly, the characteristics of the university English lesson. One participant, the teacher, stood and read aloud from a textbook in a manner which may or may not have been audible to other participants. Other participants, the students, spent most of the lesson sitting in front of the teacher, possibly paying attention but possibly engaged in activities which had no bearing on the subject being 'taught'. With very few exceptions, therefore, English lessons involved one person who talked, and a large number of observers who were free to move around the classroom, talk to their friends, write letters, pay attention to the teacher, or day-dream, as they wished. The performer did not hope for absolute attention to every word which was uttered, and the audience did not expect to be called upon to give that attention. Yet the audience which behaved in this way was not being disrespectful.

One's overriding impression from observing these lessons was that the teachers and students were participating in a ritual. In other words, English lectures were repeated performances of one basic ritual in which the fact that the various participants had come together was of much greater importance than the actual content. This ritual could take place so long as one priest-teacher was present as sole performer and so long as any number of acolyte-students were present as partially attentive witnesses. Occasionally, the witnesses were invited to provide responses to an utterance from the performer, but this was not obligatory for every participant. The performance of the ritual did not demand unseemly expressions of devotion or concentration from any of the participants, although the acolyte-students were never lacking in respect for their priest-teacher.

There are, I believe, similar phenomena which can be discovered in other aspects of Indonesian culture besides education. After describing these phenomena and pointing out the parallels, I wish to propose an explanation of the role which they play.

The shadow puppet performance

It has been suggested (Coleman 1987a) that there may be a parallel between the university English lesson and a performance of the Javanese *wayang kulit* or shadow puppets, and I wish to explore that parallel in more detail here. The *dalang* or puppet master sits cross-legged before a screen with a light placed above his head. (The *dalang* is always a man.) The intricate two-dimensional parchment puppets, representing gods, heroes, demons and clowns, are held up so that their shadows fall onto the screen. The *dalang* manipulates all the puppets and speaks the parts of all the characters in the story. The performances, which accompany wedding ceremonies, circumcisions and other important family or community events, begin at about nine o'clock in the evening and continue, without a break, until dawn. The members of the audience may sit either behind the *dalang*, in which case they can watch him at work, or on the opposite side of the screen to the *dalang*, in which case they can see only the shadows of the puppets on the screen.

Foreign observers of *wayang kulit* performances are frequently struck by the informality of audience behaviour. For example, Van Ness and Prawirohardjo (1980: 3ff) give the following description:

> Many of the onlookers will come and go from the performance area as they wish ... Many will quietly engage in conversation over sweet Javanese tea, often gossiping about the characters as if they were real ... There are always some who choose to doze

off after the first hour or so, to be awakened with a jolt by the raucous clanging of the fight scenes.

A very similar description is given by Scott-Kemball (1970: 38):

> The audience ... chat among themselves, look around to see what is going on, eat if they feel hungry, and even have a quick nap.

Although the members of his audience may come and go and even fall asleep, the *dalang* continues his performance unperturbed. Both the irregular attentiveness of the audience and the *dalang*'s imperturbable performance despite that varied attentiveness are emphasised by Becker (1979: 230):

> One of the first things a *dalang* learns is that not everyone will respond to a *wayang* in the same way. There is no assumption that everyone will be interested in the same things at the same time; someone will always be dozing. The setting for a *wayang* is noncompulsive, more like a Western sports event than serious theater. It is not shameful or embarrassing to sleep through what someone else is enjoying.

The parallel between the *wayang kulit* performance and the university English lesson does not end here. The respect which students have for their teachers is also very similar to that which the audience has for the *dalang*. Early in the nineteenth century, Raffles observed that 'The *Dalangs*, who manage and conduct these amusements, are treated with considerable respect' (1978: I, 339), and nothing has changed since then. Indeed, the parallel between the *dalang* and the teacher has been commented upon by Van Ness and Prawirohardjo (1980: 44).

The public address

A second parallel with the English lesson is to be found in the *sambutan* or public address which is given by a *pejabat* (government official) during ritual occasions such as opening ceremonies for new public buildings or closing ceremonies for training courses. *Sambutan* are also given during modern – rather than traditional – wedding receptions in certain areas of Indonesia. (Though in the case of wedding receptions the speaker need not be a government official, it is still desirable that the *sambutan* should be given by someone whose role and status are clearly identifiable and who is deserving of respect from the audience.)

The features with which we are now becoming familiar are to be found in the public address as well. One performer, the *pejabat*, addresses an audience which is deeply respectful towards him or her by virtue of his or her status. The audience may pay full attention, little attention, or no attention at all to what is being said and indeed many members of the audience will spend much of the duration of the ceremony chatting busily together. Yet the performer is unperturbed by the fact that many members of the audience are overtly paying no attention.

Interpreting the ritual

Now I do not wish to stretch the comparison between these three cultural phenomena – the university language lesson, the shadow puppet performance and the public address – too far. I must also ensure that the nature of the relationship between the three types of performance is clarified. Thus it is necessary to insert two qualifications at this point.

First of all, I am not suggesting that there is a causal link between any two of these phenomena. For example, *wayang kulit* is found primarily in Java and Bali, whereas the data which I have been using here was gathered in a different part of Indonesia where *wayang kulit* is almost unknown. It is therefore not my intention to argue that student behaviour in university English lessons in one part of Indonesia was influenced by or was the product of audience behaviour during *wayang kulit* performances in another.

Secondly, the comparison is obviously not perfect in every detail. This can be illustrated in several ways. *Wayang kulit* audiences are often already reasonably familiar with the stories which are being performed, whereas the observed undergraduates were presumably not yet familiar with the content of their English lessons.[6] Also, the *dalang* is usually perfectly audible, whilst the English lecturer was sometimes inaudible. And of course the *wayang kulit* audience is under no obligation to be present at all, unlike the undergraduate audience which risked penalties for non-attendance.

So I am certainly not claiming that any one of the three phenomena of university English lesson, *wayang kulit* performance or *sambutan* is a type of either of the other two. Nevertheless, despite these qualifications, the three all clearly have several features in common. They centre around one conspicuous and highly respected individual, the performer, who must be continuously present. An audience is always present, but the members of the audience may or may not pay attention to the content of the presentation. For the audience, there seems to be no difficulty in reconciling lack of attentiveness with respect for the performer. The performer, on the other hand, is apparently not worried by the fact that the audience may not be paying full attention. In other words, all three phenomena appear to be members of one class of social event.

Having reached this point, we must now ask what functions events of this type have. It was suggested earlier in this section that the university English lesson is perhaps a ritual. What about the *wayang kulit* performance and the *sambutan*? What are the functions of these activities if their respective and respectful audiences may yet fall asleep?

The *wayang kulit* performance serves to create a beneficent atmosphere, both temporally (before, during and for some time after the performance) and spatially (throughout the area in which the audience is sitting and even, to some degree, for as far as the *dalang* is still audible). According to Scott-Kemball (1970: 39), the members of the audience know that witnessing a shadow play means 'they are protected from all evil things, because they are within the field of the benevolent influence that spreads outward from the screen.' Geertz agrees with this description of the function of *wayang kulit* performances. He goes on to explain how audience informality can be interpreted in relation to this function (Geertz 1976: 269; first published in the 1950s):

> ... anyone attending a *wayang* is safe from all harm at least as long as it is going on and probably longer. Thus the giving or attending of a *wayang* is in part ... a ritual defensive act ... and one often sees a *wayang* going on but no one really paying much attention to it, the point being not the content of the story but the ritual efficacy of the performance.

A description written some twenty years later (Van Ness and Prawirohardjo 1980: 4) is basically the same. For the Javanese, there is no paradox in paying deep respect to the performer and yet behaving in a 'pleasantly chaotic' manner while he performs:

> ... the informality of the environment is essential. The majority really knows beforehand what is happening in the play, and the fact that it is being played is the important thing, not whether everyone watches it all the time.

In short, 'the *wayang* performance has become a ritual ceremony' (Moebirman 1973: 57) and it creates a benevolent atmosphere in its vicinity.

The *sambutan* is a more recent and, unfortunately, a much less well-documented phenomenon, even though it probably occurs more frequently in daily life than the *wayang kulit* performance. Nevertheless, it is not difficult to see that the function of the *sambutan* does not differ greatly from that of a shadow puppet performance. The *sambutan* is required to ensure the smooth functioning of a seminar, the well-being of those who are to work in a new building, or the success of a marriage. The ceremony of which the *sambutan* forms part would be very much less effective were the address not given.

A related function of the *sambutan* is to re-emphasise the *status quo* and the relative rank of all those who are present. Palmier (1969: 153) describes the preparations for a series of *sambutan* to be given on the occasion of the opening of a cattle breeding station and highlights the ways in which the relative status of the different *pejabat* who were expected to attend the ceremony was reflected in these arrangements. It may also be significant that the evening news broadcast on TVRI, the state television service, consists overwhelmingly of extracts from *sambutan* which have been given by government ministers and officials in different parts of the country during the day.

The parallels between the university English lesson, the *wayang kulit* performance and the *sambutan* are striking, and the ritual functions of the latter two are clear. It therefore seems reasonable that we should look in this direction for an explanation of the function of the English lesson. As I have already indicated, I do not mean to suggest that there is any causal link between the three; my argument is, rather, that these are three separate phenomena which have several characteristics in common and which therefore are likely to have similar functions.[3]

I am proposing, then, that at the time that these observations were made universities in Indonesia were providing an intensive training for future government officials. They were inculcating a highly developed sense of status and an awareness of the proprieties required for the maintenance of a stable society. The English lesson played its part in this long socialisation process. In fact, Cummings seems to have reached a somewhat similar conclusion about the Indonesian education system, for he says (1982: 26), 'in the few places of careful observation, it is clear that the school is being used as a vehicle for teaching loyalty.'

Implications of the analysis

If our interpretation of the ritual function of the university English lesson is accepted, then we can be excused from having to make evaluative comments about what happens in the classroom. Certainly, the label which was attached to these weekly rituals was 'English lesson', but we can assert with some confidence that there was very little learning of English taking place during the rituals. At the same time, it may well be that some other sort of learning was happening during the rituals.

However, our analysis gives rise to two practical issues. Firstly, there is no doubt that most of the students in the institution where these observations were carried out did succeed in learning English, at least to the extent that they required it to pursue their major studies. If that is the case, where did learning of English take place if it was not in fact in the language classroom? The second question is a forward-looking one. Knowing, as we now do, that the English lesson has a largely ritual function, is there nevertheless any way in which we can make use of this opportunity to help students to improve their language ability? These questions will be explored in this final section of the chapter.

How is English learnt?

Research into the first of our questions – about where the learning of English really takes place – is still at an early stage (Coleman 1991, 1993). It seems likely that Indonesian university students actually do their learning in four ways: in peer groups, visits to lecturers' homes, practice opportunities and small-scale tuition.

Informal study groups, centred around a student who is recognised by his or her peers as being bright in a particular subject, are very common, especially in the period immediately preceding examinations or when an assignment has to be completed. For the majority of students this is probably the most important learning procedure.

Many students visit their lecturers at home. Some conscious and deliberate teaching-learning of a subject takes place during these visits, but, equally importantly, students seem to use the visits as opportunities to 'tune in' to a lecturer's wavelength more delicately than is possible in the classroom.

Opportunities to practise a skill are probably important learning occasions. These may be timetabled and provided by the institution (e.g. laboratory practice for chemistry students), but many students also seek out opportunities for practice outside the university. Some students, for example, go to extraordinary lengths to track down foreigners on whom they can practise their English.

Small private language schools (*kursus*) flourish throughout Indonesia. The tuition or coaching of small groups (*les privat*) is also extremely common; this usually takes place in the teacher's home. Both of these formats cater for the general public, but university students frequently participate.

Further investigation is needed before the significance and relative importance of these four learning procedures can be established. What is clear, however, is that alternative learning routes are available for students, although each one of these alternatives requires some investment of energy, initiative or even finance by learners.

Making use of the English lesson

Let us assume that, in a situation such as that which we have described, we wish to develop procedures which will help university students to learn English more effectively. What courses of action are open to us?

The first alternative would be to maintain the conventional format of the English lesson (i.e. one teacher and many learners) but try to 'improve the teaching' which takes place during the lesson. This is unlikely to be successful, for this would be merely tinkering with the ritual. In fact, when this approach was adopted in the university in which most of my observations were made, teachers found that they were constantly slipping back into the old ways, despite genuine efforts to 'teach' more effectively. Largely, it seemed that this was because the students were not prepared to behave any differently from the way they had always done in English lessons. Indeed, as the students saw it, if they had behaved any differently (for example, by being critically attentive, or by putting questions to the teacher) they would have been guilty of showing a lack of respect. It is difficult to avoid the conclusion that the conventions of the lesson were so strong that all the participants involved – both teacher and students – found it impossible to act outside the roles with which they were familiar (the roles of passive, inattentive, respectful student or active, ineffective, respected teacher respectively). Once teachers and students found themselves in the context of an English lesson it was practically impossible for them to adopt new roles. The strength of these conventions obliged the participants to behave as they did.

The second possible way of promoting genuine learning would be to exploit and promote the four extramural learning procedures (peer group, visits to lecturers' homes, practice opportunities and small-scale tuition). This avenue has hardly been explored yet (but see Coleman 1989, 1993).

As we have already discovered, the real 'function' of the English lesson ritual was almost certainly not to facilitate the learning of English at all. Thus the third alternative would be to take the revolutionary step of abandoning the English teaching ritual altogether. In short, we would have to find a way of avoiding the teaching in order that learning might start. Detailed descriptions of an experiment to do exactly this can be found elsewhere (Coleman 1987a, 1987b), and so the briefest of outlines will suffice here. The experiment took place in the same Indonesian university where most of my classroom observations had been made, and it involved many of those lecturers whom I had originally observed. What we attempted to do was to put all the participants – lecturers and students – into a type of event which could no longer be perceived as a 'lesson'. If this could be achieved, we reasoned, then there was a possibility that participants would not find themselves falling back into those roles which are inseparable from the lesson ritual. And if conventional roles could be avoided, then there was a chance that students could do some real learning of English. We went about this by exploiting both the students' apparent lack of inhibition about moving around the classroom and their custom of working in small peer groups. So English lectures became highly interactive task-based events during which students exchanged, manipulated and interpreted large quantities of English language data. Teachers, meanwhile, took on consultative and inconspicuously managerial roles. Rather to everyone's surprise, there was no difficulty in bringing about such a revolution in classroom behaviour. The majority of students responded with enthusiasm, and test results also indicated that students did actually acquire new language skills during the course (Coleman 1992). The success of the experiment in turn suggests that the initial analysis of what it is that happens in conventional language classrooms is a valid one.

Despite the apparent success of this experiment, however, there is a very important contradiction here. If the function of the university English lesson is essentially a ritual one, then by bringing about a change in classroom behaviour we are subverting the lesson to our own ends. I am beginning to suspect that the conventional patterns of behaviour which we encounter in an academic institution have valid functions within the 'ecosystem' of that particular academic culture, however exotic some of those behaviours may appear to the outsider. Although our attempts at reform may be admirably well intentioned, our missionary zeal to do away with behaviours which are apparently inappropriate may actually have unforeseen repercussions elsewhere in the academic ecosystem.

Conclusion

In this discussion, I have tried to show that the behaviour of teachers and students in university classes in Indonesia, for all its strangeness, was actually consistent, that it had parallels in other aspects of Indonesian culture, and that it probably had a ritual socialising function. I have also shown that other outside commentators who have observed this phenomenon have not attempted to analyse it in its cultural context; consequently they have had no alternative but to condemn what they found as 'poor teaching'. However, we will be in a good position to act effectively if – instead of merely criticising as substandard anything which is unfamiliar – we are prepared to interpret *within its cultural context* everything that we find in the language classroom.

Notes

1 I was extremely fortunate in being allowed complete freedom of access to language classrooms, over a period of several years, in the university where I was working. I am grateful to the university authorities for granting this permission, and to lecturers and students for allowing themselves to be observed. Earlier versions of this paper have been read by and have benefited from the comments made by Dick Allwright, Etty Bazergan, Jean Brick, Chris Candlin, Jim Hardman, Jacqui Lineton, Nicki McLeod, Elizabeth Marden, N. S. Prabhu, the late Jacob Sabandar, Brian D. Smith and Ken Turner. The late Jacob Sabandar was my counterpart and mentor during the period when the observations described here were carried out, and my greatest debt is to him.

2 In many cases this was the students' book of *Kernel Lessons Intermediate* (O'Neill *et al.* 1971) or one of the books in the 'New Concept English' series (Alexander 1967a, b, c, d).

3 It was not only students who brought relatives with them to the classroom. A lecturer in one of the technical faculties at this university once told me that his wife always accompanied him when he lectured, although in this case, of course, there was no connection with English teaching.

4 Etty Bazergan (personal communication) tells me that in fact there were differences between student behaviour during lectures on subjects in which they were majoring (more attentive) and student behaviour during lectures on more 'marginal' subjects (less attentive). For the majority of undergraduates, clearly, English was not of central importance. Meanwhile, Brian D. Smith, in a personal communication, tells me that the type of behaviour which I observed in university language classes did not occur with the same frequency in language classes in teacher training colleges (I.K.I.P.) in Indonesia at the same period.

5 According to Hardjanan (1984), the 'eight critical problems' faced by Indonesian universities in the early 1980s were: (a) how to accommodate the huge numbers of people then demanding tertiary education; (b) finance; (c) how to develop a curriculum with an appropriate and 'relevant' balance of pure and applied science; (d) how to determine priorities (between the opposing pressures to equalise opportunities and to provide an efficient service); (e) how to deal with

uncertainty about the true value of an objective scientific approach in tackling current social problems; (f) how to decide whether universities were educational institutions only in name or whether they were actually doing the job for which they were intended; (g) how to complete the change-over to an American-style credit system; and (h) how to provide the universities with enough lecturers and the lecturers with an adequate career structure.

6 There are possible counter-arguments to this claim. For a start, university English lectures often covered ground which had already been dealt with twice before, in junior and senior high school, the reason given being that students had failed to master what they had been taught at school. To that extent, therefore, students *were* already familiar with the content of the classroom performance. A second point is that the content of a *wayang kulit* performance may in fact be just as exotic for its audience as the content of one of the observed English lectures was for its audience. The former tells of gods, demons and mythical heroes, whilst the latter talked of last trains to Bournemouth and husbands who do the washing up. However, I do not wish to make too much of either of these counter-arguments.

7 M. Hamka (personal communication) disagrees with this analysis. He argues that it is necessary to distinguish between socio-cultural events *per se* (such as *wayang kulit* performances) and phenomena associated with them (such as audience behaviour). In this case, he believes that the parallels which have been identified do not necessarily indicate that there are structural and functional similarities among the three socio-cultural events themselves. Rather, he suggests, the similarities are merely between behaviours which are incidentally associated with these events.

References

Alexander, L. G. 1967a. *First Things First: An Integrated Course for Beginners.* (New Concept English Series) London: Longman.

Alexander, L. G. 1967b. *Practice and Progress: An Integrated Course for Pre-Intermediate Students.* (New Concept English Series) London: Longman.

Alexander, L. G. 1967c. *Developing Skills: An Integrated Course for Intermediate Students.* (New Concept English Series) London: Longman.

Alexander, L. G. 1967d. *Fluency in English: An Integrated Course for Advanced Students.* (New Concept English Series) London: Longman.

Aziz, A. A. 1981. *Strategies for Communication between Teachers and Pupils in a Rural Malaysian School.* (RELC Monograph Series) Singapore: Singapore University Press for SEAMEO Regional Language Centre.

Ballard, B. 1982. 'What is this word *analysis?*' – The educational culture-shock of Southeast Asian students in Australian universities. Paper presented at the Third Study Skills Conference, Sydney University, May 1982.

Becker, A. L. 1979. Text-building, epistemology and aesthetics in Javanese shadow theatre. In A. L. Becker and A. A. Yengoyan (Eds.) *The Imagination of Reality: Essays in Southeast Asian Coherence Systems.* Norwood, N.J.: Ablex.

Beeby, C. E. 1979. *Assessment of Indonesian Education: A Guide in Planning.* Wellington: Oxford University Press for New Zealand Council for Educational Research.

Candlin, C. N. and D. Murphy (Eds.) 1987. *Language Learning Tasks.* (Lancaster Practical Papers in English Language Education 7) Englewood Cliffs, N.J. and London: Prentice-Hall International.

Chamberlain, A. and T. Teodoro (Eds.) 1982. *Studies in Classroom Interaction.* (RELC Occasional Papers 20) Singapore: SEAMEO Regional Language Centre.

Coleman, H. 1987a. Teaching spectacles and learning festivals. *English Language Teaching Journal* 41(2): 97–103.

Coleman, H. 1987b. 'Little tasks make large return': Task-based language learning in large crowds. In Candlin and Murphy, 121–45.

Coleman, H. 1989. *Approaches to the Management of Large Classes.* (Research Report 11) Leeds: Language Learning in Large Classes Research Project.

Coleman, H. 1991. Learners' strategies in tertiary-level large classes. In British Council (Ed.) *Proceedings of the Conference on Academic Communication Skills in African Universities,* 44–57. Nairobi: British Council.

Coleman, H. 1992. Moving the goalposts: Project evaluation in practice. In J. C. Alderson and A. Beretta (Eds.) *Evaluating Second Language Education.* Cambridge: Cambridge University Press.

Coleman, H. 1993. Investigating and exploiting what learners do in large classes. Paper presented at the International Conference on Communication Skills for Nigerian Federal Universities, Nsukka, Nigeria, 29–31 March 1993.

Cummings, W. K. 1982. Notes on higher education and Indonesian society. *Prisma* 21: 16–39.

Geertz, C. 1976. *The Religion of Java.* Chicago: University of Chicago Press. (First edition 1960.)

Hardjanan, A. 1984. Delapan masalah kritis di universitas. In Miharjo 1984.

Hill, L. A. 1954. *The Teaching of English in Indonesia: Problems and Suggestions.* Jakarta and Groningen: J. B. Wolters.

Johns, A. H. 1979. The turning image: myth and reality in Malay perceptions of the past. In A. Reid and D. Marr (Eds.) *Perceptions of the Past in Southeast Asia.* Singapore: Heinemann Educational for the Asian Studies Association of Australia.

Miharjo, N. (Ed.) 1984. *Bunga Rampai Pendidikan Harian Kompas 1981–1984.* Ujung Pandang: mimeo.

Miharjo, N. (Ed.) 1986. *Bunga Rampai Pendidikan Harian Kompas 1984–1985.* Ujung Pandang: mimeo.

Moebirman 1973. *Wayang Purwa: The Shadow Play of Indonesia*. Jakarta: Yayasan Pelita Wisata.

O'Neill, R., R. Kingsbury and T. Yeadon. 1971. *Kernel Lessons Intermediate: Students' Book*. London: Longman.

Palmier, L. H. 1969. *Social Status and Power in Java*. (London School of Economics Monographs on Social Anthropology 20) London: The Athlone Press.

PKG (Pemantapan Kerja Guru). 1992. *A Guide to PKG English In-Service Training*. Jakarta: Direktorat Pendidikan Menengah Umum.

Raffles, T. S. 1978. *The History of Java*. Kuala Lumpur: Oxford University Press. (First edition 1817.)

Riyanto, A. and H. Coleman (Eds.) 1994. *Proceedings of the International Conference on Indonesian Secondary Education, University of Leeds, 27th–29th March 1994*. (Leeds Occasional Papers on Education in Indonesia, Number 1) Leeds : University of Leeds School of Education.

Sadtono, E. 1983. *Penguasaan Bahasa Inggris Dosen di Indonesia*. Malang: Institut Keguruan dan Ilmu Pendidikan.

Salleh, M. bin H. 1982. Cross-cultural comparison in classroom interaction. In Chamberlain and Teodoro, 145–57.

Scott-Kemball, J. 1970. *Javanese Shadow Puppets*. London: Trustees of the British Museum.

Stanfield, R. 1977. *Report on English Teaching Situation at Hasanuddin University, May–June 1977*. Unpublished report for Australian-Asian Universities Co-operation Scheme.

Sutabutr, C. 1986. Patterns of classroom interaction in the teaching of English in Thai schools. Paper presented during the RELC Regional Seminar on Patterns of Classroom Interaction in Southeast Asia, Singapore, April 1986.

Tomlinson, B. 1990. Managing change in Indonesian high schools. *English Language Teaching Journal* 44(1): 25–37.

Van Ness, E. C. and S. Prawirohardjo. 1980. *Javanese Wayang Kulit: An Introduction*. Kuala Lumpur: Oxford University Press.

5 Large- and small-class cultures in Egyptian university classrooms: A cultural justification for curriculum change

Adrian Holliday

The scenario

The setting of this chapter is undergraduate classes in Egyptian faculties of education. The students are training to be secondary school English teachers, and are doing English language as part of a BA in education. From the late 1970s to 1991, there was an ODA (Overseas Development Administration) project, managed by the British Council, located at Ain Shams University, Cairo, to improve the teaching of English generally. It worked in co-operation with a USAID (United States Agency for International Development) project, managed by the Fulbright Commission. The undergraduate English project was part of this wider project. Other parts included an undergraduate Methodology project, an undergraduate Literature project, and an in-service training project. Responsible for each of these projects was a British Council or Fulbright 'consultant', who was supposed to work with volunteer Egyptian colleagues to improve the respective curricula. Various aspects of the Ain Shams project have been discussed in Bowers (1987) and Holliday (1991a, 1991b, 1992 and 1994b).

There are approximately 18 faculties of education in Egypt. Problems recognised by all parties included a shortage of Egyptian lecturers and large classes, which sometimes reached the 500 mark. Many of the lecturers commuted to provincial faculties from the capital and often found it difficult to meet their timetable requirements. The Fulbright branch of the project also employed American lecturers to teach in many of the faculties of education, along with the occasional British VSO (Voluntary Service Overseas) appointee; and these alleviated some of the staff shortages. After the termination of ODA involvement in 1991, the Fulbright Commission has continued to increase its supply of American lecturers, working independently of Ain Shams University. The complex reasons for the termination of the Ain Shams project are beyond the scope of this chapter. However, a contributing factor may have been that the curriculum change was insufficiently appropriate to the social context to be sustained.

Two possible aspects of this are touched on in this chapter:

1 the apparent effectiveness, but deeper social inappropriateness of expatriate classroom methodology, and
2 the failure of a committee approach to curriculum development to allow individual Egyptian lecturers to develop their own socially appropriate methodologies.

Any of the 'solutions' presented here came far too late in the day to be properly explored or to achieve credibility in the eyes of the funding agency. However, this chapter does not aim to present solutions to save a particular curriculum project, but rather to explore the overall need to situate curriculum development within an ethnographic understanding of the influences of the wider society on the classroom.

As 'consultant' for the undergraduate English project, I observed 70 classes over a period of three years, some of which were taught by Egyptian lecturers, and some by British and American expatriate lecturers. The observations took place at 17 faculties of education. Ten Egyptian lecturers, five American Fulbright personnel, and two British VSO lecturers were observed. Thirty-five classes were taught by the observer as guest lecturer, 17 of which were also observed by the class's Egyptian lecturer. Twenty-seven undergraduate student groups were observed. The observation data cited in this study is taken from a wider corpus in Holliday (1991a); and some of it is also used in Holliday (1994b).

The observations were part of a means analysis comprising an ethnographic investigation into the various classroom, institutional and professional-academic cultures, which I carried out to help me determine what sort of curriculum change would be appropriate. The rationale behind this investigation was that curriculum change often fails when instigated by a curriculum developer who has insufficient understanding of the deeper protocols within the local social context. Investigation of the social context is therefore needed to reduce this risk of failure. An ethnographic approach is suitable for two reasons. First, it looks deep at the dynamics of social context. Second, its qualitative, interpretive nature helps one to realise the complexity of social context, and to put curriculum development in perspective (see Holliday 1991a; 1994b: 203).

A social dilemma

The parameters of my curriculum development task were themselves problematic in that they could not escape cultural bias. Ethnography was important to help me understand the nature of this problem and to find a route through it. Three parameters can be labelled as follows.

1 The aims were to improve the effectiveness of language teaching in the preparation of Egyptian English teachers.
2 This implied that language teaching needed improvement.
3 Furthermore, according to my brief, and also to my own professional orientation, the effectiveness of language teaching was equated with practical classroom activities that involved the students.

Different paradigms

Although the second parameter, that language teaching needed improvement, had been agreed upon by the host institutions and the curriculum project, it was uncertain how far the nature of the improvement in terms of the third parameter, classroom activities, was understood by each party, and indeed shared. Beneath the surface agreement, the different educational cultural orientations of the two parties were likely to produce very different notions of 'effective teaching'. The project was influenced by the private language school ethos of 'ELT' originating in Britain, Australasia and North America, which I term BANA, driven by an instrumental need to provide clients with defined language skills. The educational culture of the host institutions, which I call TESEP, standing for *te*rtiary, *se*condary and *p*rimary education, derives from a very different and very varied world-wide state education ethos which is driven by broader-based social and political needs (Holliday 1994a, 1994b: 12, 73). I argue that BANA currently exercises a technological superiority over TESEP, which is fuelled by a BANA professional-academic culture which has spread its influences world-wide, especially through aid projects similar to the Ain Shams project (1994b: 73). I was therefore aware that my work, especially with regard to the parameter of classroom methodology, but also my whole professional orientation, might well be contributing to this professional-academic imperialism. (The notion of 'imperialism' is similar to that argued by Phillipson 1992, but I find his terminology slightly patronising. Phillipson's term 'Centre' seems to imply an inherent superiority over a docile 'Periphery' – a docility which certainly did not exist in the Egyptian context I shall describe.)

The TESEP Egyptian lecturers would therefore see 'effective teaching' completely differently from the way in which the BANA project saw it. They had Ph.D.s in Linguistics or Literature, and were given the formal acclaim for such by both colleagues and students with the title 'Dr' (Holliday 1991a: 300–12); and they no doubt sincerely believed lecturing in these theoretical university subjects to be necessary in the *education* of future teachers. I use Bernstein's (1971) term *collectionist* to describe this more didactic, subject-oriented point of view – derived from the notion of a *collection* of subjects. The project, on the other hand, felt that the job of the lecturers ought to be the teaching of language *skills* to be used in the classroom by future teachers. I use Bernstein's term *integrationist* to refer to this skills-based point of view – essentially inhabiting an *integrated* curriculum (Holliday 1994b: 72). A further factor in these different perceptions was that there had been a marked change in the whole nature of university English language education characterised by falling standards, rising student numbers (Hopwood 1982: 140; Rugh 1985: 238–9). In effect, there had been a decline in linguistic standards among the students, running alongside the increase in numbers, which required practical language teaching. The project argued that the Egyptian lecturers' perceptions of their jobs, which might have been appropriate in the days before the decline, when trainee teachers would enter university with good adequate English, was now out of date (see also Wahba 1990). Soueif's (1992: 92) novelistic account of being a student at Cairo University before the decline in the early 1970s, and then of what it was like to teach in the newly large classes with the declining linguistic ability of their students (1992: 451) illustrates this change, and the predicament of Egyptian lecturers.

The need for ethnography

The difference between the Egyptian lecturers' basic approach to education and the project's approach was thus a key variable in the social context. Without understanding this context, curriculum change could never work. There was thus the need for an ethnographic approach, to look not only at local cultures of the host institutions, but also at the culture of curriculum development and its implications within the local social context. The social context had to be looked at not only in terms of local cultures of the host institutions, but also in terms of the 'foreign' cultures surrounding the analysis itself, providing the ethnography with a healthy *reflexivity* (Hammersley and Atkinson 1983: 14).

What therefore could be seen in the social context which might give *some* guidance as to how the curriculum developer might proceed – or indeed, not proceed? The analysis which follows represents a search for signs. It looks only at a small aspect of the social context (described more extensively in Holliday 1991a and 1994a). Its interpretive, qualitative nature gives it the status of heuristic hypotheses.

Small- and large-class cultures

During the course of the observations it became apparent that there were significant differences between the indigenous culture of very large

89

classes of between 50 and 450 students, and the culture of small classes of fewer than 50 students. This 'large-class' standard is intuitive, and depends on a range of factors other than number of students, such as physical conditions and seating (Shamim 1993). It is my own opinion that in Egypt the 'natural break' between small and large university classes, in terms of the different types of classroom culture which they each produce, seems to be at 50. I use the term 'indigenous' not to refer to a situation which was prior to or untouched by foreign influence. Such a situation would be impossible to find in Egypt, where expatriate teachers and foreign educational influences have been a normal feature for a very long time (Herrera 1992: 1–3). I therefore use the term to refer to classes with Egyptian lecturers.

The differences between the large- and small-class cultures made the question of classroom methodology particularly interesting. In indigenous small classes, the lecturers were not using the BANA skills-based, discovery-oriented, collaborative methodology which the project would have liked. Nevertheless, what they were doing may well have been more productive because rooted in a tradition that seemed to work within that particular classroom culture. However, in classes with over 50 students there was a marked change in the type of rapport observed. In the large-class culture there was a distance between lecturer and students that reduced rapport and showed evidence of tension. Apart from the over-crowding and poor acoustics in the large classes (Holliday 1991a: 223–8), this state of affairs was not surprising considering the relative newness of large classes. Another contributing factor might have been that Egyptian lecturers were not trained in classroom management techniques that might have helped them solve the large-class problem.

Good rapport in small classes

In the small-class culture, although it was teacher centred, there seemed a sense of harmony, with good rapport between lecturer and students, and signs that learning was going on. It seemed sensible to hypothesise that good rapport and harmony in the classroom would encourage learning (Collier 1979), and that therefore there was no need for curriculum change in small classes. Indeed, when indigenous small classes were compared with small classes taught by expatriate lecturers, it became apparent that the introduction of a BANA methodology could well be counter-productive.

Classroom instructions and protocol

Classes with Egyptian lecturers contained a lower percentage of explicit instructions regarding classroom procedure than classes with expatriate lecturers. This was seen particularly in the contrast between two classes, both with 40 students, in the same room, one taught by an Egyptian lecturer, and the other by an expatriate lecturer. (In the ensuing observation descriptions, the names used for the lecturers are fictitious, and the gender in each case has no relation to reality. I use fictitious names and alternate male and female to facilitate readability.) In the class of the expatriate lecturer, Alan, I observed:

> An extremely organised lesson ... with a large amount of time reviewing old and explaining new procedures (this being only the third session in the year ...), moving very clearly, step-by-step, with a sharp, but controlled 'OK' between each one. (Observation notes)

Alan's complex two-page handout was not unusual by British or American teaching standards. Similar use of instructions could be seen in other expatriate classes. For example, another lecturer was 'sergeant-major-like in setting up lesson procedures', and also in maintaining these procedures as the lesson progressed with explicit checks on student behaviour – 'making the students actually stay in the room until all the sentences had been copied' at the end of the lesson (Observation notes). The use of instructions to separate lesson stages could also be seen in the lesson of a third expatriate (Observation notes).

However, the lesson of Dr Asya, the Egyptian lecturer was 'very different. ... No time was spent on explaining procedure – everyone seemed to know what to do and got on with it from the moment of start' (Observation notes). Another example of classroom procedures already being established was observed, with a very different teaching style, in the lesson of another Egyptian lecturer. 'The lecturer had a very good, business-like relationship. A very careful routine had been established and was carried out in a very disciplined manner' (Observation notes).

In discussion with Dr Asya, after her lesson, I asked about the differences in instructional style between hers and Alan's lesson. She said that:

> She had explained the procedures very carefully in the first lecture and that this was enough, and that, yes, she was in a better position [as an insider] than Alan ... who constantly reconfirmed procedures, to know *when* her students had got

the message and therefore when she could stop reconfirming. (Observation notes)

Dr Asya linked her observations of what Alan did with wider influences within the society he came from:

> She added that she and her compatriots were always annoyed in the United States when they went to airports, train stations etc. where they were constantly being retold what the procedures were. She said that this insulted their intelligence. (Observation notes)

In other words, Dr Asya claimed that Egyptian lecturers had an insider advantage over expatriates, because they were better in touch with the methodological needs of the students. In contrast, the expatriates' mode of giving instructions seemed alien and annoying. One of the issues here was the timing of classroom instructions. In giving instructions too frequently, the *protocol* of the classroom culture was broken in the sense that the students were treated as less than competent. Something similar is seen in Collier (1979) in which expatriate teachers of Eskimo children break the natural rhythm to which the children have been used:

> Anglo [American] teachers generally ran their classes on a schedule that gave relatively short periods of time to each activity. Transition points are clearly defined and sharp. Eskimos handling similar processes structured the processes differently. Things took longer and the transition between activities were less sudden and distinct. (Collier 1979: 43)

Opaque local protocols

It can be hypothesised from these two pieces of data that a reason for the counter-productiveness of BANA teaching style was that expatriate lecturers were out of touch with deeper aspects of the Egyptian university classroom culture. They may have been immune to many of the protocols which inhibited Egyptian lecturers in adopting innovative classroom practice, and thus have had a false picture of what sort of innovation was appropriate. There were signs elsewhere in the observation data that Egyptian students were very hospitable to outsiders, and were not therefore likely to tell their expatriate lecturers when they were breaking protocol (Holliday 1991a: 256-60, 1994b: 150).

Evidence of classroom cultural forces, perhaps influenced by the wider society, which expatriate lecturers, as outsiders, found difficult to perceive, could be seen elsewhere. Communication took place in the classes of Egyptian lecturers which was difficult for myself as an observer to understand. For example, in Dr Asya's class:

> Anyone walking in would have thought there was chaos because a lot of students were talking at once and the lecturer did not always seem to be in control; ... [she] asked some students to be quiet, but not some others who appeared to be talking out of turn; ... one particular student in a group which always seemed to be talking out of turn was clearly in contact with the lesson because she often contributed very relevant comments; ... the end of the lesson was left, apparently, without a concrete conclusion. (Observation notes)

During Dr Fuad's lesson with an unusually small class of about twelve:

> Most of the students were involved and enthusiastic learning certainly seemed to be going on. ... What was remarkable was the level of voice noise in this lecture, both from lecturer and students, which was so low that I had great difficulty hearing what anyone was saying. I was sitting on the back row of a class that consisted of only three rows of students. [Dr Fuad] was walking back and forth only a few feet from the front row. It seemed that everyone could hear each other, and that therefore there was a communication going on which I could not tap. (Observation notes)

In the discussion with Dr Asya, after her class:

> She said that she sensed my wonderment at what was going on sometimes ... and said that, yes, she knew exactly what was going on and that, yes, it was culturally normal to be talking and listening at the same time ... and that although some students were talking a lot, perhaps only 60% about the lesson, they were very much in touch. The ones she told to be quiet were really off the point. (Observation notes)

Although these examples contain much which may have been due to idiosyncratic teaching styles, Dr Asya's students' ability to talk and listen simultaneously on the one hand, and the quietness of Fuad's classroom on the other, both seem to represent a gregariousness which was seen elsewhere in the classroom observations (Holliday 1991a: 237–40) and in life outside the classroom (e.g. wedding guests talking and moving about the church while the wedding was going on, and similar behaviour among audiences in cinemas etc.), and suggests that there were rules of communication within the Egyptian classroom culture which were hidden from the outsider.

Rapport in large classes

I have so far suggested that effective teaching was going on in indigenous classrooms with fewer than 50 students, despite the fact that they were not of the BANA teaching style initially preferred by the project. One would therefore be inclined to be restrained in introducing curriculum change.

Breakdown in rapport

The situation in large classes seemed, however, to be very different. Here, an apparent breakdown in rapport between lecturer and students suggested a need for curriculum change.

For example, Dr Nasser's class, with 150 students, was:

> A polished production, in which the students were the chorus ... helping to construct the lesson, of which the lecturer was definitely the architect, but it was not clear whether or not the design was in the learning interest of the students. The students were never in a position to negotiate what the lecturer put on the blackboard: they appeared instead to be anticipating each step of the lesson according to a prescribed pattern. ... The finale was a very lecturer-centred role-play, ... but it was clear that the outcomes were limited according to what had been taught before. ... Then [at the end of the lesson the students] ... are told to march out one group at a time. The whole thing was like a military rally. (Observation notes)

Another (in my view less competent) class, with 120 students, was:

> Very lecturer-centred. Whole lecture consisting of the lecturer pacing the podium plucking sounds demonstratively ... from the air, asking the occasional question of a student to elicit an illustration of his point. Twice a student was asked to come to the front and write on the blackboard. ... The lecturer pays little attention to the student's contribution, makes no attempt to communicate with the students. Signs of student boredom, though they seem completely deferential. ... The students are mainly watching passively. Have books open, presumably

waiting for the lecturer to refer to it – he never does. (Observation notes)

Both these classes (to me) displayed a more mechanical, distant relationship between the lecturer and students, with the 'lesson' more of a performance for the students to follow than responding to student-lecturer interaction. This state of affairs approximated to what Coleman (1987: 98) terms a 'teaching spectacle', where the students are spectators to a distant show.

Thus, in large classes, the relationship between Egyptian lecturer and students seemed more distant. This time I hypothesise that this corresponds with a breakdown in contact between lecturer and student, created by a loss of the close proximity when the lecturer is faced with a large-class situation with a large number of students, many of whom are physically far away (Holliday 1991a: 250–4).

Evidence that classroom behaviour in small classes was influenced by a 'high contact' national culture (see Watson and Graves 1973 and Morain 1986) was seen in the way in which students preferred to sit close together despite there being plenty of space in the rest of the room. For example:

> Two students arrived shortly after the beginning of the class. It was interesting that despite plenty of space in the room, all the students sat next to each other in the front row, in adjacent seats. On two occasions an arriving student sat on a seat without moving the bag and books of a student already seated in an adjacent seat, merely pushing them slightly to allow room to sit. (Observation notes)

The factor of distance in the large classes was compounded by poor acoustics, which was a feature of most classrooms observed, but which became especially difficult in classes of over 50, where loud shouting or the use of a microphone was necessary for most lecturer-student communication (Holliday 1991a: 223–5). The breakdown in rapport in large classes was brought home to me at the beginning of a class which I was going to guest teach. I was surprised when the class lecturer:

> Literally pushed me into the lecture hall to a group of 300, telling me she might have left for home before I finished. She did not introduce me to the students and did not herself really appear in front of them. I got the impression she had no great rapport with them. (Observation notes)

Indeed, she seemed almost frightened. The warmth and hospitality with which I was normally received into classes (Holliday, 1991a: 256–60) was completely missing. This was not surprising, as, when I got into the class, I found myself 'on a stage at least a foot above the heads of the seated students. ... I had to literally climb down stairs [at the side of the stage] to get down to the students' (Observation notes).

Maintenance of rapport

Significantly, this loss of student-lecturer rapport was not so evident with expatriate lecturers. In a class of 150, with some students standing down the aisles due to overcrowding, Beatrice 'succeeded in getting the students to work ... in informal groups, and the fact that the students were working was shown by a diversity and open-endedness in their responses' (Observation notes). The same lecturer was filmed on video, in the same room, with about 80 students. The film shows that about 50% of the class was taken up with informal group work.

In expatriate lecturer Dawoud's crowded class with 450 students, with many standing, some of whom had to use the walls to rest their notebooks on, there was evidence of students organising themselves in 'community' learning, in which collaboration extended beyond group work to other learning-related activities in the classroom, with the lecturer very much in a decentralised role (Holliday 1991a: 358–62, 1994b: 155) – approaching Coleman's definition of a 'learning festival' (1987: 98). This lecturer also managed to carry out role-play sessions under similar circumstances. However, it was noted that this lecturer's 'success' in coping with the situation was 'largely because the lecturer appeared confident and clear about what he was doing'.

I also managed to create a similar learning environment, under similar conditions, in many of my own guest lectures. However, it was difficult to know to what extent I was being carried by the advantages of hit-and-run, one-off situations. Also, it needs to be remembered, as noted above, that expatriate lecturers were to some extent immune from classroom or other cultural pressures. Nevertheless, the ardours of long-term teaching gradually eroded this advantage for many expatriates, and constant problems were noted (Holliday 1991a: 367–71). The most immutable problems were to do with the physical logistics of the classroom conditions, and not with cultural factors. In one class, which I taught on a regular basis for a year, I had only 60 students, but the appalling acoustics made the class seem much larger and severely slowed down the whole classroom process:

> Much time seemed to be taken up making the necessary repeti-
> tions because of the bad acoustics. To make it known to the rest
> of the class what an individual student was saying, it was often

> necessary to walk as close as possible towards the student (so that
> I could hear what she was saying), and repeat to the rest of the
> class (with my louder voice) what was said. (Observation notes)

Most of these problems were apparently solved by expatriate lecturers, through methodological ingenuity, to the extent that marked improvements in the students' practical language skills, in the classroom, were observed. Two cases illustrate this. When Egyptian lecturer, Dr Layla, was observed teaching one of the groups of students which Dawoud also taught:

> It was difficult to imagine that this was the same group. ... As
> well as being quieter and less active ... the students were not
> displaying as much competence either in English or classroom
> process; and their lecturer apologised both before and after for
> her 'weak' students. (Observation notes)

Secondly, during a staff development seminar, when Egyptian lecturers were shown the video film of Beatrice's class, one lecturer, not believing how well the students were doing, said that 'he thought the lesson had been rehearsed, or that the students were not average, that they must have been taking extra English' (Observation notes).

Here can be seen the conflict between the two very different views of what constitutes 'effective teaching' referred to briefly above ('Different paradigms'): that of a *collectivist* attitude, which has difficulty appreciating the value of the skills-based teaching style characteristic of the *integrationist* expatriate classes.

A rational versus a traditional approach

Ethnographic observation thus seemed to reveal that, whereas within *small* classes Egyptian lecturers seemed able to maintain an effective, though culturally idiosyncratic teaching style, and expatriate lecturers failed to make the established BANA methodology socially appropriate, in *large* classes local approaches seemed to be failing, and expatriate teaching seemed to be succeeding. In this part of the chapter I intend to offer a possible explanation for this state of affairs in terms of a sociological model.

Small- and large-class cultures

The features displayed by the indigenous small-class situation suggest a classroom culture quite different from that of the large-class situation.

The small-class culture seems to be based on natural, implicit community and personal relationships. This type of culture can be compared to a *Gemeinschaft*, or 'small', 'original form of society', in which the forms of behaviour are 'taught by the clan, age and sex group' (Martindale 1961: 271, 429, citing Vierkandt 1928 and Riesman 1950 respectively). These forms of behaviour constitute 'a complex embodying of the natural will', and have the characteristics of 'a collective ... insofar as its members think of grouping as a gift of nature created by a supernatural will' (Martindale 1961: 83, citing Tönnies 1957). It is characterised by *traditional* forms of behaviour which have 'thorough adherence to customary ways of behaving' (Murphy 1986: 149–50, using Weber's terminology).

On the other hand, the large-class culture precipitates the need for a new, consciously organised, explicit, classroom management. This type of culture can be compared to a *Gesellschaft*, or 'large' society – characterised by *rational* forms of behaviour 'in which the validity of social usage is found in the logicality of its fit with other usages', and is 'modern' in the sense that it involves rationalisation after the event, rather than the adherence to prescribed recipes for action (Murphy 1986: 149–50, using Weber's terminology). In other words:

> A society or total complex of social relationships which embodies the rational will is called a *Gesellschaft* .... . To the degree that consciousness of authority arises from class relationships, the collective tends to assume the characteristics of a *Gesellschaft*. (Martindale 1961: 83, citing Tönnies 1957)

Thus, in the small-class culture, I wish to argue that the Egyptian lecturers follow *traditional* classroom processes, which belong to attitudes about human interaction which are beyond and prior to professional, pedagogic issues of the classroom. This traditional approach has a deeply rooted rapport and protocol which is difficult to reproduce by the expatriate lecturer. On the other hand, the expatriate lecturers need to *rationalise* their approach to deal with what to them is a novel classroom culture. They would do this anyway because, according to the integrationist paradigm ('Different paradigms' above), they are trained to work out their methodologies consciously for the purpose of the pedagogic job to be done. Because they are outsiders to the small-class culture, they cannot participate in the traditional rapport, and they have a *Gesellschaft*-type relationship with the culture. Hence, in the small-class culture the expatriate lecturers can do little to improve – and will possibly damage – the situation.

However, the large-class culture forces an entirely different situation. With the breakdown in the proxemics necessary for the natural, community approach, the Egyptian lecturers' traditional approach no longer works, and produces an ineffective rapport. This notion is supported by Abou-Lughod's unpublished study of the effects of urbanisation in Egypt cited in Safty, Palmer and Kennedy (1985). She reports the difficulty which people in many walks of life have in coping with 'anonymity and secondary contacts' of urban life to which they are not used, as they leave the more intimate contacts of the village behind (Safty, Palmer and Kennedy 1985: 235).

The rationalised approach of the expatriate lecturers, however, enables them to make the best uses of the classroom resources available in the new large-class culture and so to do better than the Egyptian lecturers. One resource they make good use of is the natural ability of the students, from life outside the classroom, to co-operate informally to solve problems. Students co-operating to take turns sitting down, frequently observed in overcrowded classrooms, could be compared to seated passengers on crowded public transport holding the bags of standing passengers, and passing them out of windows after their owners had alighted (Holliday 1991a: 237–40). This co-operation was observed amongst students throughout small- and large-class situations, and seemed to enable them to cope with the crisis of poor classroom conditions. Although proximity between Egyptian lecturer and students had broken down in large classes, the students showed evidence of having preserved a proximity between themselves sufficient to support this co-operation. Indeed, the degree of student co-operation might have thrived in large class situations. Anawati's MA thesis on Egyptian boy-girl student relationships, cited in Safty, Palmer and Kennedy (1985), claims that the now common 'colleagueship and friendship' between sexes was unknown at the beginning of the 20th century (Safty, Palmer and Kennedy 1985: 215). Rugh (1985: 283) suggests that 'non-kin' collaboration in the Egyptian work place has increased with urbanisation. She argues that whereas in the old village society non-kin friendships were encouraged between young people from approved families, for the purpose of finding future marriage partners, the anonymisation of city life makes this difficult, and the club, the work place and the university classroom now provide such 'safe' relationships. Thus, the new overcrowded educational norm (Rugh 1985: 256–60) might well have bred co-operation among highly motivated students as they develop new forms of solidarity to cope with a relative distance from the source of teaching. The students, unlike their Egyptian lecturers, thus appeared able to cope with the transition from the small- to the large-class culture. The project capitalised on this phenomenon in the introduction of group work in large classes (Holliday 1991a: 404, 1994b: 184, 202, 1994c).

The need for new, rationalised traditional forms

Nevertheless, despite the success of the expatriate lecturers, it is unlikely that they could be as successful as the Egyptian lecturers would be if they too rationalised their approach to deal with the large-class culture. This is because the rapport between the expatriate lecturers and their students in the large-class culture, although making use of the students' traditional forms of interaction, could never fully understand or harmonise with these traditional forms. The large-class culture with the expatriate lecturer would be no more than an ultra modern, undeveloped, simplistic society, with no shared traditions, and artificial, imported rules. The rationalised approaches introduced by the expatriate lecturers therefore had questionable long-term effectiveness because they were not *rooted* in the traditional forms and thus did not connect at a deep level with the local culture. *Tissue rejection* would eventually take place, in that over the longer term the innovation brought from outside would be rejected because it would be insufficiently meaningful and acceptable, at a deep, cultural level, to the host environment (see Hoyle 1970; Holliday 1991a, 1993 and 1994b: 134).

The exception to this rule would be expatriate lecturers who had an unusual understanding of the local culture, or who had an unusual gift in cultural sensitivity. Collier (1979: 42, 45, 48) refers to the latter in an expatriate teacher who belongs to a minority group in his own country, and who has therefore developed this gift. Dawoud, in my own data ('Maintenance of rapport by expatriate lecturers' above), displayed this ability, perhaps because, although a naturalised American, his country of origin had a culture which in many ways is cognate with the local culture in the study (Holliday 1991a: 358–61, 1994b: 156). Such a teacher would be able to mix a rationalised approach with a deeper knowledge of local tradition.

I therefore wish to hypothesise that only a new, rationalised – yet traditional – approach, could be fully effective in the *Gesellschaft* culture of Egyptian university large classes. Exceptions apart, *only* local lecturers would be able fully to achieve this, because it would require a rationalised building and re-allocation on an existing traditional basis. This should therefore be the projected goal for successful curriculum innovation. The Egyptian lecturers would have to enter into a new *paradigm* of educational awareness. This might well require a movement away from the traditions of collectionism towards a more skills-oriented, integrationist approach – but only if they found this appropriate on rationalising the situation. Paradigm change of this nature is always problematic because it requires the overthrowing of traditions which have been the basis of teacher identity and status. However, the *crisis* of the large-class situation, and the anomalies created in the old paradigm when the existing traditional approach ceases to fit the exigencies of the new *Gesellschaft*, make this necessary.

Indeed, crises of this nature are often the cause of paradigm change throughout society (Kuhn 1970: viii; Schutz 1964: 95). As with paradigm change elsewhere, the conscious rationality of the new approach may only need to be temporary: the new rationalised-traditional approach would eventually become traditional, and a new professional-academic culture would be formed.

Conclusions

There are both substantive and methodological implications for curriculum design in what I have said in this chapter.

The role of imported teaching styles

Substantively, the role of expatriate lecturers and imported teaching styles is in question. Both of these forms of curriculum improvement may appear to succeed in the short run, although it appears from the evidence I have presented that there is reason to doubt their effectiveness in both the short and long term.

This does not mean that expatriate lecturers and imported teaching styles should not be employed, but that their role in curriculum innovation should be looked at critically. In Holliday (1991b) I describe how the experience of expatriates was used by Egyptian lecturers who wished to develop their own (rationalised-traditional) methodologies. A good example of this can be found in Azer (1990), which is also discussed in Holliday (1994b: 184). He took the rationalised methodologies developed by the expatriates in the project, compared them back with what he knew about the traditionally rooted protocols of the Egyptian classroom culture, and developed his own methodology from the synthesis of the two. Interestingly, during this development process, in which he carried out his own ethnography, Azer discovered things about what his students would and could do which he had not appreciated before. He was thus also learning about the new *Gesellschaft* large-class culture. Ethnography is not just for outsider expatriates to find out about 'foreign' cultures, but also for 'indigenous' teachers to find out more about their own changing classroom cultures. The process of joining rationalisation and tradition requires a rediscovery about the latter.

A need for a phenomenology of change

Methodologically, I feel it is significant that this substantive conclusion could only be reached through looking at what actually goes on, at a deep, cultural level, during the process of curriculum change.

Some writers in English language education (e.g. Swales 1980 and Coleman in Chapter 4 above), and more who write about curriculum reform generally (e.g. Hoyle 1970, Eggleston 1980, Kelley 1980, Tomley 1980 and Shipman, Bolam and Jenkins 1974) report evidence of curriculum innovation not meeting the deep requirements of the host educational environment. All of them refer to personal, cultural, social structural or institutional reasons for this failure, which are sufficiently deep as not to be perceived by the curriculum developer, either at the planning stage, or perhaps throughout implementation. Fullan (1982: 4) puts this failure down to a 'neglect of the phenomenology of change'. Sociolinguistic procedures for planning English language curricula are well developed; but procedures for seeing what happens at a deep level during the process of English language curriculum change are not.

The observations made in this chapter, employing essentially ethnographic procedures, are the result of an endeavour to look at, and to develop procedures for looking at, this phenomenology.

References

Azer, H. 1990. Can a communicative approach to university grammar cope with large classes? *Occasional Papers in The Development of English Language Education* 12. Cairo: Centre for Developing English Language Teaching, Ain Shams University.

Bernstein, B. 1971. On the classification and framing of educational knowledge. In M. F. D. Young (Ed.) *Knowledge and Control*, 47–69. London: Collier-Macmillan.

Bowers, R. (Ed.). 1987. *Language Teacher Education: An Integrated Programme for ELT Teacher Training*. (ELT Documents 125) London: Modern English Publications.

Coleman, H. 1987. Teaching spectacles and learning festivals. *English Language Teaching Journal* 41(2): 97–103.

Collier, M. 1979. *A Film Study in Classrooms in Western Alaska*. Fairbanks: Center for Cross-Cultural Studies, University of Alaska.

Eggleston, J. 1980. Action and reaction in science teaching. In Galton, 81–94.

Fullan, M. 1982. *The Meaning of Educational Change*. Ontario: The Ontario Institute for Studies in Education Press.

Galton, M. J. (Ed.) 1980. *Curriculum Change: The Lessons of a Decade*. Leicester: Leicester University Press.

Hammersley, M. and P. Atkinson 1983. *Ethnography*. London: Tavistock.

Herrera, L. 1992. Scenes of schooling inside a girls' school in Cairo. *Cairo Papers in Social Science* 15(1). Cairo: American University in Cairo Press.

Holliday, A. R. 1991a. Dealing with tissue rejection in EFL projects: The role of an ethnographic means analysis. Lancaster University: Unpublished Ph.D thesis.

Holliday, A. R. 1991b. From materials development to staff development: an informed change in direction in an EFL project. *System* 19(3).

Holliday, A. R. 1992. Tissue rejection and informal orders in ELT projects: Collecting the right information. *Applied Linguistics* 13(4): 404–24.

Holliday, A. R. 1994a. The House of TESEP and the communicative approach: the special needs of State English Language Education. *English Language Teaching Journal* 48(1): 3–11.

Holliday, A. R. 1994b. *Appropriate Methodology and Social Context.* Cambridge: Cambridge University Press.

Holliday, A. R. 1994c. *Large University Classes in Egypt: The Application of a 'Distance Learning' Methodology*. Working paper 17. Leeds: University of Leeds, International Network for Class Size Studies (INCLASS).

Hopwood, D. 1982. *Egypt: Politics and Society 1945–81*. London: George Allen and Unwin.

Hoyle, E. 1970. Planning organizational change in education. *Research in Education*, May, 1–22.

Kelley, P. J. 1980. From innovation to adaptability: The changing perspectives of curriculum development. In Galton.

Kuhn, T. S. 1970. *The Structure of Scientific Revolutions*. Reprinted and enlarged. Chicago: University of Chicago Press.

Martindale, D. 1961. *The Nature and Types of Sociological Theory*. London: Routledge & Kegan Paul.

Morain, G. G. 1986. Kinesics and cross-cultural understanding. In J. M. Valdes, (Ed.) *Culture Bound*, 64–76. Cambridge: Cambridge University Press.

Murphy, R. E. 1986. *Culture and Social Anthropology: An Overture*. Englewood Cliffs, N.J.: Prentice-Hall.

Phillipson, R. 1992. *Linguistic Imperialism*. Oxford: Oxford University Press.

Riesman, D. 1950. *The Lonely Crowd: A Study of the Changing American Character*. New Haven: Yale University Press.

Rugh, A. 1985. *Family in Contemporary Egypt*. Cairo: American University in Cairo Press.

Safty, M., M. Palmer and M. Kennedy 1985. *An Analytic Index of Survey Research in Egypt*, Cairo Papers in The Social Sciences 8, Monographs 1 and 2. Cairo: American University in Cairo Press.

Schutz, A. 1964. The stranger. *Collected Papers* 2: 91–105. The Hague: Martinus Nijhoff.

Shamim, F. 1993. Teacher-learner behaviour and classroom processes in large ESL classes in Pakistan. University of Leeds: Unpublished Ph.D. thesis.

Shipman, M. D., D. Bolam and D. R. Jenkins. 1974. *Inside a Curriculum Project*. London: Methuen.

Soueif, A. 1992. *The Eye of The Sun*. London: Bloomsbury.
Swales, J. 1980. The educational environment and its relevance to ESP programme design. In British Council (Ed.) *Projects in Materials Design*, 61–70. (ELT Documents Special.) London: The British Council.
Tomley, D. 1980. The selection of curriculum content: issues and problems. In Galton, 33–50.
Tönnies, F. 1957. *Community and Society* (trans. C.P. Loomis). East Lansing: Michigan State University Press.
Vierkandt, A. 1928. *Gesellschaftslehre: Hauptprobleme der philosophischen Soziologie*. 2nd ed. Stuttgart: F. Enke.
Watson, O. M. and T. D. Graves. 1973. Quantitative research in proxemic behaviour. In M. Argyle (Ed.) *Social Encounters: Readings in Social Interaction*, 34–46. Harmondsworth: Penguin. Reprinted from *American Anthropologist* 68, 1966: 971–85.
Wahba, M. 1990. Literature and the teaching of English in an Egyptian university. In M. Abousenna (Ed.) *Proceedings of The National Symposium on Teaching English in Egypt: Linguistics, Literature and Culture, 1989*, pp. 1–10. Cairo: Centre for Developing English Language Teaching, Ain Shams University.

6 Learner resistance to innovation in classroom methodology

Fauzia Shamim

A natural impulse of many people is to meet force with force; that is, to overcome the opposing forces by exhorting, appealing, arguing, urging, inducing and scolding. Increasing pressure against the opposing forces usually will increase the resistance pressure, and as a result, tension will be heightened. Frequently (but not always), the wisest and most effective course of action is to focus on ways of understanding and reducing resistance rather than trying to overwhelm it. (Watson and Glaser 1965: 42 cited in Havelock 1973: 131)

Introduction

The process of educational change is a complex one involving multiple and interrelated factors that may influence it at different stages and at different levels. Educational change can be both planned and unplanned. It can be initiated by an insider (principal, teachers) or by an outside change agent (e.g. a superintendent). Many of us believe that a teacher-initiated innovation at the grassroots level of the classroom is more effective as it is often introduced directly in response to an immediate problem in the specific context of the classroom. An innovation initiated by the teacher in the classroom is usually within the boundaries of the desired objectives of the syllabus, though it can also take the form of redefining the desired objectives in terms of what counts as knowledge and learning. This redefinition of learning objectives necessitates a change in classroom methodology or in the route to learning. Consequently it requires a redefinition of teacher/learner roles while remaining broadly within the parameters of the syllabus and the prescribed textbooks.

In this chapter I present a case study – an account of my experience in trying to introduce innovative methodology into my classroom in Pakistan. However, this attempt to innovate was met with a great deal of resistance from the learners; this resistance was manifested in both overt and implicit forms of behaviour. An examination of the authority structure and the norms of interaction in two contexts in Pakistani society reveals that there were parallels between learners' beliefs and assumptions about the definition of knowledge and learning and the norms of appropriate classroom behaviour, on the one hand, and on the other, the culture of the larger community, whose norms they share as members of the community. More important, there was found to be a lack of 'fit' between the learners' perceptions of knowledge, learning and teaching-learning behaviour in the classroom, derived from the culture of the wider community, and the assumptions of the innovation which predisposed the learners negatively towards the proposed methodology. Consequently the dissonance between the two cultures became a major impediment to the successful implementation of the innovation. Thus learner resistance can be explained with reference to the clash between the beliefs and assumptions of the learners, entrenched in the culture of the community, and the 'culture' of the innovative methodology.

Introducing innovative methodology in the classroom: Confessions of a teacher

What follows is an account of the problems I faced in trying to introduce an innovative approach to teaching and learning, based on the communicative methodology of language teaching, in my other subject classes.

Impetus for change

The traditional style of teaching in Pakistan is largely teacher centred and based on the lecture method. The learners are passive listeners with virtually no opportunities to become active participants in the teaching/learning process. During a lecture the learners religiously note down every word of the lecture (or as much of it as they can) to faithfully reproduce it in the examinations. This style of pedagogy on the one hand does not allow the learners to be creative and independent in their thinking, while on the other, it encourages the rote learning of vast amounts of material which are useful only on the day of the final exams.

I was always uneasy about the effectiveness of this style of pedagogy used in Pakistani classrooms for the learning of concepts and enabling the learners to apply this knowledge in problem solving in different situations outside the classroom. This uneasiness with the present state of teaching and learning in Pakistan became the prime motivator for my desire to introduce an alternative methodology in my classroom.

Choosing a solution: an alternative methodology

Not having the experience of teaching in any other way than the way I was taught, I began my search for an alternative approach to teaching in books and articles on ELT methodology. However, it was only after following a one-year training programme in the theory and practice of English language teaching – a programme which relied heavily on the process approach to learning and teaching – that I gained enough confidence to initiate the use of this approach in my classroom.

Implementing the change

Introducing a change in methodology in my English language classes would be difficult, I believed, because of the prescribed textbooks, the demands of the formal system of examinations, the irregular frequency of meetings with my class due to unscheduled holidays, but, most importantly of all, because of the large numbers in the class. In order to avoid the 'effects' of having a large class (see Shamim 1993), I began by experimenting with innovative instructional and management techniques in a small class of ten postgraduate students doing a course in Linguistics and Language Teaching. Since, after graduation, the majority of these students would be teaching English, I felt that we could talk about the effects of the innovative methodology on the teaching/learning process, through their experience as learners. I also hoped that an ongoing discussion of the teaching/learning process could be initiated in the classroom through 'metacommunication' activities (cf. Breen and Candlin: 1980).

I told the students at the outset that I would like to experiment with a different approach to teaching and learning from that which they had been traditionally exposed to. I told them that this would require a redefinition of our roles as teacher and learners. However, if they were not happy with anything we could discuss the problem and work together on finding a solution that would be acceptable to both parties. I spent a lot of time initially – and often at the beginning of each class – in explaining, setting up and discussing the new procedures for classroom behaviour. A comprehensive outline of the course, divided according to weeks, was also distributed along with an indication of readings on each topic. A system was introduced to make readings available to the group a week in advance of each topic. Selected books were borrowed from the library and placed on a reserve shelf in the classroom with one of the students volunteering to take care of the loan register for easy availability. (The non-availability of books and reading material is often used as an excuse by the learners for not doing the assigned readings.)

In the first session, after outlining the course objectives and going through other procedural details, I asked the students to work in groups and brainstorm to produce a poster on their conception of the factors involved in the teaching/learning of a language. Fortunately, it was a course in the psychology of learning so the students did not see the task as irrelevant to the rest of the course. The instructional format consisted of one one-hour lecture followed by a two-hour workshop-discussion session per week on each topic. If the university closed down due to some unforeseen circumstances or classes could not be held due to other reasons such as student unrest, it was agreed that the course plan would be followed without reference to the calendar year (so the week 2 workshop session could be held any time as long as it followed the week 2 lecture).

Learners' resistance to innovation

Occasionally, both inside the classroom and in informal contexts outside, students were invited to reflect on whether the objectives established at the beginning of the term were being achieved or not. The students frequently complained about the demands made upon them as learners in terms of the amount of assigned readings and the contribution which they were expected to make in seminar and workshop sessions. Often, indirect ways were used to show frustration and unhappiness with the methodology being used. Hence, on at least one occasion during the term all except two students decided to stay away from class. (These two students could not be informed by their friends, in time, about the boycott plan, I learnt later.) However, this did not deter me from carrying on with the class schedule. The students were provided with a set of guiding questions to help them in their reading and later to facilitate discussion in the class. Despite this, often the majority of students came to a seminar without having done their assigned readings on the topic, and they did not hesitate to tell me so. In fact, this was followed by requests for me to give a lecture instead. I found myself walking out of the class a couple of times in sheer frustration and anger. I often wondered if it would be better in the end to give in to their request for more lectures. At least it might ease the situation of conflict that I could feel building up in the class. It was more frustrating because they refused to discuss these issues with me.

I faced similar problems in introducing group work and getting the students to accept the idea that learning could take place *even without explicit direction from the teacher.* Initially, when I gave a group task, I tried to walk around to see if any help was required. The groups stopped talking as soon as I came too close to them, or they asked me for my opinions on the issues that they had been asked to think about. So I tried to leave the class sometimes on different pretexts, but I found on my return that, in fact, no work had been done during my absence. Finally, I compromised by 'watching' over them from my seat at the front of the class while reading a book or doing some other work. This unobtrusive policing of the learners by keeping an eye on them, as it were, from my vantage position in front of the class restored my authority, it seemed, while giving them an opportunity to work in a relatively uninhibited way. Surprisingly when I followed this procedure tasks were accomplished more quickly and efficiently than when I was trying to circulate around different groups to see if they needed any help.

As examinations approached and learners began to show signs of panic, I had to make other compromises, such as increasing teacher talking time during discussion sessions. I gradually found myself assuming more and more authority in the classroom and this seemed to make the learners happy and relaxed. It was indeed ironic that the techniques I had been trying to use to create, supposedly, a non-threatening and relaxed atmosphere in the classroom had, in fact, become a potential source of tension and conflict.

Consequences for the teacher

As the learners continued to complain about the lack of time and the heavy demands made on them by the course, I felt terribly exhausted and wondered if, by introducing this new methodology, I was creating psychological barriers to learning rather than facilitating the process which had been my aim in the first place. I also started wondering for how long I could take this personal 'wear and tear' and whether it was really worth the effort since the learners certainly seemed to prefer the traditional method of teaching and learning.

Towards an understanding of learners' resistance to change

Is resistance to change similar to that which I faced in my classroom an unavoidable part of the process in instituting change? What is the basis of learners' beliefs and assumptions about knowledge, learning and the etiquette of classroom interaction? Can this resistance by my learners be explained with reference to gaps in the planning and implementation of the innovation, or is it due to the cultural orientation of the learners derived from the culture of the wider community which conflicts with the ways of behaving, thinking and learning assumed by the new methodology? It could certainly be argued that learner resistance to the innovation could be a consequence of the teacher's lack of skills and capabilities in initiating and managing change. It could also be argued that the learners were not adequately prepared for the radical changes in behaviour required by the innovative methodology (e.g. assuming responsibility for their own learning). However, learner resistance could equally well be the consequence of the disjunction between the beliefs and assumptions of the learners derived from the culture of the wider community and the specific 'culture' of the innovation.

The following discussion is just a preliminary attempt to find answers to some of the above questions and to reflect upon clients' reactions to change in general and the reaction of my learners in particular.

The role of the learners as change agents

Planners and outside change agents see the role of teachers as highly significant in terms of the successful implementation of change. For example, whenever a change in the curriculum is planned, a lot of thought and attention is given to the resocialisation of teachers in new modes of thinking and behaving. On the other hand, the role of learners – perhaps because they have low status – is by and large ignored in planning and decision making concerning the introduction of an innovation. Though recently a number of strategies for learner training have been developed, with the aim of helping learners to think about their learning process and to develop independent study habits, learner training programmes, generally, do not consider how the learners' perception of an innovation could either facilitate or impede the successful implementation of change. (An exception to this is the introduction of a learner training programme by Nolasco and Arthur 1990, to facilitate the implementation of communicative language teaching in secondary schools in Morocco. The programme was developed only after the teachers expressed their inability to introduce communicative methodology in the reality of classrooms with 40 or more students.) The vast majority of teacher training and orientation programmes in relation to learner training programmes before a planned innovation is introduced suggests that learner acceptance of a proposed change is largely taken for granted.

Generally speaking, there is nothing to prevent the learners or users of an innovation from being included in the discussion about the benefits of a proposed change prior to introducing the change. However, in practice the logistical difficulties of involving learners in any meaningful negotiation in the planning stage, especially in a teacher-dominated classroom, often induce teachers to initiate the change first (as I did) and then hope that the innovation will be accepted once the learners realise the benefits of the innovation during the process of change. (Even if learners are included in the decision-making process the discussion is often restricted to consideration of the techniques and strategies for implementing change rather than the 'value' of the change in terms of its effects on learning and achievement. The negotiation, it must be remembered, is always carried on within the framework set up by the teacher.) However, as is evident in the case study above, learners do not always passively accept an innovation. In fact, learner resistance can be a very effective barrier to change. This resistance can be manifested explicitly in overt forms of behaviour and/or by following a policy of 'silent non-co-operation' in the classroom. The failure of learners to share the teacher's perception of the benefit of the innovation can lead to a situation of constant conflict between the teacher and the learners in the classroom (as shown through the case study) and force the teacher to compromise or even totally abandon the innovation effort half-way, in the interest of harmony.

The importance of culture in the process of change

Spindler and Spindler (1987), in their long-term study of the effect of curriculum change on classrooms in Schönhausen Grundschule and later in their work in Roseville elementary school and community in the USA, found that the implicit, tacit levels of culture are most important in the process of change:

> They are what explain puzzling persistencies that are there, over time under a surface level of manifest change, sometimes even apparently dramatic change. And they are what explain most satisfactorily some startling differences in classroom management and student-teacher behaviour in the German and American schools. (Spindler and Spindler 1987: 3)

Holliday and Cooke (1982) underline the same problem with reference to ESP projects. Hence they argue for an 'ecological' approach to ESP project and curriculum design. It is suggested, rightly in my opinion, that a means analysis of the teaching/learning context in the host country should be conducted before specifying syllabus objectives, the selection of materials, etc., 'to make it (the ESP plant) take root, grow, bear fruit and propagate in the local soil' (Holliday and Cooke 1982: 124). The argument is based on the assumption of a mismatch between the local culture and the culture of the imported methodology as reflected in the project. Similarly, Holliday (1984) makes a plea for research into the subculture of the classroom before any methodological innovation is introduced. However, this has not received much attention from planners and practitioners in English language teaching. Thus according to Krasnick (1988: 27):

> In the ESL profession as a whole, almost all of our effort has been expended on refining teaching techniques and revising teaching materials. The overall effect is more and more to define cultural and interactional issues out of existence by focusing on problems which are perhaps easier and more convenient to approach. The fact that cultural and interactional forces do not call attention to themselves ... does not mean that they do not exist. It may simply be that we do not recognize their existence.

Holliday (1991) also points out that while implementing a planned educational change the data that influences all decision making is often derived from 'formal' sources and is quantitative in nature. This information about the number of pupils, teachers, teacher-pupil ratio, contact hours, etc., though very important in itself, unfortunately does not tell us anything about how the change will be perceived by the participants and how it might conflict with the views of learners (and/or teachers) about what constitutes learning and the total approach to learning and knowledge prevalent in the wider community. It is generally assumed (as I assumed) that somehow,

1 'acculturation' will naturally take place; and that
2 learners will be ready and willing to adopt totally new ways of thinking and learning and new patterns of classroom behaviour even if these are incongruent with their existing views.

Hence co-operation is taken for granted rather than considered to be an issue for further research or negotiation. However, as shown by Heath (1982), in her study of the classroom behaviour of children in Trackton, a black resident community in the South Eastern US, an understanding of the styles of interaction prevalent in the culture of the community can help explain the behaviour of students in the classroom.

Heath sought to find out why learners reacted to teachers' questions either with silence or in a way different from that which teachers expected. The questioning behaviour of white American teachers was studied in the classroom and in their homes with their own children. This was compared with the questioning behaviour prevalent in the homes of the black children and the community outside. It was revealed that whereas questions in class were used largely for naming items or labelling things in books and pictures and for regulating classroom behaviour, especially with respect to classroom routines and attention to learning skills, questions served very different functions in the community outside. Firstly, questions occurred far less frequently in adult-child interactions in the Trackton community than in the homes of the teachers. In fact, in the Trackton community, 'children did not hold high positions as information givers or question answerers, especially in response to questions to which adults already knew the answers' (Heath 1982: 116). Instead, questions were used to build up an analogy or likeness between two things. Thus, for example, the response 'Doug's car, never fixed', given in terms of a non-specific comparison, was a perfectly appropriate answer to the question 'What's that like?' (referring to a flat tyre on a neighbour's car) (Ibid.). When teachers were made aware of this discontinuity between their questioning behaviour in the classroom and the interaction patterns prevalent in the community they tried to change their questioning patterns in the classroom. As a result, students were found to be more active in responding.

As the case study shows, although I, as a teacher, was convinced of the benefits of the innovative methodology for my learners, the practical difficulties of involving learners at the planning and decision-making stage forced me to initiate the change first, hoping that learners would accept the change when they saw its benefits during the process of change. However, as described earlier, I failed to appreciate the effect of cultural forces on the learners' beliefs and assumptions about authority structure and the distribution of roles and responsibilities in the classroom. The fear and misapprehension that arose due to teacher-learner power equalisation in the classroom, the reconceptualisation of knowledge and learning proposed by the innovative methodology and the insecurity of a relatively 'open' classroom were some of the factors that posed a potential threat to the learners, not only in terms of disrupting the security of the established structure of the classroom event but also in terms of a disruption of the traditional norms of interaction in social contexts outside the classroom.

The innovative methodology which I was trying to introduce required a major redefinition of the authority structure in the classroom and was largely incongruent, I realised later, with the culture of the community. The learners' anxiety about the stability of roles and responsibilities in the classroom, on the one hand, and the disruption of the essential norms of behaviour in the well-established social order, on the other, proved to be a greater force than the proverbial authority of the teacher in the Pakistani classroom. Also, once the teacher broke the contract, as it were, by stepping out of her traditional role and changing the routine structure of the classroom event, this seemed to provide a sanction to the learners to indulge in forms of behaviour that would be termed deviant in the framework of a traditional classroom.

Thus the effect of context, both ethnohistorical and immediate (home, teaching/learning in other subject classes, behaviour patterns in the family, and other social networks), on classroom processes cannot be underestimated. Learners in Pakistan, as in any other community, do not live in a social vacuum. In fact, before taking up their role in the classroom, they are participants in a cultural milieu and their beliefs and assumptions about modes of behaviour and knowledge are structured by the culture of the community in which they operate. The question here is not whether the cultural patterns of the community are good or bad or whether they should be encouraged or reversed in the classroom. The fact is that they are there as important variables that influence the way learners perceive, classify and judge (and often reject) the innovative methodology. Thus the cultural patterns need to be taken into consideration by practitioners, planners and policy makers alike.

The authority structure and norms of interaction in Pakistani society: Two examples

How are learners socialised into their role as learners? What is the source of their beliefs and assumptions about the structure of the classroom event and their rights and responsibilities as learners in the classroom? One obvious answer is that teachers teach as they were taught and in the process socialise learners into well-established patterns of classroom behaviour. Hence, norms of teaching/learning behaviour are set up in a community. However, though this approach offers interesting insights into how traditional forms of behaviour and interaction patterns are established in the community, it does not help us in finding out why learners in a particular community behave in the classroom as they do.

In this section of the chapter I will look at the etiquette of interaction in some social settings in the community in Pakistan – the home and family, and the work situation – in an attempt to trace the continuity of these patterns in the classroom. This analysis will help us understand some determinants of learners' resistance to change. It will also help us see why even the most er.thusiastic of teachers are forced to 'give up' innovations that require styles of interaction in the classroom which are radically different from those prevalent in the community.

The home and the family

The home or the family as the basic social unit is still the most important variable in the life of an individual in Pakistan. Elders in the family command great respect and their advice is sought on important family matters like arranging a marriage.

Children are encouraged to live with their parents even after they become financially independent and get married. At home, there is a very rigorous idea of rights and obligations. Hence it is the right of the parents to:

1 look after and provide for the children till they can earn for themselves and even after that if the parents have enough resources;
2 advise children on all matters pertaining to everyday life, e.g education, choice of career, selection of a marriage partner. This advice is binding on the children and failure to follow parental advice is deemed as irresponsible behaviour and is negatively sanctioned by friends and other family members.

Logically following from this right of the parents to make important decisions on behalf of their children is the notion of their responsibility for the consequences of these decisions. Hence, if a son or daughter graduates with high grades, it is the parents who are congratulated first. Similarly, even a slight misdemeanour by a child can bring shame or a bad name to the whole family.

The 'children' also have very well defined rights and duties:

1 There is a tacit understanding that children (even after they are adults) will not
  a go against the wishes of the parents or 'disobey' them;
  b show disrespect by presenting a reasoned or rational argument even if they do not fully agree with the decisions of the parents. (In fact they will show their deference and respect for their parents/elders by remaining silent.)
2 Children, whether they are still young or already adults themselves, are not considered equal partners in a conversation with elders. Showing too much curiosity and asking the elders (especially if they are not close members of the family) a lot of questions is considered impolite.

The work situation

By 'work situation' here we are referring only to educational contexts, although much of what is said is generalisable to other work situations. In the work context, the ability to make decisions is considered the prerogative of those who are in the higher echelons of power. The very idea of including junior members of staff in discussion about important matters is abhorrent and seen as a threat to authority. People lower in status cannot be equal partners in a conversation. So even when a 'democratic' head seeks to invite opinions from his employees they are reticent in giving their honest opinions. In fact, the responses are usually framed in accordance with what they believe is the current socially acceptable thinking on the issue. More specifically, employees will agree with the boss's beliefs and ideas. Hence, in committee meetings and discussion sessions junior members of staff make very little contribution in terms of creativity and original ideas. In fact, committee meetings have a social rather than an administrative or an academic function. They are basically used to gain the acceptance by the members of decisions that, in principle, have already been taken before the meeting is called. (This might be stated clearly at the beginning of a meeting. Even otherwise, there is an implicit understanding among committee members that only cosmetic changes will be made to a proposal presented by the chairperson who is senior in rank and authority, especially if he or she is also the person who has convened the meeting.) Members often come to the committee meetings without a clear idea of the agenda or of their role as contributors to the 'deliberations'. Consequently, they are unable to make any meaningful contribution to the decision-making process.

Discussion

Thus the general patterns of interaction in the home and work context in Pakistan indicate that, first, 'Authority is external and imposed upon the individual' (Spindler and Spindler 1987: 161).

Second, unquestioning obedience to authority, whatever the source of this authority may be (e.g. rank, age and/or status), is considered the hallmark of 'good' behaviour and rated very positively by society. Hence a good employee does not question the decisions of the employer and a good child follows parental wishes and commands rather than his/her individual preferred way of thinking and behaving.

Third, the advice of superiors is interpreted as an order which is binding on those lower in rank or authority. It is believed that people younger in age, and consequently lacking in experience, need to be constantly guided and advised by those who know 'better', i.e. elders, superiors, etc. The development of an independent mind, especially in the young, is positively discouraged and interpreted as 'offensive' behaviour and a threat to parental and other forms of authority.

Now let us look back at the case study with which this chapter began, to see how these ideas implicit in the culture of the community were manifested in the behaviour of the learners as a consequence of my efforts to introduce innovative methodology in my classroom. In the wider community, silence is equated with deference to authority, and the authority of anyone higher in rank or status is complete and absolute. In the classroom situation the teacher is an authority figure due to their age and superiority in knowledge, and so it follows necessarily that pupils in the classroom should remain largely silent and speak (minimally) only when they are told to do so by the teacher. Moreover, the teacher is considered a repository of knowledge, the only resource in the classroom except the textbook. In fact, the teacher often acts as a mediator between the coursebook and the learners, interpreting text and explaining meaning as he or she takes the students through the mysteries of the text (cf. Shamim 1993). Thus the teacher, by virtue of rank and status, controls what goes on in the classroom. Following from this role of the teacher is the definition of responsibilities. The teacher is considered responsible for the what and how of all teaching/learning in the classroom.

Conversely, the majority of teachers view the learners as 'empty vessels' who should make their best efforts to 'take' (learn) whatever they can from the teacher. The same teachers further believe that learners being low-status – like children in a family or junior members of staff in an organisation – need explicit direction and help from the teacher in order to learn. Consequently, they do not place much faith in learners' ability to take responsibility for their own learning or to make any meaningful contribution to the process of 'creating knowledge' in the classroom.

Furthermore, in the traditional classroom, learner talk is indicative of disruptive behaviour and a lack of teacher control. Learning will take place, it is assumed, if the learners remain quiet while listening carefully to the teacher. To ensure this the teacher usually sets up a fixed and rigid structure for all events in the classroom. In addition, as mentioned earlier, in all classroom discourse, the teacher has higher rank and status and is considered superior in terms of knowledge, experience and judgement, whereas the learners are 'lesser' partners in the interaction. These traditional patterns of classroom behaviour which are in consonance with the norms of behaviour in the wider community were reflected in my learners' demand for more lectures and their unwillingness to participate in workshop-discussion sessions and reading seminars.

Let us take another example. Because the questioning of authority, whether parental or political, is discouraged in the home and community, students were very uncomfortable when invited to participate in the process of negotiation to create shared meaning in the classroom, since this necessarily involved asking a lot of real questions both by the teacher and the students. Likewise, as they were accustomed to receiving explicit directives (dos and don'ts) both at home and in traditional classrooms, an opportunity for them to chart their own course to learning independently, as it were, created a lot of anxiety.

The authority of the teacher in a Pakistani classroom, like the authority of the parents in the home situation, is traditionally the source for the structuring of all interaction in the classroom. However, when the teacher 'abdicated' her traditional role of authority, the learners felt extremely insecure in their new-found freedom. Moreover, it is likely that the relatively unstructured nature of the communicative classroom, requiring the learners to redefine their own role and responsibilities as learners (and those of the teacher) in the classroom, created a 'value conflict' (cf. Dalin 1978). One way to resolve this conflict would have been an effort on the part of the learners to readjust their perception of their role in other similar 'unequal' encounters in the community outside the classroom. However, as the culture of the community largely favoured the traditional style of teaching and learning and as the teacher had, in any case, broken the 'contract' by disrupting the routines and structure of the traditional classroom, it seems that, in this situation of apparent chaos created by the innovation, the learners found it easier to override the authority of the teacher in the classroom by rejecting the innovation than to readjust their ways of thinking, believing and behaving to make them congruent with the demands of the innovative methodology. An observation that can be made at this stage is that learners' compliance with the authority of the teacher in the classroom in Pakistan seems to be functional only in terms of the social organisation and shared norms of interaction in the traditional classroom. Thus, as shown in the case study, when the teacher tried to create a new social order, in response to the demands of the innovative methodology, the learners considered themselves 'free' from their 'contract' of appropriate classroom behaviour and were, therefore, not hesitant in showing their dissatisfaction with the innovation.

Summary and conclusion

The case study in this chapter has examined efforts to introduce change in one classroom in Pakistan. It has also looked at the interaction patterns in two different settings in the community in Pakistan, i.e. home and family and the work situation. Parallels between interaction patterns in the community and teacher/learner behaviour in traditional classrooms suggest that incongruity between the assumptions of the proposed methodological innovation and the cultural orientation of the participants in the classroom situation, which is essentially a microcosm of the wider community, could help to explain the resistance not only of my learners but also the negative predisposition of other teachers and learners in Pakistan to the introduction of a communicative methodology in their classrooms.

Though a number of explanations could be offered for learner resistance to change (as was seen in my classroom), the discussion above indicates that the lack of 'fit' between the 'users' (learners) and the assumptions of the innovative methodology was largely a result of 'value conflict'. On the one hand, learners' beliefs and assumptions about the norms of appropriate classroom behaviour shown to be entrenched in the culture of the community clashed with the assumptions of the innovative methodology. On the other hand, the affinity between their expectations of the etiquette of teacher/learner behaviour in the classroom and the culture of the community made it easier for them to reject the innovation. This disjunction between the beliefs and assumptions of the learners derived largely from the community whose members they were and whose norms they shared, and the assumptions of the innovative methodology thus proved to be a major barrier to the effective implementation of the innovative methodology. Learner resistance to the innovation was just one of the manifestations of this phenomenon.

In conclusion, three observations can be made about introducing educational change in general. They are as follows:

1 The need for behavioural change is not limited to teachers. Students, parents and communities also have to change for the successful implementation of an innovation.
2 It is easier to implement a change that is congruent with the ways of thinking and believing and the norms of interaction prevalent in the culture of the community.
3 An innovation, if it clashes radically with the culture of the community, should be adapted to the local culture before being introduced. Conversely, acceptance by clients should be gained through different methods before the change is introduced.

Also, there are some questions that we, both as practitioners and as planners, need to ask ourselves at this stage:

1 Will those superior in rank and status be willing to tolerate a diminution of their status due to this readjustment of rights and obligations required by an innovation?
2 Are people lower in status willing and ready for this change? But most important of all:
3 Will the community accept such a radical shift in responsibilities and concepts of choice and control in the context of home, family and other social networks?

These and other related questions that have to do with a change in the total structure of relationships in society need to be asked when introducing a methodological innovation. If we agree that culture is transmitted through schools and that schools are responsible for the secondary socialisation of the child, and that the school and community constantly interact with and upon each other to establish cultural norms, then the introduction of an innovative methodology in the classroom should be seen as a source of potential conflict between two cultures. Attempts must be made to address this issue explicitly rather than treating it as a constraint at a later stage of implementation (Holliday 1984).

Implications for teacher training

Teachers, who are often described as 'agents of change', need to be made aware, as a necessary part of their initial training, of the potential problems arising out of a dissonance between the culture of their learners and the assumptions of an innovative methodology. According to Katz and Kahn (1975: 36):

> ... we persist in attempting to change organisations by working on individuals without redefining their roles in the system, without changing the sanctions of the system, and without changing the expectations of other role incumbents in the organisation about appropriate role behaviour.

It is assumed in teacher training programmes that an innovation can be successfully implemented by training the teachers in a different 'mindset'. The dynamics of change are neither discussed nor are the potential barriers to change pointed out. This leaves the teachers unprepared to face the problems that follow their efforts to implement change in the relative isolation of their own institutions and classrooms. Even if the teacher believes in the benefits of an innovation and is committed and willing to invest the extra time and effort in implementing a desired change, those efforts could be aborted by a number of factors, such as learner resistance. The teacher, being unaware of these problems, is usually left totally exhausted in trying to overcome this resistance while at the same time losing faith in the benefits of the innovation.

Thus it is important for teacher trainers to encourage participants in teacher training programmes to discuss both overt and 'hidden' barriers to the successful implementation of change in their own teaching/ learning contexts. This will not only make trainees aware of potential sources of conflict but it will also enable them to develop strategies and tactics to deal with anticipated problems in initiating and managing change in their own classrooms. It will also facilitate the initiation of a dialogue between teachers, parents, educationists and decision makers for a greater understanding of these issues and possibly lead to indigenous solutions that will be sensitive to the culture of the community.

References

Breen, M. P. and C. N. Candlin. 1980. The essentials of a communicative curriculum. *Applied Linguistics* 1: 89–112.

Dalin, P. 1978. *Limits to Educational Change*. London: The Macmillan Press Ltd.

Havelock, R. G. 1973. *The Change Agents Guide to Innovation in Education*. New Jersey: Educational Technology Publication.

Heath, S. B. 1982. Questioning at home and at school: a comparative study. In G. Spindler (Ed.) *Doing Ethnography of Schooling*, 102–31. New York: Holt, Rinehart and Winston.

Holliday, A. R. 1984. Research into classroom culture as necessary input into syllabus design. In J. Swales and H. Mustafa (Eds.) *English For Specific Purposes in the Arab World*, 29–51. Birmingham: University of Aston in Birmingham.

Holliday, A. R. 1991. Dealing with tissue rejection in EFL projects: The role of an ethnographic means analysis. Lancaster University: Unpublished Ph.D. thesis.

Holliday, A. R. and T. Cooke. 1982. An ecological approach to ESP. In A. Waters (Ed.) *Issues in ESP*, 123–43 (Lancaster Practical Papers in English Language Education. Vol. 5.) Oxford: Pergamon Press.

Katz, D. and R. Kahn 1975. Organisational change. In J. V. Baldridge and T. E. Deal (Eds.) *Managing Change in Educational Organisations: Sociological Perspectives, Strategies and Case Studies*, 35–74. Berkeley, California: McCutchan Publishing Corporation.

Krasnick, H. 1988. Cultural factors in the classroom: Teaching English to Trukese. *RELC Journal* 19: 21–8.

Nolasco, R. and L. Arthur. 1990. You try doing it with a class of forty! In R. Rossner and R. Bolitho (Eds.) *Currents of Change in English Language Teaching*, 188–96. Oxford: Oxford University Press.

Shamim, F. 1993. Teacher-learner behaviour and classroom processes in large ESL classes in Pakistan. University of Leeds: Unpublished Ph.D. thesis.

Spindler, G. and L. Spindler. 1987. Schönhausen revisited and the rediscovery of culture. In G. Spindler and L. Spindler (Eds.) *Interpretive Ethnography of Education: At Home and Abroad*, 143–67. New Jersey: Lawrence Erlbaum Associates.

Watson, G. and E. M. Glaser. 1965. What we have learned about planning for change. *Management Review*, November 1965.

7 The effect of institutional and national cultures on examinations: The university in Kenya

Mary Muchiri

Introduction

Examiners make a number of assumptions when setting examinations. These assumptions are intimately related to the shared understanding of the examiner and the student about what is expected of both parties in the context of the specific educational institution. The assumptions may include the following:

- the examiner's expectations regarding contènt, depending on what is considered to be legitimate knowledge in the particular discipline;
- the type of responses expected (for example, whether the students are supposed to challenge the views of their lecturers or not); and
- what is understood by the various concepts referred to in the examination.

These assumptions in most cases reflect both the attitudes of the individual examiner and the practices of the wider society in which the institution is located. They may either be in line with the practices of society at large or they may constitute a reaction against such social practices. This is because the sub-culture of the university is the culture of the educated élite, who, in addition to being members of that wider society, are also exposed to values of the even wider international community through their academic work. Moreover, the institution is a microcosm of the wider society, not only in its reflection of social practices but also in representing the conflicts that exist in the wider society between its many sub-cultures.

The process of trying to explain why certain things happen in a particular society is a complex one. This is because there are multiple causes for any specific instance of social behaviour. However, one may be able to identify typical behaviours and, by association with other behaviours, come to a general conclusion regarding parallels and relationships between behaviours (even while acknowledging that any identified relationships may not be *causal* in nature).

As a member of the Communication Skills department[1] at Kenyatta University, I was charged with the responsibility of helping students to improve their study skills, test-taking skills being an important aspect of those skills. If I was to help students from all disciplines, as I was expected to, I had to find out what was already happening. I was concerned, for example, with how students were being prepared for examinations by their subject lecturers, and in what ways the current practices influenced what the students did during the whole process of assessment. (The complete process includes not just the interpretation of examination questions but preparation for examinations and the type of feedback which students receive.) In order to help the students improve their test-taking skills I also felt that it was necessary for me to understand what skills the students were expected to possess in the different subject disciplines.

In this chapter, we will examine some practices employed by students and staff of Kenyatta University with regard to examinations. These practices are then related to what actually happens in the wider Kenyan society and to what is *supposed* to happen (according to the view of national culture which is expressed through the national goals of education).[2]

In order to investigate these issues, we will look at examination questions and students' responses to them, as well as staff and student questionnaires and interviews. Four main aspects of the examination process are discussed here. These are the methods of preparing for examinations employed by both staff and students, the interpretation of examination prompts by students, the moderation and marking of examinations by lecturers and the methods of giving feedback to students.

Analysis of the prompts and student responses, though useful in suggesting general areas of student weaknesses, is not enough to show why these problems were being experienced. Through the questionnaires we can ask specific questions about the actual practices used and the assumptions underlying these practices. However, it is not always easy to identify the motives which lie behind questionnaire responses, and so interviews are also important as a means of clarifying these assumptions and probing further the reasons for some of the answers.

The concept of institutional culture is taken to include both the explicitly stated policies of assessment at Kenyatta University (such as what format the examination should take) and all the implicit assumptions that staff and students made about the purpose and practice of doing examinations (for example, whether students should include their own material or simply reproduce what is given during lectures).

Kenyatta University is the main institution for training secondary school teachers in Kenya. The students spend the first year doing specialist courses in their content[3] departments. During the second year they do courses on teaching methods and then they take the final examination (which is the one I used for analysis). After this examination they are supposed to be fully prepared to go for their teaching practice. Then they have one more year of theory in their content departments before qualifying as graduate teachers.

In 1990 the 8-4-4[4] education system was introduced in Kenya. This system gives students only four – instead of six – years of secondary education before entering university. 'A' level examinations have also been abolished under the new system. Consequently, by the time students enter university, they have had fewer years of learning and using English than used to be the case, even though English is the sole medium of instruction at the tertiary level. Since 1990, therefore, a compulsory course in communication skills has been introduced for first year university students.

The national goals of education

Although there are always mismatches between written policies and actual practices, policy documents are some of the most important forms of evidence to which one can refer in order to discover what education is expected to achieve in any nation. I have therefore used the Kenyan National Goals of Education as an indicator of how the education system sees 'national culture'. I am aware that these are only stated goals and that they are rarely achieved. Therefore, in cases where the goals and actual practice differ, I have used the practice to represent the true national culture.

The National Goals have been drawn up by the government in an attempt to reconcile many traditions, including those of the different ethnic groups of Kenya as well as those based on modern Western ideas. For example, the concept of 'nation' itself only came about as a result of the colonial administration that drew arbitrary boundaries on the map and forced people with their own different systems of education to be regarded as one nation. Also, as Ngugi points out, in almost all societies there is a dominant element whose views are usually equated with the national culture:

> Within nearly all nations today the centre is located in the dominant social stratum, a male bourgeois minority. But since many of the male bourgeois minorities in the world are still dominated by the West we are talking about the domination of the world, including the West, by a Eurocentric bourgeois, male and racial minority. (Ngugi 1993: xvii)

Kenya has six national goals of education: national unity, national development, individual development and self-fulfilment, social equality, respect and development of cultural heritage, and international consciousness. It is clearly very difficult to use an examination system to assess whether these goals have been achieved. For example, one of the important aspects of the goal of 'national development' is *adaptability to change*, as the following quotation illustrates:

> ... adaptability to change cannot be interpreted to mean a passive undiscriminating acceptance to all change. What is meant is the development in the country's *youth* of an *enquiring attitude towards traditionally established values*. The *children* should be able *to blend the best of the traditional values with the changed requirements that must follow rapid development* in order that they may build a stable and modern Kenyan society. (Ministry of Education 1986; emphasis is mine)

This is clearly a noble objective but one that is not easy to develop or to assess through an examination. An added problem arises from the fact that these objectives were formulated relatively recently, yet the system of education that is supposed to foster them was not originally designed with such goals in mind. The Kenyan system of education is based on the British system and was introduced during the colonial period mainly for the purpose of training African clerical staff to work in the colonial government offices.

Although some changes have been introduced since independence, the system remains basically the same. The main aim of the students, then, is to acquire a certificate that will enable them to get a job or a place in an institute of higher learning. This 'exchange value' of education and the great competition for certification – the 'Paper Qualification Syndrome' – has been extensively discussed by Sambili (1993). According to Sambili (1993: 16):

> An educational qualification has a predominant exchange value if its use is perceived by those who possess it to be in what it can be exchanged for, such as higher education or training opportunities that in turn facilitate the acquisition of better salaried jobs.

It is no longer easy, then, to see much similarity between the current British system of education, which emphasises individual development and contribution, and that in Kenya. This is because the Kenyan system has developed independently, in response to the actual social needs of the Kenyan people. In this sense the practices at Kenyatta University can no longer be associated with the original colonial system, except in the sense that they may be seen as manifestations of attempts by the staff and students to meet their social and pedagogic needs within its basic structure.

Practices that reflect the national culture

Let us look now at the ways in which academic staff and students prepare for examinations, the ways in which students interpret examination questions, the moderation and marking of examinations and the way in which feedback is given to students.

Preparation for examinations

Most members of staff who teach the content courses assume that it is enough for them just to teach content. They feel that students have taken many examinations before coming to the university and therefore they should know what is expected of them. A few lecturers, however, feel that it is necessary to help the students acquire test-taking strategies, such as the ability to analyse a question in order to give a full response and to allocate time appropriately. When asked what problems students have in interpreting examination questions, members of staff say that they believe the students find difficulties in interpreting instruction words, technical vocabulary, complex grammatical constructions and quotations, in that order.

The Communication Skills teachers, on the other hand, feel that students need a lot of help in understanding both the format and the language of the examinations. This is because they perceive the students to have a much lower mastery of the English language than did the former 'A' level university entrants; they feel that the students are also less prepared for university in general. However, both assumptions are based purely on the lecturers' intuitions and the students contributed little to the debate.

What do the students think? Contrary to many of the lecturers' views, the students themselves say that they need help in order to respond to examinations appropriately. They say that the most difficult aspects for them to interpret are complex grammatical constructions, technical vocabulary, quotations and instruction words, in that order. This is almost exactly the opposite of the order in which the staff members rate the difficulties.

The students also point out the importance of past examination papers in helping them to predict the questions for which they should revise. They try to identify what the lecturers emphasise during lectures and they use lecture notes and handouts as the most important resources during revision. This again is different from what the lecturers think, because they are of the opinion that library books and laboratory or field notes are the most important resources for students.

Students report three main ways of preparing themselves for examinations. The majority of students use mainly their lecture notes and handouts, any other notes taken from course books, and, in some cases, notes from library books. These are used to make detailed model answers to past questions which they expect to appear again in the examination. The notes are then memorised for reproduction during the examination. These notes are referred to as 'Mwakenya', especially if students take them into the examination room and copy them, as sometimes happens. 'Mwakenya' is an underground political movement and the use of the name by students is an indication that they recognise that use of the notes is not approved of by the administration. (This practice is not limited to Kenyatta University, apparently. While attending a conference in Nigeria, in 1993, I was informed of a similar practice there known to the students as 'Ecowas', the abbreviation of 'Economic Community of West African States'.)

In the second approach, students discuss the model answers in groups and adopt the answer supported by the majority, rather than depending on their own ideas and those taken from the various sources used. Another variation to the group notes procedure is one in which some students do not bother synthesising all the notes into 'Mwakenya' but, instead, they just memorise lecture notes and handouts without necessarily discussing them in groups.

Students adopting the third approach are identified as the 'Survival Group'. This group meets and compiles a single set of notes to be taken into the examination room by one of the members of the group; this is then consulted by all the others in turn. This practice is called 'Xeroxing' or 'dubbing'. The notes occasionally make use of sources other than lecture notes and handouts, although this happens rarely since the members of the group are described as being not interested in learning but are just interested in passing the examination.

These practices are described by the students as being the result of the way in which staff tend to test only what has been covered in lectures and the reluctance of some lecturers to encourage students to do their own research in the library. These practices are also attributed to the facts that staff have very large classes to deal with and that there are insufficient resources for the students to use.

Two aspects of this situation are worthy of our particular attention. The first concerns the respective roles of lecturers and students, and the second relates to the students' tendency to co-operate with each other.

Firstly, it is interesting to note that in the national goals the words *youth* and *children* are used throughout to refer to learners. This is a clear indication that those who formulated the goals were confident that they knew what the youth needed, since they were in a position of authority, being the elders of the nation. Traditionally, the elders were the leaders of society and whatever they decided was done without question. During the colonial period, they were replaced by the colonial administrators, who were in turn replaced by the African governments after independence. The latter have retained the authoritarian attitudes of the colonial governments, so that any criticism, whether constructive or not, is interpreted as treason.

These same roles are usually extended throughout the system of education. The role of the teacher is that of the 'elder' while the student is the 'child'. It is not surprising, then, to find a tendency by staff members to do everything for the students in order to make sure that they pass the examination, and for the students to take lecture notes as their main source of information.

Consequently, the students are usually not consulted about anything. Decisions are made on their behalf, even at the university level where most of the students are no longer children but are adults capable of making contributions to the way things are done. This patriarchal attitude on the part of the lecturers leads to conflict, because the students have a conception of the university as a place where one becomes free from parental authority and develops into an independent thinker.

It is clear, from the differences between the staff and student opinions about the need to teach test-taking strategies and the use of resources, that the students are never consulted on these issues. It is also clear that the assumptions which the staff make are not necessarily correct.

A second area of interest is the practice of the students in collaborating during revision for examinations. Students do not see knowledge as an individual commodity. (As Jin and Cortazzi 1993 found among Chinese students studying in Britain, these students generally consider matters from a 'collective' point of view whereas the British tutor sees the strength coming from the personal interest of an individual'.) The idea of unity, which is one of Kenya's national goals, is emphasised in all social spheres. For example, 'Harambee' – which means 'pulling together' – has been the rallying call since independence. We have all sorts of 'harambee projects'.

It is not surprising, then, that students do not see the academic sphere as being different from other spheres of life; consequently 'pulling together' in the context of examinations is at times treated by students as if it was as legitimate as it would be in other contexts. However, as in the case of the respective roles discussed above, we can see a conflict between this concept and the essentially individualistic system in which the students have to operate. One is expected to pass examinations as an individual and so, when 'collaboration' occurs in the examination room, it becomes 'cheating'; when knowledge is not acknowledged as belonging to an individual, in writing, it becomes plagiarism.

Students from mainly collective societies find these concepts difficult to grasp. For example, Sambili (1993: 234) points out that there are very strong social pressures from the people whom school leavers call 'tall relatives' (meaning important relatives) which influence their choice of employment:

> It was observed in this study that socio-cultural factors were dominant in shaping student behaviour. Examples of these socio-cultural factors were: the cultural stigmatisation of self-employment … peer pressure and parental expectations of their children's academic performance and securing of employment opportunities.

There have even been cases in Kenya of clever students taking public examinations for their friends. This is not seen as 'cheating' but as helping a friend or a member of the family. This is another very strong concept among collective societies. The one who has must share with those who do not have, especially in the context of the extended family. In a predominantly individualistic system, on the other hand, this is interpreted as impersonation and is punishable, even by imprisonment.

Students' interpretation of examination questions

From the examiners' prompts and from students' actual responses, we can see that students find it more difficult to respond to less structured prompts because these do not provide a format for the answer. (Pollitt *et al.* 1985 report a similar finding.) On the whole, the students tend to respond in point form rather than use essay-type continuous responses with introductions and conclusions. They give general responses to specific prompts and often confuse main points with supporting details. There is little or no individual student contribution, hence there is considerable similarity between the responses which students give to the same prompt. The content of students' answers to different questions within the same subject area sometimes overlaps; this is even found in the answers which they give to examination questions from different disciplines.[6]

All of the above findings are indications that both the institutional and national cultures are important not just in fostering certain attitudes in students and staff but also in the actual interpretation of questions in examinations. This means that when students respond to examinations set in other cultural environments, they may be at a disadvantage, unless the expectations of that institution are made explicit. This concurs with Jin and Cortazzi's (1993) findings about Chinese students studying in Britain.

The moderation and marking of examinations

Kenyatta University uses external moderation for both undergraduate and postgraduate examinations. This practice is becoming less and less effective and more and more costly as the number of undergraduate students continues to increase. Moreover, the system forces staff to set examinations long before they teach the content to be tested, thereby making teaching very examination-oriented. Nevertheless, the system continues to be used because the authorities seem to have a deep mistrust of staff members' ability to manage examinations without some form of policing.

The students confirm that they share the fear that, left alone, the members of staff may not be fair to all students. The students report different forms of unfairness during marking. These are attributed to the fact that the staff are dealing with very large numbers of students and so do not have enough time to mark all the scripts carefully. Some unfairness and bias is, however, seen by the students as being associated with the same types of prejudices that are found in the wider Kenyan society, such as ethnicity, gender and personal grudges. When I asked one member of staff what the reason for the secrecy in examinations was, this was the reply:

> The only reason is that there are people who want to cover their inadequacies. Because if you know you marked someone's work and you are very genuine about the marks, you shouldn't fear. You can make mistakes, but you shouldn't fear the challenge, if somebody tells you that you have made a mistake. You should be able to admit (that you were wrong and you are ready to be corrected).

For me this quotation exemplifies the Kenyan socio-political culture. Like many other undemocratic systems, to criticise any politician or any other person in authority is interpreted as a challenge to their authority. This is also an example of the conflict between the stated policy – in the educational goal about 'adaptability' already quoted – and actual practice in education.

However, challenges are beginning to appear in both cultures, as a result of recent changes in which Kenya adopted a multi-party political system.[7] Both politicians and educationists have to adapt to a situation where they are required to be more accountable to the general public. In the case of lecturers at Kenyatta University, it may be expected that more and more students will demand investigation or remarking of their examinations; this should help to make marking and the awarding of grades more transparent.

An added problem, however, is the tendency of the Kenyan community to personalise professional issues. Like the politicians, the educationists seem to make no distinction between their personal and professional responsibilities. Education, in fact, is not seen as being on an equal footing with other professions such as law or medicine. The lecturers, therefore, need to demonstrate that their working practices are transparent and accountable in order for both the students and the administrators to recognise them as professionals and stop treating them with suspicion.

Feedback on examinations

Both staff and students are in agreement that the main reason why no feedback is given to students after examinations is because of the fear that students may raise questions about their grades. This creates problems for staff members who are not used to being accountable for their marking. The experience of students with regard to the feedback given for continuous assessment assignments seems to strengthen this claim; when some staff members were asked to justify marking which was apparently unfair they were unable to do so. As one interview respondent told me:

> They don't give any adequate kind of answer to some of these problems. Or ... if you press so much, they'll have to at least adjust and give you more marks.

The two cultures in conflict

We have seen how examination practices at Kenyatta University parallel phenomena found in wider Kenyan society. We have also seen that, at times, conflicts between different interests occur. I shall now give a few more examples of the type of conflict that arises from the fact that the university sub-culture is partly influenced by the wider international academic culture as well as different elements of the national culture.

The national goals paint a picture of unity and equality; however, the students see inequalities in all aspects of Kenyan social life, especially because of corruption with regard to the distribution of employment opportunities, training opportunities and wealth. It is common knowledge among Kenyans that, in addition to a certificate, one must also have the 'right'[8] names and come from the 'right' place and have proper connections with 'tall relatives' before one can get a job. The term that best summarises this practice is 'magendo', a Kiswahili word that refers to corrupt practices (usually bribery).

These practices are viewed as 'injustices' by students who have been taught to think in terms of modern Western democracy. As a result there are frequent student riots in the universities. Such behaviour, however, is seen by the authorities as a betrayal of 'African Solidarity' and attributable to the influence of foreigners; from the point of view of the authorities it clashes with the stated goal of 'building a stable and modern Kenyan Society' based on justice for all.

There is, therefore, a conflict between the two national goals of national development and individual development. Although students belong to a collective society, they also belong to an international academic community which is primarily concerned with the development of the individual. As a result, practices such as reproducing lecture notes in examinations – which enable students to acquire certificates but which do not help them to acquire self-confidence and skills – are seen by many as frustrating. Moreover, the 'exchange' value of the certificates is diminishing because of increasing unemployment, as Sambili (1993: 243) points out:

> Self employment will become increasingly the main direction of employment and livelihood for the majority of educated Kenyans.

In the near future, employers will no longer be interested in mere certificates but they will want proof of what the prospective employee can do. Also, with increasing costs of production, the recommendation from a 'tall relative' may no longer be sufficient. Furthermore, the cost of education is being shifted onto the individual student more and more, in line with the policy of 'cost sharing'. For example, the students at state universities have begun to pay a part of the tuition fees, in addition to repaying government loans for the rest of the money needed for their university education. It is, therefore, likely that students will demand to have more for their money's worth, especially in what Sambili (1993: 16) calls the 'use value' of education:

> ... an educational qualification has a predominant use value if its use is perceived by those who possess it to be in the immediate application of the skills it embodies in a given type of employment.

A final example of the conflict between African and Western national cultures is more general. The primary school syllabus (Ministry of Education 1986) states:

> Education should respect, foster and develop Kenya's rich and varied cultures. ... It should also instil in the youth a sense of respect for unfamiliar cultures.

While it is difficult to assess through an examination whether this goal has been achieved, it certainly seems to encourage students to choose what is culturally appropriate for them as individuals. The university, for many students, is the first place for them to exercise such freedom, because it is here that they meet people from different national cultures as well as from non-African cultures.

This cultural heterogeneity gives rise to the conflict already mentioned above, in which certain staff members still behave as if there was only one ethnic group, their own, and then give those who belong to that group higher grades. It is also a source of conflict for those individuals who see the national culture as encouraging ethnic hatred in Kenya. In trying to be free from the ethnic prejudices prevalent in the national culture, these people are perceived as betraying their particular group, while those who belong to other groups treat them with suspicion.

Implications for higher education in Kenya and in other developing countries

Much research has been done on different aspects of students' responses to examinations (see, for example, Horowitz 1986; Okong'o 1990; Hounsell 1984; Kroll 1990; O'Brien 1992). At the institutional level, studies like those by Bartholomae (1985) and Jin and Cortazzi (1993) have shown that students in different parts of the world enter the university with different expectations and that the staff members of different institutions also have different demands on students. For example, Bloome (1993) identifies the 'apprenticeship approach' in which learning as a cultural practice takes place through collaborative actions with a more knowledgeable or capable other. In the higher education context this approach results in the interpretation of the lecturer as the knowledgeable one while the student is mainly a recipient of rather than a contributor to knowledge. This is the approach employed by many lecturers in developing countries, and, as we have seen, it results in rote learning and the reproduction of facts in examinations.

As the developing countries become more and more a part of the modern world, these attitudes will need to change in order for their 'youths' to be able to contribute to the development of their modern states. Failure to change will inevitably mean a greater dependence on the Western world whose ideas in education and technology currently dominate these developing countries.

One of the main changes will have to be a greater involvement of students, especially at the university level, in the process of decision making concerning even such matters as what they should learn and how they should be examined. Though changes of this type cannot be expected in the immediate future, it is hoped that studies such as the present one will serve to raise awareness of what will be required if all concerned parties are to prepare themselves for the change. Failure to prepare for change may lead to a decline of the traditional university as more and more students look to other alternatives such as the Open University and private universities which can provide courses more suitable for their individual needs.

In the absence of explicit advice on how to interpret examination prompts, the students have used their own experience of practices during examinations to develop ways of preparing themselves. Many of these strategies involve working in groups. While we should appreciate this collaboration among students as a way to help them share knowledge and resources, at the same time university students need to be made aware of their membership of the wider academic community and they need to be initiated into its conventions. It may be that as they become more aware they will learn to be proud of their own work and to stop parroting others. Since knowledge is mainly disseminated through writing, students need to be confident in using that medium. In that way both individual and social development may be expected to take place.

Lecturers, on the other hand, need to encourage students to refer to a range of different sources and to stop employing practices such as that described to me by a librarian at Kenyatta University:

> We have a problem with some lecturers who only give specific references and they say 'read this book in the short loan'. So that's where they are narrowing the students' approach to looking for information. They don't want anything else. Even alternative titles because the lecturer insisted they must use those references. It is a major problem in my experience.

This behaviour is also associated with the fact that staff have no time to find out what is in the library because they spend most of the time setting and marking examinations. Some students feel that academics are narrow-minded:

The problem is that some lecturers get excited about one text and they will not accept anything else that anybody says. There is a narrow-mindedness that tends to restrict scholarship and it is a pity.

Another reason why lecturers may have no time to read and write is the fact that many of them have to combine lecturing with what is referred to as 'Jua Kali' (Hot Sun) enterprises. This is a general term for all the attempts which an individual makes to earn something extra to supplement his or her salary. These activities range from selling eggs to opening a consultancy in town. This happens mainly because the lecturers are poorly paid in comparison to their colleagues in the private sector. Combined with the fact that most politicians behave as if they were experts in education (something which they cannot possibly do with regard to other professions), this lowers the professional status of educationists. If governments in developing countries really believe in the value of education for the development of their nations, the most effective way of showing it would be by respecting the teaching profession.[9]

Conclusion

The institutional culture of Kenyatta University is currently facing both immediate logistical problems and longer term attitudinal problems. There is an urgent need to overcome a practical crisis, while in the long term there may be a need to change some of the attitudes which prevail both within the university and in Kenyan society at large.

Many of the practices which have been described here are seen by most staff and students as being temporary and undesirable. They are associated with the current crisis resulting from student over-enrolment and the consequent shortage of learning facilities. Both students and staff feel that this crisis could be overcome if only appropriate numbers of students were admitted and adequate resources were provided. If at the same time one of the two systems[10] was adopted exclusively, academic staff feel that they could set, mark and give proper feedback to the students. With the pressure off, they would be able to encourage the students to do independent work.

Although the immediate changes which have been called for are desirable and necessary, I feel that there is also a need for more radical changes if Kenyatta University – and probably many other African universities – is to be prepared for the new challenges which face institutions of higher learning in all parts of the world. These more fundamental challenges were summarised, during a review of assessment at Lancaster University (Knight 1993), to include new demands in dealing with:

> Academic audit, quality assessment, larger student numbers, students from non-traditional backgrounds, validity and reliability of assessment and effectiveness in terms of time and contribution to the learning process.

These challenges will have to be faced in Kenyatta University as well, but, in addition, we need to deal with issues of transparency, accountability and the development of manpower for nation building in the new era of multi-party politics. For these long-term changes to occur at least three basic questions must be addressed.

What kind of education are we advocating at the university?

The Kenyan system of education was established with the purpose of fulfilling British colonial needs and it has not changed much since independence. The changes that have occurred at the tertiary level have been brought about as a result of exposure to other systems of education, especially the American system, through those Kenyans who have studied abroad. Consequently these changes have not been based on a true understanding of what Kenyans really need. Moreover, the recent changes that have taken place in the 'parent' systems of the United Kingdom and the United States of America have not always been appreciated by Kenyan educationists. Many practices have therefore continued in Kenya which have been found inadequate or have been discarded elsewhere.

Are the assessment methods currently being used appropriate for testing the type of knowledge, skills, and attitudes that we are teaching?

The answer to this second question must imply a willingness to try different types of assessment methods rather than being satisfied only with what we have always done. Of special interest to me is the need to involve our students more and more by letting them take responsibility for their learning, as they assume more self-confidence in other areas of social life in what is supposed to become a more democratic society.

The concept of the lecturer as the 'moving dictionary' will also have to change and greater recognition be accorded to the need for collaboration by both students and staff as knowledge makers. These changes must be based on a real understanding of what Coleman, in Chapter 4 above, calls the educational 'ecosystem'. This leads in turn to my third question.

Of our current practices, are there some that we could exploit more than we are doing already, before we think of introducing new ones?

Our awareness that institutions are part of wider society must lead us to the realisation that some of our institutional practices are part of that wider culture. I have in mind, for example, the co-operative nature of Kenyatta University students as they prepare for examinations. Further investigation into such practices (for example, through student interviews and protocols) may reveal positive ways in which they can be incorporated into the official learning and assessment procedures of our institutions.

Notes

1 This is one of the departments that were recently established in all state universities in Kenya (and in many other African universities) to try to help students cope with their studies by providing them with communication and study skills in English as a Second Language, the medium of instruction for all subjects at university.
2 The goals are provided as an appendix to give a full picture, but only a few are discussed in this chapter.
3 'Content departments' is the term used to distinguish the departments responsible for teaching subject content from those in education, that is, those responsible for teaching methodology.
4 The 8-4-4 system was introduced in 1990, at the tertiary level, so that the students now have four instead of three years of tertiary education.
5 The examples that Jin and Cortazzi (1993) give to show the differences between 'collective' and 'individualistic' tendencies in society are that a Chinese student shows his or her 'collective' criterion for choosing a research topic in that it is based on the needs of others, while personal motivations would probably inspire a British student.
6 This is probably as a result of confusing what is learnt in Subject Methods (the examination which I analysed) with another one known as General Methods. General Methods deals with general concepts of teaching and learning as opposed to Subject Methods which deals with the methods of teaching the individual subject.
7 Since independence, in 1963, Kenya has adopted a one party political system. The first democratic elections were held during early 1993.

8 'Right' in this case is interpreted to mean 'coming from the ethnic groups of the ruling class' or 'having connections among members of that class'.

9 See Nwaokolo (1993) for a full discussion of this problem.

10 The current system used at Kenyatta University is a combination of the American unit system and the British term system. This creates problems for both staff and students because final examinations have to be done at the end of every term.

References

Bartholomae, D. 1985. Inventing the university. In M. Rose (Ed.) *When a Writer Can't Write*. London: The Guilford Press.

Bloome, D. 1993. The social construction of intertextuality and the boundaries of school literacy. *Changing English* (1): 168–78.

Horowitz, D. 1986. Essay examination prompts and the teaching of academic writing. *ESP Journal* 5 (2): 107–20.

Hounsell, D. 1984. Students' conceptions of essay writing. Lancaster University: Unpublished Ph.D. thesis.

Jin, L. and M. Cortazzi. 1993. Cultural orientation and academic language use. In D. Graddol, L. Thompson and M. Byram (Eds.) *Language and Culture*, 84–97. Clevedon, Avon: Multilingual Matters Ltd.

Knight, P. (Ed.). 1993. Lancaster Review Toolkit. Lancaster University: Unpublished working paper.

Kroll, B. (Ed.) 1990. *Second Language Writing Research: Insights for the Classroom*. Cambridge: Cambridge University Press.

Ministry of Education. 1986. *Syllabus for Kenya Primary Schools*. Nairobi: Government Printer.

Ngugi wa Thiong'o. 1993. *Moving the Centre: The Struggle for Cultural Freedoms*. London: James Currey.

Nwaokolo, P.O.E. 1993. Social perception of the status of teachers in Nigeria with particular reference to vocational teachers: A case study of Edo and Delta States of Nigeria. Lancaster University: Unpublished Ph.D. thesis.

O'Brien, T. A. 1992. Writing for continuous assessment and examination conditions: A comparison of undergraduate performance. University of Manchester: Unpublished Ph.D. thesis.

Okong'o, G. A. 1990. A linguistic study of examinations: Some salient features for Kenyan English for Academic Purposes programmes. University of Birmingham: Unpublished Masters dissertation.

Pollitt, A., C. Hutchinson, C. De Luca and N. Entwistle. 1985. *What Makes Exam Questions Difficult?* Edinburgh: Scottish Academic Press.

Sambili, H. J. 1993. A case study of employment related experiences of Kenya's first 8-4-4 graduates. Lancaster University: Unpublished Ph.D. thesis.

Appendix

Kenyan National Goals of Education (Ministry of Education 1986)

1 *National Unity*

Education in Kenya must foster a sense of nationhood and promote national unity. Kenya's people belong to different tribes, races and religions, but these differences need not divide them. They must be able to live and interact as Kenyans. It is a paramount duty of education to help the youth acquire this sense of nationhood by removing conflicts and by promoting positive attitudes of mutual respect which will enable them to live together in harmony and to make a positive contribution to the national life.

2 *National Development*

Education should meet the economic and social needs of national development equipping the youth of the country to play an effective productive role in the life of the nation.

a *Economic Needs*

The system of education in Kenya should produce citizens with skills, knowledge, expertise and personal qualities that she requires to support her growing economy. She is building up a modern and independent economy which is in need of adequate domestic manpower to support it. She requires both self-employed manpower and manpower in paid employment.

b *Social Needs*

Education in Kenya must prepare children for those changes in attitudes and relationships which are necessary for the smooth process of a rapidly developing modern economy. There is bound to be a silent social revolution following in the wake of rapid modernization. Education should assist our youth to adapt to this change.

However, adaptability to change cannot be interpreted to mean a passive indiscriminating (*sic*) acceptance of all change. What is meant is the development in the country's youth of an enquiring attitude towards traditionally established values. The children should be able to blend the best of the traditional values with the changed requirements that must follow rapid development in order that they may build a stable and modern Kenyan Society.

3 *Individual Development and Self-fulfilment*

Education should provide opportunities for the fullest development of individual talents and personality. It should help every child to develop his (*sic*) potential interests and abilities. A vital aspect of individual development is character building. Education should foster sound moral and religious values in order to help children to grow up into self-disciplined, self-reliant and integrated citizens.

4 *Social Equality etc.*

Education should promote social equality and foster a sense of social responsibility within an education system which provides equal educational opportunities for all. It should give the children varied and challenging opportunities for collective activities and corporate social service.

5 *Respect and Development of Cultural Heritage*

Education should respect, foster and develop Kenya's rich and varied cultures. It should instil in the youth of Kenya an understanding of past and present culture and its valid place in contemporary society. It should also instil in the youth a sense of respect for unfamiliar cultures.

6 *International Consciousness*

Education should foster positive attitudes to other countries and to the international community. Kenya is part of the international community. Her people do not live in a vacuum. They are part of the complicated and interdependent network of peoples and nations. Education should therefore lead the youth to accept membership in this international community with all the obligations and responsibilities, rights and benefits that this membership entails.

Part 3   Changing places and the language classroom

Brigid Ballard, Martin Cortazzi and Lixian Jin, the contributors to Part 3 of the collection, share an interest in higher education with the four authors of the chapters in Part 2. Cortazzi and Jin, and Ballard, however, are primarily concerned with helping people move between academic systems. Ballard is involved in helping international students (and particularly people from Southeast Asia) to adapt to study in her own institution, the Australian National University in Canberra. Cortazzi and Jin, on the other hand, examine what happens when Western teachers move into the Chinese academic system.

In 1988, Coleman made the following suggestion:

> To some extent ... the possibility that systems of higher educa-
> tion may not be performing precisely the same functions in
> different societies is obscured by the similarity of the nomenclat-
> ure which is employed. In almost all academic systems, for
> example, it is very easy to identify *entities* which can be labelled
> 'student', 'lecturer', 'administrator', 'examination', 'seminar',
> 'term' (or 'semester'), 'degree', and so on. Similarly, it is
> relatively easy to identify *processes* in most academic systems
> which can be labelled 'research', 'passing' (and 'failing'),
> 'studying', 'teaching', and so on. However, we must not allow
> the similarity of these labels to disguise the possibility that their
> referents are not identical. (Coleman 1988)[1]

Later, Coleman related this suggestion to the concept of 'doxa', borrowed from Bourdieu (1977) to signify all those beliefs and practices which are so fundamental and so self-evident to the members of a society that they are never discussed, never questioned, never consciously accepted or rejected:

> ... almost all academic systems share the same rhetoric:
> 'students', 'exams' and 'lectures', for example, are probably
> universal. Nevertheless, despite the existence of this shared

terminology, the differences between the doxa of one academic system and the doxa of another may be more fundamental than we care to think. (Coleman 1991: 14)

In an unpublished paper, Krasnick (1994) picks up this suggestion and expands it into a detailed study of the misunderstandings and misinterpretations which arise when Indonesian academics are preparing for postgraduate study in Canada. His investigation looks at three different types of what he terms 'cultural *faux amis*': events, roles, and written genres. 'Seminars' and 'discussions' are examples of types of event taking place in academic contexts which may have very similar names in Bahasa Indonesia (*seminar* and *diskusi*) but which may arouse very different sets of expectations among Canadian and Indonesian academics. Similarly the role of the 'professor' (*profesor* in Bahasa Indonesia) probably differs quite considerably in Indonesian and Canadian universities and, as Krasnick points out, there may be a mismatch between an Indonesian student's expectations of the *profesor* and a Canadian professor's own perceptions of his or her responsibilities. In academic writing, Krasnick indicates that terms such as 'introduction' (*introduksi*) may also arouse confusingly different sets of expectations in the minds of Indonesian and Canadian academics.[2]

When there is a danger of such misunderstanding, what action can be taken? Krasnick discusses the question of whether an academic cross-cultural communication course should be taught, either separately or integrated in some way into a more general language skills course. He argues that an academic cultural competence course is necessary, although much of the responsibility for implementation must be left to the students themselves. He therefore hints that the people who move from one academic culture to another must become 'junior anthropologists'. According to Krasnick, there are, however, difficulties associated with taking too strong a 'cultural' line in pre-departure or pre-sessional training. Firstly, language teachers themselves have an overriding concern with how to say things, and much less with what is to be said. As we will see below, Ballard makes a related point when she observes that most study skills training is 'reproductive' in nature, rather than 'analytical' or 'speculative'.

Secondly, Krasnick argues that students very often do not consider that culture learning is an important part of successful overseas study. This observation has been confirmed by a study carried out by Trevor Grimshaw, who looked at the experiences of Indonesians studying at the University of Leeds and compared these with the content of the pre-departure programme offered by the British Council in Jakarta:

[I] would like to make a further observation based on ...

experience of teaching on predeparture courses. .... the students on such courses tend not to think very much about the situation to which they are heading. They are so concerned with the immediate future – and in particular the IELTS Test – that any discussion of the UK is almost considered a digression. (Grimshaw 1993: 17)

Grimshaw identifies a number of ways in which Indonesians are taken aback when coming to Britain to study, including managing relations with lecturers, processing information, identifying sources of information, interacting with students of other nationalities, and interacting with British people. None of these issues is dealt with in their pre-departure training.

In Chapter 8, Ballard's contribution to this debate builds on the considerable body of her earlier work – drawing on her extensive experience in helping Asian students enter the Australian academic system – in which she has consistently argued that there are fundamental differences between academic cultures in terms of expectations and forms of behaviour. These differences interfere when movement from one academic context to another takes place (see, for example, Ballard 1982, 1984, 1989 and Ballard and Clanchy 1991). The differences are also highly complex – indeed she warns us against looking at them in terms of a 'fixed dualism or dichotomy by which different societies can be classified and simplistically stereotyped'. Ballard proposes that education systems can be characterised by their attitudes to knowledge which fall somewhere along a continuum between conservation and extension. An education system which falls towards the 'conservation of knowledge' extreme will emphasise a 'reproductive' approach, whilst a 'speculative' approach is likely to be found in systems which fall at the 'extension of knowledge' extreme. An 'analytical' approach will characterise systems which fall somewhere between the two extremes of the continuum.[3]

Ballard's argument is that, ironically, the academic skills courses held in Australian universities are, by their very nature, unhelpful, because they tend to adopt a reproductive approach. The rest of the university, meanwhile, is likely to demand at the very least an analytical mode of behaviour – if not a 'speculative' one – from its students. The English language class, therefore, largely reinforces inappropriate study behaviours, rather than acting as the prompt or catalyst which can help students to question those behaviours. As Kramsch (1993: 11) observes, 'Neither second nor foreign language education have any tradition of dialectic thought.'

One of the ways in which Ballard supports her startling assertion that the English language class is counter-productive is to highlight the differences between questioning in the language classroom and questioning in the real academic classroom. In very few language classrooms, she suggests, do questions have the function of probing, raising issues, developing ideas and 'extending the intellectual boundaries of the discourse'. She also reminds us that writing may have many different functions – as has been argued by Street (1984, 1993) in his work on cultural variability in the roles which literacy carries – ranging from 'the public record of appropriate behaviour' to 'a vehicle for the analysis and extension of knowledge'. Students who carry with them one such perception of the function of writing – honed, probably, through many years of practice – are bound to experience severe difficulties when thrown into a system which demands that writing should perform quite different functions. We are reminded yet again, here, of Krasnick's 'cultural *faux ami*' argument.

We return, then, to the same question: what are we to do to facilitate the movement between academic cultures? Krasnick, as we have seen, has proposed that a greater role needs to be given to sociocultural analysis in the EAP classroom. Ballard's proposal is similar, but she spells it out in somewhat greater detail. What is needed, she suggests, is not a course in 'English for Academic Purposes' but, rather, a programme in 'English for Intellectual Purposes'. EIP courses would focus on 'the nature of cognitive acts required by specific tasks or assignments set within a distinctive academic context or discipline' and would be much less concerned with language form than is currently the case. The first priority must be to introduce academics who are moving between cultures to the intellectual demands of university work in the target situation and only then provide them with opportunities to develop and practise the language which is needed to satisfy those demands.

In this way, Ballard's proposals require language teachers to develop in three novel ways:

1 They must familiarise themselves with the intellectual and educational culture of the target situation.
2 They must familiarise themselves with at least one general intellectual approach of the sciences, the social sciences or the humanities.
3 They must change 'their own teaching behaviour from a reproductive to an increasingly analytical style' – by example.

Ballard claims – and there is no gainsaying the assertion – that her proposals constitute 'a challenge for language teachers which could extend the professional basis of language teaching in interesting new directions.'

The analysis presented by Cortazzi and Jin in Chapter 9 resonates with many of the earlier chapters in this collection. They consider the cultures of learning which permeate behaviour in language classrooms in China and are particularly interested in the clash of expectations which occurs when Chinese students are taught by Western teachers, thus reminding us of one of the issues identified by Holliday in his examination of Egyptian university classrooms in Chapter 5.

Cortazzi and Jin go further than this, however, and trace the roots of behaviour in university classrooms back to students' earliest educational experiences in kindergarten and primary school. They thus provide an overview of the complete educational system in China (paralleling LoCastro's survey of education in Japan in Chapter 3). They argue, very effectively, that although classroom behaviour as manifested at different levels in the system may *appear* to vary in certain respects, there are in fact continuities throughout the system.

Most significantly, classroom behaviour at all levels reflects a constellation of socio-economic features in Chinese society. The range of these features is extraordinary and includes:

- the need for children to have memorised 2,600 written characters by the age of 13;
- the duty of schools to counteract the tendency of families to over-indulge their children (since each family is permitted just one child);
- the ancient belief that enlightenment comes only after full mastery of whatever is being studied.

Cortazzi and Jin recommend that where language learners and teachers do not share the same culture, a process of 'cultural synergy' – based on the model of accommodation theory – is required. The objective of this process is to raise the cultural awareness of *both* parties involved in the classroom process. Here we have, therefore, another radical proposal to place beside Ballard's argument that the language classroom should become more analytical and less reproductive in character.

Notes

1 Compare Pennycook's observation that 'despite the apparent commonality in the terms "teaching/learning English" ... [situations may be] so diverse that they can only be discussed in terms of their specific contexts' (1994: 5).

2 In discussion of the concept *profesor*, Krasnick observes that his students frequently request permission to visit their instructors at their homes. As we saw in Chapter 4, Coleman records a similar phenomenon at a different institution in Indonesia and tentatively interprets it

as evidence of students seeking an opportunity to adjust themselves to the lecturer's expectations and style. Elsewhere (Coleman 1993), it has been suggested that this desire to visit lecturers at home may spring from a need felt by the most highly motivated students to become 'individuals' in the eyes of their lecturers, particularly when they are studying in very large classes; if the lecturer recognises one as an individual then it is possible that some at least of the lecturer's attention may be directed towards one during the lesson. In fact, this desire on the part of students to get to know and understand their teachers is not peculiar to Indonesia. See, for example, the evidence provided by Roberts *et al.* (1992: 7) that students in colleges of further education in London are also aware of the importance of their relationships with their lecturers. Indeed this study found (1992: 17) that a student's ability to manage his or her relationship with the teacher constituted one of three essential components which contribute to overall success (the others being 'managing assessment' and 'managing learning'). Moreover:

> ... students who have established a relatively good relationship with the teacher but who have not tuned in successfully to the overall teaching mode do relatively better in the final assessment than those who do not have this good relationship. (Roberts *et al.* 1992: 46)

So in this case the question is not whether seeking to establish good relationships with teachers is a culturally specific phenomenon. The problem for students moving from one academic system to another is, rather, how one can look for and find *culturally appropriate ways* of achieving such relationships.

3 There is a clear parallel, incidentally, between Ballard's three-fold 'reproductive-analytical-speculative' distinction and the five-level model, proposed by Dahlgren (1984), which ranges from 'structural' through 'relational' to 'extended abstract'.

References

Ballard, B. 1982. Language is not enough: Responses to the academic difficulties of overseas students. In H. Bock and J. Gassin (Eds.) *Communication at University*. Melbourne: La Trobe University.

Ballard, B. 1984. Improving student writing: An integrated approach to cultural adjustment. In R. Williams, J. Swales and J. Kirkman (Eds.) *Common Ground: Shared Interests in ESP and Communication Studies*, 43–53. (ELT Documents 117.) Oxford: Pergamon Press.

Ballard, B. 1989. Overseas students and Australian academics: Learning and teaching styles. In B. Williams (Ed.) *Overseas Students in Australia: Policy and Practice*, 87–98. Canberra: IDP.

Ballard, B. and J. Clanchy 1991. Assessment by misconception: Cultural influences and intellectual traditions. In L. Hamp-Lyons (Ed.) *Assessing Second Language Writing in Academic Contexts*. Norwood, N.J.: Ablex.

Bourdieu, P. 1977. *Outline of a Theory of Practice*. Cambridge: Cambridge University Press.

Coleman, H. 1988. The appropriacy of teaching study skills. Paper presented during the conference on 'Studying with English', University of Bristol, 5–6 January 1988.

Coleman, H. 1991. The testing of 'appropriate behaviour' in an academic context. In P. Adams, B. Heaton and P. Howarth (Eds.) *Socio-Cultural Issues in English for Academic Purposes*, 13–23. (Review of ELT vol. 1, no. 2.) London: Modern English Publications.

Coleman, H. 1993. Investigating and exploiting what learners do in large classes. Paper presented at the International Conference on Communication Skills for Nigerian Federal Universities, Nsukka, Nigeria, 29–31 March 1993.

Dahlgren, L.-O. 1984. Outcomes of learning. In F. Marton, D. Hounsell and N. Entwhistle (Eds.) *The Experience of Learning*, 19–35. Edinburgh: Scottish Academic Press.

Grimshaw, T. 1993. Adjusting to life on a British campus. Jakarta: Unpublished report prepared for the British Council.

Kramsch, C. 1993. *Context and Culture in Language Teaching*. Oxford: Oxford University Press.

Krasnick, H. 1994. The role of 'cultural *faux amis*' in teaching academic cross-cultural communication. Unpublished paper. Yogyakarta: Canada-Indonesia Predeparture Program, Universitas Gadjah Mada.

Pennycook, A. 1994. *The Cultural Politics of English as an International Language*. Harlow: Longman.

Roberts, C., C. Garnett, S. Kapoor and S. Sarangi 1992. *Quality in Teaching and Learning: Four Multicultural Classrooms in Further Education*. Sheffield: Training, Enterprise and Education Directorate, Department of Employment.

Street, B. V. 1984. *Literacy in Theory and Practice*. Cambridge: Cambridge University Press.

Street, B. V. (Ed.) 1993. *Cross-Cultural Approaches to Literacy*. Cambridge: Cambridge University Press.

8 Through language to learning: Preparing overseas students for study in Western universities

Brigid Ballard

Introduction

Teachers of English as a second or foreign language normally measure their success in terms of the success of their students in passing language tests or in achieving a specified level of communicative competence, particularly oral and reading competence. In colleges and universities the gearing of the course design, the construction of materials and the styles of instruction to the achieving of such benchmarks may be valid for teaching large generalist classes. There is, however, one group of students with very specific English language needs who are not adequately catered for in such traditional language classes: students who are learning English in order to study overseas in an English medium Western university.

These students are usually highly motivated language learners and among the most successful students in the classroom. They see language classes as the doorway to their future studies and their careers. Yet when they emerge at the end of their course with a satisfactory TOEFL or IELTS score and proceed triumphantly to university in Britain, North America or Australia, they find that studying in English is significantly different from learning English and that the academic success to which they have become accustomed is now much more elusive and hard to achieve. Too often their language learning has taken place in a vacuum, divorced from the intellectual context of their other studies. In the language classroom they have been rewarded for linguistic accuracy, for correctness in the reproduction and manipulation of language and structures; now they are required to move beyond this focus on language in its own right to using language as a tool and a medium for thinking. Such students provide a particular challenge to the language teacher who, in attempting to meet their language needs, has to develop a syllabus which relates English not merely to the social culture of English-speaking countries but also to the broad intellectual culture and the specialised 'sub-cultures' of the university.

The truism that learning a new language involves learning a new culture informs the syllabus for most language courses. As our foreign language students memorise greetings, practise dialogues about shopping, sightseeing or visiting homes, and follow all the routine lessons, they are also explicitly provided with cultural explanations for the situations and behaviours they are learning to mimic. Most language textbooks and audio-visual materials now include notes on cultural points alongside all the vocabulary lists, linguistic patterns and exercises.

Our students bound for overseas universities, however, are not moving only to a foreign country but also to a distinctive educational culture which can be unexpectedly different from the one in which they have been nurtured. Therefore their language training needs to be designed and structured to take account of these educational differences, alongside the differences in social culture.

In this chapter I want to focus the attention of those who develop and teach English courses on the difficulties confronting foreign language and foreign culture students when, shaped and polished by their English language classes, they finally appear alongside local students in a classroom or laboratory in a Western university. In their earlier language classes they were encouraged by a language teacher who was sympathetic to students struggling to express themselves in a foreign tongue. Now they are likely to be faced with a lecturer who has very little knowledge of the home countries of these foreign students, very little patience with their special problems, and only irritation with their language difficulties. This lecturer will be mainly concerned with presenting the content of the course and with leading the students to raise constructive questions about this content. There will be little incentive to modify the syllabus or assessment requirements to suit the needs of the foreign student minority; and there will be (often justifiable) appeals to 'maintaining academic standards' whenever such suggestions are raised. Inevitably it will be the foreign students, not the system, that must make the necessary adjustments.

So how are these foreign students to survive, and to succeed, in the real life of the university degree course? And how can language teachers develop courses which will assist these students in making a successful transition to this new environment? Clearly these students have already made the crucial first step in the adjustment process: they have acquired sufficient competence in English language to satisfy the university authorities that they are capable of following the degree course for which they are now enrolled. These students are the success stories of the EFL courses, the pride of their EAP/ESP/ETP teachers. They know more about the gerundive, about passive constructions and the use of the subjunctive than most native speakers.

Despite such formal knowledge, however, the use of English will continue to be a problem for these students, and their lecturers and supervisors, throughout their studies. In our experience in the Study Skills Centre at the Australian National University, problems with language serve as a ready-made excuse, used by both staff and students, for poor academic performance. 'I am not getting good grades – it must be because of my English', the students cry as they seek out supplementary English assistance; 'They are doing poorly – it must be their weakness in English', the lecturers cry as they herd these students to the nearest available Language Centre. Nor does this situation necessarily reflect badly on their prior language learning, for language acquisition is inevitably developmental, with each new situation evoking a further variation in linguistic competence. A preliminary language course can only cover the most common situations and in the most general terms.

Yet the explanation that 'poor English' is the basic cause of the academic problems of most overseas students is clearly inadequate; and, in our experience, additional English courses seldom resolve their problems either. Masked by language problems lie the much deeper problems of adjusting to a new intellectual culture, a new way of thinking and of processing knowledge to meet the expectations inherent in the Anglo educational system. Foreign students come not merely from other language backgrounds but, more importantly, from other cultural backgrounds.

In the following discussion, I will first examine some of the cultural differences which affect attitudes to knowledge both within our own society and across different societies. The insights generated from this examination will then be applied to the styles of teaching and learning that are characteristic of the English language classroom; and finally some suggestions will be made about developing a more appropriate syllabus and teaching style in English language classes for students from other languages and other cultures who are preparing to study in Western universities.

Cultural influences on approaches to learning

In our work as study skills advisers in an Australian university we meet a wide range of overseas students enrolled in first degree and postgraduate courses and coming from many different countries, though predominantly from Asia and the Pacific region. On the basis of our experience with these students and with the academic staff who teach them, we have become increasingly interested in the cultural influences on attitudes to knowledge, and therefore on styles of teaching and of learning, which characterise the educational process (Ballard and Clanchy 1984, 1991a). Figure 1 sets out a model of the relationships between cultural

Attitudes to knowledge:		Conserving ————————— Extending ——>		
Learning approaches:		Reproductive <———>	Analytical <———>	Speculative

Teaching Strategies	Role of teacher	• almost exclusive source of
		  – knowledge
		  – direction/guidance
		  – assessment
			• co-ordinator of learning resources
			• questioner, critical guide, gadfly
			• principal source of assessment
				• more experienced colleague and collaborator
				• preliminary critic and adviser
				• patron

	Characteristic activities	• transmission of information and demonstration of skills • overt moral and social training	• analysis of information and ideas within interpretative frameworks • modelling of/demand for critical approach to knowledge and conventions	• discussion/advice on ideas and methods on individual basis • modelling of hypothetical and creative thinking • collaborative search for new ideas

	Assessment	• tests of memory recall and practical demonstration of skills
		• emphasis on replication
		• geared to ranking
			• assignments/exams requiring critical analysis and problem-solving emphasis on:
			  – originality
			  – quality of interpretation
				• independent research – thesis and papers of publishable quality
				• 'contribution to the field of knowledge'

	Aim	• simple ('unreconstructed') transfer of knowledge and skills
		  ⇓ ⇑
			• independent and critical styles of thinking
			• development of capacity for theory and abstraction
			  ⇓ ⇑
				• development of speculative, critical intelligence
				• expansion of knowledge base (theory, data, techniques)
				  ⇓ ⇑

Learning Strategies	Type	• memorisation and imitation ⇓ ⇑	• analytical and critical thinking	• speculating, hypothesising
	Activities	• summarising, describing, identifying, and applying formulae and information	• questioning, judging and recombining ideas and information into an argument	• research design, implementation and reporting • deliberate search for new ideas, data, explanations
	Characteristic questions	• what?	• why? how? how valid? how important?	• what if?
	Aim	• 'correctness'	• 'simple' originality, reshaping material into a different pattern	• 'creative' originality, totally new approach/new knowledge

Figure 1 *Influence of cultural attitudes to knowledge on teaching and learning strategies (Ballard and Clanchy 1991a: 13)*

attitudes to knowledge and the development of different teaching and learning strategies.

There are two assumptions underpinning this model. The first is that there are attitudes to knowledge which emphasise the conservation of knowledge and attitudes which emphasise its extension, and that both types of attitude are to be found, in differing degrees, at work in all cultures and societies. We are positing a continuum of attitudes, not some fixed dualism or dichotomy by which different societies can be classified and simplistically stereotyped. As we well recognise, individual students in all cultures can vary their attitudes to knowledge, and therefore their current study behaviour, according to the intellectual task facing them and the level at which they are working.

Nevertheless, and this is our second underlying assumption, there are also dominant tendencies within cultures about socially appropriate attitudes to knowledge. It is these traditional attitudes, which can lie at significantly different points along the continuum, that gradually shape the preferred educational processes within different societies at different moments in their history (Ballard and Clanchy 1991a).

Within our own Western education system we would expect to find the reproductive approach dominant in our primary and secondary schools. Here the teacher is the source and the director of knowledge who selects and transmits information and demonstrates appropriate skills; and the students seek, through memorisation and imitation, to reproduce what they have been taught. The good teachers are those who present their material clearly, in a well organised sequence, and who can relate the personal experience of the students to the lessons being taught. Good students pay attention, do their homework, and demonstrate in tests and exams how 'correctly' they have mastered the materials they have been taught. For example, in a Maths class students are taught to use a particular formula and are then tested in terms of how accurately they can repeat this procedure. In a History class they may be given notes on a particular historical event, for example a list of five causes of the French Revolution, and in an exam they will get high marks if they can reproduce these same five points.

The analytical approach would be generally characteristic of our undergraduate education where there is a progressive shift to a more critical style of learning. Here the aim is to develop independent and analytical styles of thinking and the capacity for handling theory and abstraction. Knowledge is no longer fixed but is open to question and criticism, and a key role for a lecturer is to open up the uncertainties, paradoxes and complexities inherent in every topic being studied. Teachers are no longer the sole authoritative source of knowledge; instead, they now guide and challenge their students to develop their own ideas and judgements. Good students learn to question and evaluate all they hear and read. They are expected to recombine ideas and information about a controversial issue to support and develop their own 'original' argument or interpretation. Our Maths students must now construct arguments to justify the application of a particular formula to new situations. Our History students must now produce a 2,000-word essay on the causes of the French Revolution which will draw on lectures, tutorials and critical reading of a wide range of books and articles which each present a different interpretation, based on different assumptions and different weightings of evidence. Each essay should reflect the critical judgement of the individual writer about the significant causes of the events of 1789.

We reach the speculative approach in our postgraduate courses, particularly in research degrees. Here the criterion for a successful thesis is that it 'makes a significant contribution to knowledge' and the prevailing assumption is that knowledge is constantly open to extension, revision and change. The supervisor of a research student combines the roles of senior colleague and preliminary critic; and learning takes place, often on an individual basis, through discussion, experimentation and reflection. The Maths scholar formulates new problems or creates new solutions; the History scholar unearths new sources of evidence or develops new explanatory theories.

Of course this explanation is necessarily simplified. For example, there are many ways in which the divisions overlap: we may get analytical and even speculative approaches in the final years of secondary school, just as some university courses may be highly reproductive in approach as, for example, in science courses where students have to learn new basic skills and information. And, as we know from the work of Marton and his Gotenburg colleagues (Bowden 1986), an individual student may in one course be relying on reproductive (surface) learning strategies and in another on analytical (deep) strategies, depending on the intellectual demands of the set task and on the student's own motives in meeting those demands. Nonetheless, the notion of a continuum of (culturally influenced) attitudes to knowledge and approaches to learning does much to explain the underlying problems students have in moving from one level to another within an education system. The shift is not merely a matter of deepening knowledge but also involves changing intellectual strategies: the scholarly aims are different, even the typical questions which are raised vary from one level to another.

The same continuum of attitudes is to be found in other cultures but the dominant attitude to knowledge may vary and so shape the educational process differently. All societies produce analytical minds and creative thinkers. No cultural system has a monopoly on scholarly achievement. However, in many non-Western societies there is a much stronger emphasis on the conserving attitude, producing a greater reliance on reproductive learning. Sometimes this approach derives partly from lack of educational resources. If there are few books, little lab equipment, and large classes, then inevitably the teacher and the textbook must constitute the basic sources of knowledge. And if progress is largely assessed by attendance and by easily processed multiple-choice tests of factually based material, then students will adapt their learning strategies accordingly. But underlying the problems endemic to under-resourced educational systems lie the pervasive social attitudes to knowledge, to authority and to tradition which distinguish one culture from another and which favour particular styles of learning. For example, the reverence for the Koran in Islamic societies colours the way in which it is considered possible to handle a written source. In some Buddhist societies, where respect for the teacher is a duty which follows those of respect for the Buddha, the Law and the monks, the dynamics of the classroom are shaped by the impossibility of questioning, much less contradicting, the teacher. In Japan the subordinate role of the student overrides any attempt to develop independent or individual views. In these societies the roles and reciprocal duties of student and teacher are clearly understood and respected; and the classroom is not a venue for critical questioning or argument.

This is not to claim that all Asian classrooms are conducted solely in terms of reliance on sacred and ancient texts, any more than all Western classrooms are characterised by Socratic dialogue. Yet the classroom does reflect the values of society in many subtle ways. In a society that emphasises respect for the past and for the authority of the teacher, the behaviour of both teachers and students will mirror these values. A society that rewards independence and individuality will produce a very different classroom etiquette.

So long as students remain within their own educational systems, differences in intellectual approach between school and university, between one degree and another, between one discipline and another are relatively easy to accommodate. In Western societies, school leavers may take time to adjust to the new demands of university study, science students taking a humanities unit may find the different styles of analysis or discourse disconcerting, the leap from undergraduate coursework into independent research can be confusing as well as exhilarating; but these different demands are, to some extent, expected and students generally recognise that new situations require new learning strategies. For foreign students transferring into the Western system, however, the problems of adjustment are much more acute because their past social and educational experience may not have prepared them either to recognise or to accept the need for change in their study behaviour.

When a Japanese student was asked by his Politics lecturer, 'What is your opinion about these two conflicting interpretations of the reasons for the Great Depression?', his reply, 'But I do not have an opinion – I am a student' reflected a genuine cultural bewilderment. (We will look at this case in more detail below.)

Most commonly we find that overseas students cling tenaciously to the learning strategies that have worked so well for them in the past. They assume that hard work correlates with success, and so if they do poorly in an early test in a course they are prepared to work even longer hours to improve their grade – the problem is that if they are working in a reproductive rather than an analytical style, their grades will still not improve significantly. Their difficulties lie in the disjunction of expectations about the styles of learning that are required, and the excuse of poor language competence merely glosses over these more basic problems.

Learning in the English language classroom

The one experience all foreign language students share is their training in English language. This is their ticket to admission to a Western university. It also provides, potentially, their first taste of Western styles of teaching and learning. Yet how well does the style of the language classroom in fact prepare these students for their future studies?

If we apply our model of styles of teaching and learning to the language classroom, we quickly recognise that most language teaching falls within the reproductive approach. Necessarily so, in that students are learning a new language in which they must have mastery of the basic vocabulary and structures in order to be assessed as competent. Yet there is a real tension between the ways in which the students are expected to learn in language classes and the ways they must study in their later university courses.

Consider the contrasts, set out in Figure 2, based on the four communicative skills which underlie most language learning syllabuses. Again, the contrasts identified are necessarily simplified – indicative rather than exhaustive characteristics of the two sets of classroom objectives.

A more detailed discussion of these four language modes will show the differing purposes to which each is put in the language classroom and in the academic context.

Mode	Language class aims	Academic class aims
Listening	total comprehension	selective of content
	capacity to 'store' whole text	selective 'storage'/note-taking
	attention to discrete language features, e.g. pronunciation and sentence construction	critical responsiveness to content
Speaking	production of accurate sentences	expression of complex ideas
	accurate pronunciation and intonation	raising relevant questions/ criticisms
Reading	generation of correct linguistic structures	development of ideas
	manipulation of appropriate registers	command of appropriate style of argument
Writing	generation of correct linguistic structures	development of ideas
	manipulation of appropriate registers	command of appropriate style of argument

Figure 2   Contrasting aims of language classes and academic classes

Listening

Listening skills are among the first to be emphasised in the language classroom. Whether students are listening to the teacher, to language tapes or to each other, they are encouraged to train their auditory sense so that they can achieve total comprehension of what is being said. Listening is also the avenue to oral imitation, so that students are consciously listening for pronunciation and intonation, for sentence construction and idioms, for language usage. They are tested for this skill by comprehension questions and by their capacity to reproduce the formulaic utterances they hear. Inevitably what is said in such contexts is less important than how it sounds.

In university lectures and tutorials, however, listening skills are directed to quite different ends. Now students must listen with critical attention to gain specific information or understand a particular line of argument. Although overall comprehension is important, more essential is the capacity to process the spoken material so as to extract from it the points that are relevant to the student's own needs – maybe for use in an essay, or to open up a criticism or discussion, or to fill in gaps in existing knowledge. The listener plays an active role in determining what is important in the lecturer's presentation.

So foreign language students bring to lectures a set of largely inappropriate listening skills. They try to 'hear' and then write a full record of everything that is said. They complain that the lecturers and other students 'talk too fast' and so they cannot keep up with all that is said. They plead to be permitted to tape lectures so that they can go over and over them later in order to extract every last meaning from each sentence. Their aim is to achieve total recall, and if given a chance they will quote their lecturers verbatim in later essays. Yet such a reproductive approach is seldom appropriate to either lectures or tutorial discussions. Lecturers always insist that the 'good student' is one who listens closely and makes only occasional notes on selected points from the presentation, who in tutorials is capable of picking up the significant point in a discussion and developing it further. The 'parrot-like student' is given scant credit.

However the foreign student comes to such classes with experience only of reproductive listening, both from school and from English language lessons. In fact the English language classroom largely reinforces, rather than acts as the first step away from, inappropriate learning habits. What could have been a valuable opportunity to induce some shift in learning styles, in an 'exotic' language class where students are predisposed to mimic new behaviours, is missed. Instead the opportunities for confusion and for misdirected learning strategies are perpetuated. The intellectual shift that is inherent in the concept of selective and critical listening remains unaddressed.

Speaking

The more active speaking skills remain the most common focus of English language classes, the very hallmark of communicative competence. However, consider the activities that characterise the acquisition of oral English skills: patterned questions and responses; prepared talks on simple topics of general interest; maybe a debate, in which the speakers prepare their speeches and present, as firmly as possible, one side of a controversial (but usually trivial) topic. Students are praised for the clarity of their pronunciation and the accuracy of their syntax, that is for their control of spoken language.

In university courses speech is the medium for exchange of ideas, for argument, for the development of new points of view. The patterns that underlie exchanges are the intellectual patterns of argumentative discourse, rather than discrete speech acts or carefully graduated models of linguistic interaction. And in this situation most foreign language students find themselves tongue-tied and dumb. While they are still attempting to produce linguistically acceptable utterances, the class discussion has moved on to other points.

Most foreign students react in either of two ways to their incapacity to join in discussions. Some explain their failure in terms of their language problems. 'I do not have the words to say what I think,' they complain. 'By the time I have worked out what I want to say, the other speakers have moved to another point.' Others say: 'I am shy to speak in public because the others may not understand what I am saying. And it makes everything slow down.' And their common response in such circumstances: 'I wait till someone else expresses what I wanted to say, and then I feel better.' But many of these students recognise an additional constraint. As one Thai student explained: 'I do not wish to be like Australian students who criticise each other and even contradict their lecturer. Such behaviour is not proper, I think.'

There is one particular speech act which typifies the different purposes of speaking in language classes and in tutorials: the use of questions. In the language classroom the teacher is likely to pose most of the questions, except when students are specifically rehearsing the interrogative or when the class is engaging in conversation practice. So the initiative for designing and raising the questions generally lies with the teacher. Moreover when the teacher or the students do ask questions, these will commonly be of two distinct types. The first is the question leading to a clarification of fact (*What did you say? Where is the book? Whose pen is this?*) and the second is the question as part of 'game playing' in which the focus remains not on the content but on the form of the reply (as in many patterned 'dialogues' or 'class conversations' in which everyone plays the language game and the actual sense of the conversation is secondary – and often deliberately hilarious). In few cases will such questions be real, in the sense that they are raising matters of substantive content and genuine interest. And in even fewer cases will they be probing questions which raise issues, develop ideas and extend the intellectual boundaries of the discourse.

Yet in the academic classroom questions about matters of 'fact' or simple clarification are relatively rare, and they are generally regarded as unproductive and merely indicative of inattention on the part of the questioner. If we refer back to Figure 1, the diagram outlining cultural influences on teaching and learning styles, the characteristic styles of questions for each learning approach are listed. As we have suggested, the most common question for the reproductive approach is 'What?', leading to simple clarification of facts. In undergraduate courses the students move to more probing and complex questions such as 'Why? How? How valid is this view or statement or finding? How important is it?' Here the student is required to take independent responsibility for both understanding and evaluating what is being presented in lectures, labs and tutorials. Questions are now designed to lead to further complexities and development of the original material – the aim is no longer reproduction but tentative validation or extension of knowledge. And in the postgraduate years our students move to the wholly speculative 'What if?', raising hypotheses and questioning the very basis of current theory, knowledge and ideas.

For a student coming from a culture in which knowledge is less open to question and criticism, the first barrier lies in the need to make a deliberate change of attitude about how knowledge can properly be handled. Once the student has overcome that cultural hurdle, then the art of generating productive questions has to be learned. Once again the linguistic problem masks a much deeper culturally-based intellectual disjunction.

Reading

The approach to reading in language classrooms also relies on a reproductive style of learning, further reinforcing the past experience of foreign students which has often been limited to reading school text-books. Many of these students come from educational systems in which there is a scarcity of library resources and even of textbooks and from a tradition in which great respect is paid to the written word. The good student will study the textbook diligently and, as far as possible, learn it by heart. Apposite quotations from traditionally authoritative sources are the sinews of argument and can be the deciding factor when a conflict of views arises. A Koranic verse, a traditional saying, or a sentence written by an eminent scholar is not open to criticism or discussion but forms the unqualified justification and validation of the point of view being presented. So close attention to the wording of a text is essential.

In the English language classroom this approach will be further reinforced. Many language textbooks include short reading passages (which are seldom intellectually challenging) that the student must translate and 'comprehend'. Such tasks involve much use of the dictionary and the answering of sequenced questions to show that the student has covered and understood the whole passage. Students are seldom required to question the passage or read it only for a particular item of information or idea. So reading is characterised by detailed language work leading to comprehension.

In an academic course, 'reading a text', or referring to sources, draws on a very different set of strategies. For example, the skill of purposeful skimming is essential when many texts have to be scoured for material for an essay or thesis or tutorial discussion. Selective close reading of key passages and critical analysis of the writer's ideas, evidence and argument provide the basis for the reader to form an independent judgement of the issues relevant to his or her purpose in reading the text in the first place. Now students can no longer read just to follow the writer's presentation; they must also read to form their own synthesis of the ideas and conclusions presented in a range of sources (Ballard and Clanchy 1988).

For a foreign postgraduate student, fresh from success in English language classes and coming from an education system in which library resources have been rare, there is often a painful adjustment to the style of reading expected in Western universities. Such a student is likely to be greeted by her supervisor soon after arrival with the vague instructions: 'Why don't you spend a couple of months in the library just reading around your subject, getting up to date with the most recent research in the journals? Then come back and we'll talk about your research topic.' This student will head, dutifully, for the library. After some days of confusion about the library system (compounded by the fact that she may mistakenly treat the reference librarian like a lowly clerk, which will not produce goodwill and co-operation), she will, probably with the help of a fellow student, work out the call numbers of the main journals in her discipline. She can then identify a range of articles that seem to relate to her field of interest and proceed to borrow the ones she is able to locate on the shelves.

By the end of eight weeks it is not uncommon that such a student will have managed to read only a dozen journal articles – but she will have studied them till the pages are in tatters. She will have annotated every difficult word, memorised every diagram, and will be able to repeat much of them verbatim. If her supervisor were to give her an examination on the contents of these articles, she would probably do very well.

But of course it would never cross the supervisor's mind to 'test' the student on what little she has managed to read over the past two months. The supervisor expects (though probably not considering it necessary to make this explicit to an advanced postgraduate student) that the student will have skimmed maybe a hundred journal articles, made sketch notes on a variety of issues, ideas, theories, findings and problems that emerge from these papers, and developed an annotated bibliography for later reference. And, most importantly, the supervisor expects the student to be ready and able to discuss these articles critically and comparatively and, through this reading, to have focused her attention on a specific area or issue which might become the topic for her own research.

When the two do meet after the eight week 'settling in' period, the mismatch of expectations about what such reading should produce inevitably leads to mutual frustration. The student has studied in the only way she knows, both from her past educational experience and using the skills she has learned in her English classes. The supervisor is at a loss because the student has not apparently made any recognisable progress at all but has merely wasted everyone's valuable time.

Such incidents are not uncommon in our experience. Once again they derive from culturally different approaches to texts, originating from different attitudes to the nature and functions of knowledge.

Writing

Writing skills are the skills most highly valued in Western universities; and they are the skills least frequently developed in language classes. Here too the mismatch between the past experience of overseas students and the expectations of Western academic staff comes into sharpest focus.

Most foreign students have relatively little experience of writing extended and systematic discourse even in their own languages, much less in English. In societies where essays are a tradition, as in Japan (Hinds 1987) or in traditional Chinese education (Mohan and Lo 1985) the discourse models and the writer's intentions are radically different from those expected of a student in a Western university (Connor and Kaplan 1987; Kaplan 1966). Where essays are required, they tend to be literary works of art rather than arguments based on the critical analysis of selected evidence. So these students have very little experience of 'thinking through writing', of using writing to develop and extend in their own independent and individual fashion the ideas, findings and theories of others.

English language classes reinforce this separation between the power of developing ideas and the act of writing. Most writing in these classrooms consists of either single sentence responses in formal exercises or the production of a couple of brief paragraphs on a very general topic. The focus is primarily on the accuracy of the syntax and spelling: when students are encouraged to look over their work before handing it in, they look for language errors, not for problems in the content or structure of their essay. And they lose marks for linguistic error, not for weak subject matter. So writing-in-English becomes a struggle with correctness of language rather than T. S. Eliot's 'raid on the inarticulate'.

In their academic courses students are expected to show in their lab reports and essays that they can systematically organise their ideas and the evidence they have selected into an argument that will produce an intellectually satisfying evaluation of some controversial topic (Clanchy and Ballard 1981, 1984). And, in their writing more than elsewhere, they must also be able to adopt the style and structure of argument appropriate to each of the distinctively different disciplines they are studying (Becher 1981, 1989; Galtung 1981; Nelson, Megill and McCloskey 1987). It is not merely content and vocabulary that distinguishes the History essay from the Botany report, the Literature essay from the Economics paper; it is also the very different scholarly traditions of argumentation and discourse structure which have developed within each discipline (Ballard and Clanchy 1989).

For the foreign language student such fundamental nuances are obscured by the struggle to write in accurate English. When these students come to our Centre seeking assistance, they commonly explain: 'I know what I want to say but I can't find the English words to say it.' Many times they will produce a piece of writing that is linguistically reasonable but which is expressing only very simplified ideas – and if the level of writing suddenly lifts, then we are reasonably safe in assuming the passage has been copied from another source (or repeated from the student's exhaustive lecture notes). What is happening here is that a focus on language is overriding intellectual concerns and the student has opted to write something correctly even if it is at a very elementary intellectual level rather than daring to express more sophisticated ideas in less than correct English.

When we encounter this problem we generally ask the student to write out the difficult ideas in his own language and then together we can work out the appropriate English expressions to convey his meaning. In such cases we find that foreign language students can nearly always recognise the most accurate English expressions from among those we suggest even though they could not generate them independently. Although students are initially reluctant to try this strategy because it runs counter to all their training in English language courses, we find it is a key step in transferring their attention from the accuracy of their language to the quality of their thinking. Of course the two must go in tandem: brilliant ideas will generally go unrecognised if they are submerged in incomprehensible syntax. On the other hand, a high level of language competence will not in itself generate sophisticated thought.

Once again the foreign students have, in their writing, also to overcome a range of cultural differences. We return to the case of the Japanese student of Politics, with very competent English and a good command of political theory, who came to seek help after his first essay had received a very low mark and much criticism from his lecturer. He had been asked for a critical comparison of the work of two leading political theorists in relation to the causes of the Great Depression. He had collected sufficient data about the Great Depression; he had plenty of information about the two scholars; he understood the force of their different theories; and he knew, from language classes, the linguistic forms and structures appropriate for signalling and making comparisons. Yet his essay had been severely criticised because he had merely written parallel accounts of the lives and ideas of each scholar without making any critical analysis or reaching an evaluation of the merits of their respective theories in relation to the Great Depression. The student was most upset at this criticism, explaining that it was not his role, as a student, to criticise or evaluate the views of eminent scholars or to tell his reader (his lecturer) what to think. Moreover, as he saw it, the purpose of a comparison is to achieve some opening for harmony between opposing views, not to pit them against each other.

Here we have a clear case of different cultural norms producing misunderstanding. This problem took some time to sort out. It was necessary to give the student some explicit instruction in the ways he was expected to analyse and evaluate the materials he had collected for his essay. First he was shown some essays by other, more successful, writers in his class in order to demonstrate the way in which an argument can be structured by analysing comparative theories. Then he was able to move away from his largely biographical account of his two political theorists towards a more critical evaluation of their ideas in terms of their explanatory powers in relation to a particular historical period. He was quite capable of these intellectual tasks; but he had not understood they were inherent in the comparative essay he had been set.

We have encountered similar misunderstandings with Asian students who have been trained to write literary appreciations rather than literary criticisms, or who prefer to falsify their experimental results if they contradict the findings of senior colleagues. Writing in many societies is regarded as the public record of appropriate behaviour, rather than as a vehicle for the analysis and extension of knowledge.

An expanded role for English language courses

Clearly students who are taking English language courses in order to prepare for studies in a Western university require special assistance which reaches beyond the normal boundaries of the language classroom. Maybe we need to develop a special English for Intellectual Purposes (EIP) syllabus which will introduce them to the intellectual skills they will require and the study adjustments they must make if they are to be successful students in an unfamiliar foreign language and foreign culture institution. This syllabus would vary from the current EAP courses in that it would focus primarily on the nature of the cognitive acts required by specific tasks or assignments set within a distinctive academic context or discipline. It would be much less concerned with the forms or structures of language acts: for example, there would not be specific lessons on 'definition', 'comparison', or 'cause and effect' presented as generalised (even deliberately 'discipline-free') language patterns. In many EAP courses a study skills component is added to a language-based course. In EIP this relationship would be reversed so that the students would be introduced first to the intellectual demands of university work and then given practice in the language structures they will require to meet these demands.

The staff of the Western university are unlikely to make the intellectual bridge for these students. Few lecturers have adequate cross-cultural experience through which to interpret the reasons for the apparent intellectual weaknesses of their foreign students. And even fewer would regard such intervention as their proper role, which they see as teaching and researching in their own field of expertise. Moreover most academic staff feel themselves under such pressures from large classes, falling standards and the need to publish that they are not likely to be prepared to vary their teaching practice to accommodate the handful of overseas students who lurk unhappily in their classes.

In desperation these students tend to seek help from other students from their home countries. In this way they can gain from the struggles of more senior students who have faced and worked their way through the problems we have discussed above. And the help these students can most usefully give is about the different styles of studying that are necessary in the new environment; the expectations of lecturers which are so often never made explicit; the best use of library, computer and lab resources; and all the survival techniques necessary for tutorial discussions, essay writing and thesis design.

Yet the support of other students or relying on an occasional flash of insight provided by a gifted and sympathetic lecturer are last ditch solutions to the problems of international students studying in Western universities. A more systematic and professional strategy is needed; and it is the English language teacher who is in the best position to provide the crucial training. If we expect the students to make all the adjustments in order to handle university study in a Western culture, then we must provide them with explicit guidance about the styles of thinking and studying that are functional in our intellectual tradition. And this guidance can be most effectively integrated with language learning in the English language classroom.

Individual language teachers will develop their own courses to suit the particular needs of their own students, but there are at least a few elements which will be common to all these separate programmes.

First, developing and teaching language classes for students going to study overseas will be an area of specialisation for selected language teachers. Part of their background or in-service training should be spent in universities, working with academic staff who teach overseas students, looking at the demands placed on foreign students, and gaining some understanding of the ways in which they cope, or do not cope, with the challenges they face. These language teachers need to make themselves as familiar with the intellectual and educational culture of the university as they are with the cultures and social backgrounds of the students they teach.

Second, the materials used for a proportion of the language classes should be drawn from the disciplines the students will study. This will almost certainly mean that the programme must have two strands: a science strand and a non-science strand. Further disciplinary sub-divisions, such as physical sciences/life sciences or humanities/social sciences, may only be feasible in a few circumstances. But the closer the language teaching can come to the actual academic interests of the students, the more motivated they will be and the more efficient the programme. This does not mean that the language teacher must also become an expert in all the disciplines of the students in the class – that is clearly an impossibility. But it is feasible for a language teacher to become competent in distinguishing the more general intellectual approaches of the sciences (e.g. Lindsay 1984; Swales 1984), the social sciences (e.g. Becker 1986), and the humanities (e.g. Megill and McCloskey 1987; Wilkes 1985), and to build the language programme from a basis of appropriate study techniques.

Finally, and most importantly, such a programme can only succeed if the language teacher makes a deliberate effort to move in his or her own teaching behaviour from a reproductive to an increasingly analytical style. One of the most effective ways of changing student behaviour is to provide an explicit model of the desired behaviour; indeed this is the traditional pattern of teaching in most language classrooms. So if students are to be prepared for an analytical and speculative approach to studies, then they must be exposed to this approach through the teaching and assessment style of their English language programme (Ballard and Clanchy 1991b). And this is not an easy shift for a language teacher to make for, as we have seen, language teaching relies heavily on the reproductive approach to learning. The reorientation process is not comfortable, either for teacher or student, and for competent language teachers used to total control in their own classrooms, it can seem particularly threatening.

I draw here on my own recent experience in helping staff in an overseas language centre develop a month long programme on academic writing for their students who were proceeding to postgraduate studies in Australia. The students were not a homogeneous group: they had varying levels of English competence; they were going to many different Australian institutions; and they came from a range of academic disciplines. The language staff were extremely competent and very enthusiastic about developing a new programme. Yet the major stumbling-block lay less in finding and developing appropriate academic materials than in convincing these teachers, who were used to being the sole source of authority in their classrooms, that they could work with materials about which some of their students would have more expert knowledge than they did. However they gradually acquired the confidence to cease trying to force these new materials into the traditional patterns of language exercises which rely on reproductive learning. Once they began to approach the materials in an analytical mode, the whole programme suddenly developed a life and validity of its own.

The lesson we learnt from this experience was that it is possible to develop a language programme in which the teachers remain the language expert, the students provide the specialised materials and context for language study, and then the teachers draw on their cultural expertise and their knowledge of Western university systems to design and interpret the classroom activities. We have found that a programme along these lines can effectively meet the needs of students who are preparing to study in a Western university. As one student from our pilot programme commented a year later, after she had successfully passed all her coursework in Australia:

> My eyes were opened on that language course when we were made to be critical of an important journal article. Then I understood that university studying was not just repetition of what other people said and wrote. Now I am inspired to suggest my own solutions in my thesis on wildlife management ...

Conclusion

English language teachers are in a unique position to assist foreign language students in bridging the gap between their previous cultural and educational experience and the demands of academic study in a Western university. Language teachers have the advantage of already being sensitive to the influences of culture on language and of language on culture. They are also, in most cases, themselves products of Western tertiary institutions and so are familiar with some aspects of the culture of the university. Even though they may not be trained as scientists or engineers, they already have the analytical knowledge and competence to unlock and interpret the characteristic linguistic patterns of these sub-cultures. They are much more aware of variation in styles of speaking and writing across disciplines than are the practitioners of the disciplines themselves, the lecturers and supervisors in each academic department.

The development of a suitable course for students who are preparing to study overseas in an Anglo university will require some shifting of the priorities and objectives of the traditional language preparation courses provided for these students. There will be a refocusing of the syllabus away from English language as the central concern and towards English as a tool for acquiring and implementing the learning and study skills appropriate to the expectations which underpin Western tertiary teaching. The language teachers themselves must be ready to shift from a traditional position of total classroom control to a more collegial approach, blending the expertise of the students in their specific disciplines with their own language-based expertise.

The development of an English for Intellectual Purposes course might usefully become the final stage of language teaching wherein the emphasis on the structure of language becomes subordinate to a focus on language as a medium for the acquisition and extension of knowledge. It is a challenge for language teachers which could extend the professional basis of language teaching in interesting new directions.

References

Ballard, B. and J. Clanchy. 1984. *Study Abroad: A Manual for Asian Students*. Kuala Lumpur: Longman Malaysia.

Ballard, B. and J. Clanchy. 1988. *Studying in Australia*. Melbourne: Longman Cheshire.

Ballard, B. and J. Clanchy. 1989. Literacy in the university: An 'anthropological' approach. In G. Taylor (Ed.) *Literacy by Degrees*, 7–23. Milton Keynes: SRHE and Open University Press.

Ballard, B. and J. Clanchy. 1991a. *Teaching Students from Overseas: A Brief Guide for Lecturers and Supervisors*. Melbourne: Longman Cheshire.

Ballard, B. and J. Clanchy. 1991b. Assessment by misconception: Cultural influences and intellectual traditions. In L. Hamp-Lyons (Ed.) *Assessing Second Language Writing in Academic Contexts*, 19–35. Norwood N.J.: Ablex Publishing Co.

Becher, T. 198⁻. Towards a definition of disciplinary cultures. *Studies in Higher Educati⁻n* 6 (2): 109–22.

Becher, T. 1989. *Academic Tribes and Territories: Intellectual Enquiry and the Cultures of Disciplines*. Milton Keynes: Open University Press.

Becker, H. S. 1986. *Writing for Social Scientists*. London: University of Chicago Press.

Bowden, J. (Ed.) 1986. *Student Learning: Research into Practice*. Parkville, Vic: CSHE and University of Melbourne Press.

Clanchy, J. and B. Ballard. 1981. *Essay Writing for Students*. Melbourne: Longman Cheshire.

Clanchy, J. and B. Ballard. 1984. *How to Write Essays*. Melbourne: Longman Cheshire.

Connor, U. and R. B. Kaplan (Eds.) 1987. *Writing across Languages: Analysis of L2 Texts*. Reading, Mass: Addison-Wesley Publishing Company.

Galtung, J. 1981. Structure, culture, and intellectual style. *Social Sciences Information* 20 (6): 817–56.

Hinds, J. 1987. Reader versus writer responsibility: A new typology. In Connor and Kaplan, 141–52.

Kaplan, R. B. 1966. Cultural thought patterns in intercultural education. *Language Learning*, 16: 1–20.

Lindsay, D. 1984. *A Guide to Scientific Writing*. Melbourne: Longman Cheshire.

Megill, A. and D. N. McCloskey. 1987. The rhetoric of history. In Nelson *et al.*, 221–328.

Mohan, B. A and W. A. Y. Lo. 1985. Academic writing and Chinese students: Transfer and developmental factors. *TESOL Quarterly* 19 (3): 515–33.

Nelson, J. S., A. Megill and D. N. McCloskey (Eds.) 1987. *The Rhetoric of the Human Sciences: Language and Argument in Scholarship in Public Affairs*. Madison: University of Wisconsin Press.

Swales, J. 1984. Research into the structure of introductions to journal articles and its applications to the teaching of academic writing. In R. Williams, J. Swales and J. Kirkman (Eds.) *Common Ground: Shared Interests in ESP and Communication Studies*, 77–86. (ELT Documents 117.) Oxford: Pergamon Press.

Wilkes, G. A. 1985. *Studying Literature*. Sydney: Sydney University Press.

9 Cultures of learning: Language classrooms in China

Martin Cortazzi and Lixian Jin

Introduction

In this chapter we attempt to understand language classrooms in China in terms of participants' own understanding of what it means to be a good teacher or a good student. Such views will form an important part of the ideological model of what teachers and learners expect from each other. This is part of a *culture of learning* which may be a determining factor on what happens in language classrooms and what is judged to be successful language learning.

By the term 'culture of learning' we mean that much behaviour in language classrooms is set within taken-for-granted frameworks of expectations, attitudes, values and beliefs about what constitutes good learning, about how to teach or learn, whether and how to ask questions, what textbooks are for, and how language teaching relates to broader issues of the nature and purpose of education. In many class-rooms both teachers and learners are unaware that such a culture of learning may be influencing the processes of teaching and learning. A culture of learning is thus part of the hidden curriculum. In many language classrooms, the teacher and students have a diverse range of cultural backgrounds, so that there may be more than one culture of learning which influences participants. Therefore it is possible that there may be largely unnoticed gaps between the expectations of the teacher and students, or between different groups of students.

Any particular culture of learning will have its roots in the educa-tional, and, more broadly, cultural traditions of the community or society in which it is located. Children are socialised into a culture of learning in their pre-school years at home and, more particularly, in the kindergarten and early years at school. This early influence is deeply imprinted on many learners and has a continuing effect into secondary school or even into university. A culture of learning is also likely to be influenced by the socio-economic conditions of that society, insofar as these affect teachers' and learners' goals and strategies. It must be recognised that student behaviour is also influenced by other social factors and practical constraints, such as age, ability, gender, the language syllabus, exams, materials, the immediate classroom context, etc. This chapter, however, focuses on cultures of learning since this topic has been largely unexplored to date.

In this chapter we examine a Chinese culture of learning largely on the evidence of statements collected from students, supported by our own observations and experience. The chapter describes the roots of a Chinese culture of learning in the language lessons in kindergarten and primary school, and traces some socio-economic influences on Chinese teachers. It gives detailed attention to Chinese students' expectations of good teachers and students, contrasted with the views of Western teachers who teach English in China. Finally, it focuses on the topic of asking questions as an illustration of different cultural approaches to learning.

The context of the present study

This study can be located within four theoretical areas in which developments are currently taking place: in *applied linguistics*, where attention is increasingly paid to learners' strategies in language learning; in *second language acquisition*, where some approaches and theoretical models pay attention to cultural factors; in *the ethnography of commun-ication*, where the importance of cultural systems of interpreting and using language is recognised; and in *language teaching*, where the role of culture has been highlighted recently. Each of these areas is considered in more detail below.

In applied linguistic research related to language teaching there has been a notable rise in interest in the topic of learners' strategies as part of the general movement towards more learner-centred approaches (Wenden and Rubin 1987; Nunan 1988; Willing 1988; Stevick 1989; Oxford 1990; O'Malley and Chamot 1990; Rubin and Thompson 1994). However, it is an overstatement to claim that 'The importance of the learner's perspective is recognized in virtually all modern approaches to the language learning process' (Tarone and Yule 1989: 134), or at least such recognition needs to be supported by detailed knowledge of the perspectives of particular groups of learners before it can be expected to have much impact on classroom practice. Learners' expectations will be influenced by their previous social and educational background, leading some learners to want a structured learning programme at variance with communicative approaches adopted by their teachers (Brindley 1989: 39). This is in large part because of their cultural background, yet in the current literature there is little discussion of cultural factors in learning strategies, or of gaps between teachers' and learners' perceptions of which strategies are appropriate. Oxford (1990) is not alone in outlining how different strategies might lead to knowledge of the target culture, but she does not consider how learners' cultures might influence their learning strategies in the first place. The notion of 'cultures of learning' is generally absent from considerations of language learning strategies and O'Malley and Chamot (1990: 165) rightly stress the need for additional research into how cultural background affects learning strategies.

In the field of second language acquisition, there are, in general, remarkably few references to cultural influences (see, for example, recent surveys by Cook 1993, Ellis 1994, Sharwood-Smith 1994, and Towell and Hawkins 1994). Two widely cited exceptions are the work of Schumann and Gardner. Schumann (1978a) has outlined an Acculturation model according to which the second language learning process is causally affected by degrees of cultural congruence between the learners' and the target language community's culture. Acculturation, the process of becoming adapted to a new culture, is defined by various types of social and psychological integration of learners with the target language group (Schumann 1978b: 29). While Schumann intended his model to account for second language acquisition, Gardner (1985: 137) sees it as being applicable to foreign language learning in schools. Gardner's own socio-educational model (1985) also highlights the crucial role of culture, proposing that 'the beliefs in the community concerning the importance and meaningfulness of learning the language, the nature of skill development expected, and the particular role of various individual differences in the language learning process will influence second language acquisition' (1985: 146). Gardner thus sees that cultural beliefs influence the general level of second language proficiency as well as influencing individual differences in achievement. His focus is on the effect of culture on the individual learner rather than on the collective, e.g. a language class or a specific cultural group of learners. Notably, neither Schumann nor Gardner gives any specific details about how cultural beliefs or degrees of acculturation affect the language classroom or how they might make up a culture of learning.

In the field of the ethnography of communication the importance of cultural variation in the use of speech in education has long been stressed (Gumperz and Hymes 1972; Saville-Troike 1982). Ethnographers have emphasised that the classroom is communicatively constituted, i.e. classroom events, social relations and roles are constructed through language. Learning is born in social interaction on the basis (partly at least) of cultural norms, values and expectations which derive from the learners' immediate community or from society at large. In this view, 'Culture is a set – perhaps a system – of principles of interpretation, together with the products of that system' (Moerman 1988: 4). Such principles of inter-pretation are crucial factors in participants' understanding of what goes on in classrooms, in what students do or do not learn. What matters is not only what happens in the classroom but how participants interpret events and what they expect to happen. The emphasis here is on how partici-pants construe the meaning and purpose of classroom activity; teachers may have one view (Woods 1980a, 1990a), students may have quite another (Woods 1980b, 1990b), even within a single culture. This has only recently come to be seen as an important issue in second language classrooms (van Lier 1988; Richards and Lockhart 1994). In language classrooms it is not uncommon to have a cross-cultural situation when the teacher is a native speaker from one culture and learners come from a different background. When students from China, for example, come to study in Britain such gaps in perceptions of the nature of academic work can be much greater than those which arise within one culture (Jin 1992; Jin and Cortazzi 1993). Whether and how teachers understand these aspects of a culture of learning is one of the keys to accomplishing practical changes in teaching and learning approaches. This has been demonstrated in insightful ethnographic studies of such minority groups as Native Americans taught by teachers from the dominant American culture (Cazden, John and Hymes 1972; Phillips 1982), but there do not seem to be similar studies of larger groups encountered more frequently by language teachers around the world. Chinese students constitute a major group of the world's learners, roughly 25 per cent, but as yet there is very little data-based research into their culture of learning, despite recent useful cross-cultural studies of Chinese communication patterns (Shih 1986; Young 1994; Scollon and Scollon 1995).

Within language teaching there has been some detailed work focusing on Chinese learners. Generally, these are small-scale studies or case studies. Typical examples are concerned with the question of whether discourse patterns in writing are transferred from Chinese to English (Matalene 1985; Mohan and Lo 1985; Alptekin 1988; Taylor and Chen 1991). Only rarely, however, do such studies relate these patterns to a larger framework of a culture of learning (Scollon 1993, 1994).

On a broader language teaching front, recent studies have emphasised the necessity of including culture in language teaching as an integral component (Valdes 1986; Byram 1989; Harrison 1990). Further, it has been argued that learners themselves should be taught to become ethnographers of a target culture, perhaps as co-learners with teachers, seeking to elicit from native speakers accounts of foreign cultures which together with other accounts can be jointly interpreted (Byram and Esarte-Sarries 1991). This raises the profile of cultural elements consider-ably and encourages observation, cognitive analysis and reflection on target cultures, but in our view it still does not go far enough. If learners are, in addition, exposed to the culture of learning of the target culture (as many learners are when they have foreign teachers), they can be encouraged to develop the metacognitive strategies of monitoring and evaluating the success of learning activities (Oxford 1990; O'Malley and Chamot 1990), but with a cultural focus, comparing foreign ways of teaching with native ways of learning. Besides developing additional learning strategies – an educational aim in its own right – this would immerse students in the ways of a target culture in the course of learning about it, while learning the language.

From the study reported in this chapter, there is some evidence that this happens when students in China have Western teachers, but the teachers seem unaware of this process. This raises two questions: first, whether teachers can adopt a more deliberate consciousness-raising approach to learning strategies so that learners can develop a reflective approach to the cultural medium of language learning. This would reverse the common approach: instead of using language as a vehicle to learn about culture, it would use cultural ways of learning to learn the language. Second, could a non-native teacher adopt a target culture of learning? In fact, in many countries, this is exactly the challenge for local teachers attempting to adopt communicative approaches from the West. If teachers wish to move toward affirmative answers to such questions a necessary preliminary is to study cultures of learning. Our research attempts this by focusing on language class-rooms in China.

In the Chinese case, children are socialised into a particularly long-standing culture of learning at an early age when they come to learn how to read and write Chinese in kindergartens and primary schools. Learning in these early years gives strong emphasis to memory, imitation and repetitive practice. This early language learning seems to share remarkable continuity with key aspects of how Chinese students will come to learn a foreign language at a later stage. Strategies which lead to success at one stage of schooling are likely to be used subsequently unless there are clear reasons for change.

That the same culture might set the framework for learning at different phases of education and across subjects is not problematic in general, but in the case of learning a foreign language like English it may be dissonant with current Western conceptions of language learning and with the target cultures of the English speaking world. It therefore makes a difference to how Chinese teachers might see communicative ap-proaches to teaching English, given that to date these have largely been developed within cultures of learning of native English speakers, or at least within those of Westerners. It makes a difference to the way in which Chinese students going to Western universities to study will learn – and learn to use – the academic English which will be so crucial to their educational success and professional training (Jin 1992; Jin and Cortazzi 1993). It makes a difference also to the way in which Western teachers in China, using Western ways of teaching, are seen by their Chinese students.

It is important to emphasise some qualifications. China is a huge country with an enormous population, its peoples are diverse in their languages and cultures, and there are important differences between north and south, and between urban and rural settings. We do not expect all Chinese learners or teachers to be the same. Nevertheless, a strongly centralised education system has been operating for some time; *Putonghua* (Mandarin) has long been taught as the unifying national form of speech and Chinese written characters are the same all over China whatever dialect is spoken. Further, when Chinese think of themselves they have in mind a number of fairly clear characteristics including conformity with a certain culture of learning. Then again, China is undergoing a period of rapid change and among young people greater individuality is becoming manifest. So, in any portrayal of a Chinese culture of learning – or of Western ones – we might expect a complex picture of many variables some of which may be in tension or even contradictory. This seems to be in the nature of a culture of learning.

In principle, there is no reason to suppose that one culture of learning is superior to another. There are different cultures of learning which may be more or less appropriate to the larger societies in which they are located, and this needs to be kept in mind when teachers or learners travel or when language teaching methodologies migrate around the world. Further, there is no reason in principle why different cultures of learning should be mutually exclusive. Rather, different ways might be reconciled or interwoven. This can be done only when we know what they are.

A good place to start considering a Chinese culture of learning is the kindergarten and primary school, since this is where Chinese learners themselves are socialised, fairly explicitly, into certain ways of learning, in groups.

Chinese kindergarten and primary classes

Chinese kindergartens take in children between the ages of two and six. A large kindergarten has several hundred children. Each class has about 25 to 30 children and at least one teacher and one teaching assistant.

Children arrive before 8 a.m. and many stay until 5 p.m. All the children belonging to one class do most activities together, including lessons for reading, writing, general knowledge, maths, music, dance and painting; physical exercises and games on the sports ground; having meals; taking a midday nap.

Let us visit some language lessons in a kindergarten in Tianjin. Children of four to five years old sit on the floor in circles learning to read Chinese. At the front a teacher sits near a piano and an assistant walks around the class ready to help any child. The children are learning to read the Chinese characters for animals. On the wall there is a poem about a little fat pig. The teacher reads it several times, then children read it in chorus. Individual children come to the front and read it, fluently, with loud confident voices. The teacher produces cards with questions written on them. The whole class reads the questions and individual children find the answers in the poem. The teacher does not give immediate feedback but first asks the class if the answer is correct or not. If it is, everybody claps in a collective evaluation of the answer. The teacher now divides the class into groups and gives each group cards with individual characters on them. The group task is to sequence the cards to make one of the sentences of the poem. This requires memory and group co-ordination. The teacher is using the task for a collective assessment of reading rather than for practice. All children are expected to maintain the same level of achievement. Slower children are helped by their peers or by the teacher. With the whole class the teacher now uses other cards with written questions about different animals, such as 'What are the tail, eyes and ears of a dog like?' The children have seen these in previous lessons. Children in chorus and individually read the questions aloud and answer them rapidly. The lesson proceeds at a smart pace, with the whole class working on the same material at the same speed. Everything is orchestrated by the teacher, strictly but in a kind manner. Every three or four minutes there is a change of activity without losing the thread of the topic: a song, an action rhyme, a dance movement around the room, picking out characters from boxes, matching characters with those on the wall, listening to a poem on a cassette. Children are consistently attentive, listening, speaking together in a disciplined chorus. They can read the characters involved in the lesson. They clearly have a sense of achievement: they are learning around 100 characters each term.

Let us now visit other language lessons in a kindergarten in Shenzhen. A male teacher is teaching English to four-year-olds. The class begins with the children singing and clapping a song. Then the teacher uses a picture with cut-out figures to present a brief dialogue between a mother and child:

'John, John, where are you?'
'Here I am, here I am, I'm in the garden.'

The teacher models this extensively with exaggerated gestures and intonation. The children repeat each part in chorus, then individually. The teacher re-enacts the dialogue with individual children and finally children repeat the dialogue in pairs taking roles. The children mimic the pronunciation, intonation and gestures exactly. The teacher then shows the class a bag, produces a series of everyday objects from it which are replaced and brought out again: 'What is this? It is a ball. Where is it now? It's in the bag.' The class listen and repeat many times with different objects, then the teacher uses the same objects, and the original picture, for a similar question and answer routine with individuals. The atmosphere is that of a highly supportive group. When children answer correctly they receive praise from the whole class. When an individual is answering, the rest of the class watch that child – not the teacher – and if the child is slow or has difficulty others help, with permission from the teacher. Children encourage each other, 'Answer it!' 'You can do it!' 'I'll help you!' The lesson finishes with a poem, an action rhyme and a song. No children have asked questions or composed their own sentences. All have clearly enjoyed the lesson and learned the dialogues. The teacher moves on to teach English to the five-year-olds. In most other schools children will have to wait until they are 13 before they begin a foreign language.

In classes for maths, music, art or dance a similar approach prevails: the teacher instructs from the front; she presents careful clear models for the children; she shows them what to learn and how to learn it; the learners all perform the same tasks at the same time; there is clear discipline, uniform attention and concentration, punctuated by varied activities. As we talk to teachers in different schools they repeatedly emphasise conformity and co-operation, communication and confidence, meaningful models and memorisation through analysis, step by step repetition, reproduction and recitation. In this culture of learning there is great consistency.

Next, we visit some primary schools in Tianjin. One has 3,000 pupils and 200 teachers, each of whom teaches one subject only. As we observe language lessons we are accompanied by several other teachers. We realise that we are not being shepherded: the teachers are also observing the class, as each one must complete 12 hours observation each term. Like the children, the teachers themselves are improving their skills through careful observation, listening and taking notes, which they will review later. We observe a Chinese reading lesson for ten-year-olds, over 60 in the class. They will spend about three hours of class time on each text in their textbook: learning the new words, going over the meaning and sentence structures, completing exercises, paraphrases and summaries. Some children will know the whole text by heart. All of them can read over 1,000 characters. By the time they are 13 they should be able to read 2,600 characters, according to the national curriculum. This considerable achievement will be largely a result of memorisation through much repetition and guided practice. Given the nature of the Chinese writing system, it could hardly be otherwise; although many characters have clues to pronunciation and meaning in their component parts, and children are taught how to use these clues, the task of learning to read Chinese will be mostly a matter of memory.

The reading lesson begins with all the learners reading aloud at their own pace. The text is about how squirrels build nests. They have prepared this reading for homework; everybody's textbook is full of pencilled notes. They are familiar with most of the routines which follow: reading aloud in rows and individually, with expression, following the teacher's model; literal comprehension questions from the teacher; looking at sentences highlighted on overhead transparencies (OHTs) to analyse the grammar; watching a video extract of squirrels moving and building nests, linked to choice of verbs; using more OHTs to see how adverbs modify meanings in the nest-building sequence; completing a written sequencing exercise with linking words; marking topic divisions in the text; reviewing the video to compose a paragraph using linking words; work in pairs to complete another paragraph; an explanation from the teacher about paragraph types, followed by classifying the paragraphs in the textbook. The use of video and OHTs is only available in key schools for economic reasons, but the other activities are typical in the use of exposition, clear models, building on what learners have prepared and learned at home. Only a small percentage of children were involved in answering the teacher's questions, yet most observed the answerers. No one asked the teacher questions. Those who spoke or read did so with fluency, clarity and confidence.

Seeing such classes, with communicative approaches in mind and an uncomfortable feeling that memorising is rote learning, Western teachers might deplore the lack of interaction and individualisation, the absence of creativity and self-expression, or dearth of personal interpretation and experiential learning. Chinese counterparts would draw attention to the large class size, the importance of discipline, the significance of giving children necessary knowledge, the pressures of the curriculum and exam system. They might remark on the role of students' individual learning and preparation at home, on how teachers stress meaning and understanding before recitation and learning, on how students who attend with concentration do indeed interact with teacher and text, in their minds. They could point out that every Chinese child is an individual with different abilities and needs, but that in Chinese society – and in the classroom – the priorities are that each person must be part of a group or community; learning interdependency, co-operation and social awareness; becoming oneself in relation to significant others; expressing that which is socially shared rather than individually felt; creating on the basis of mastery rather than discovery.

This Chinese culture of learning needs to be seen in a broader social context if recent changes and developments are to be understood.

Some current socio-economic influences on education and Chinese teachers

Chinese society influences language classrooms in a variety of complex ways but there are two major features of contemporary China which set broad limits to any discussion of current Chinese approaches to language learning: the large population and the rapidly developing economy.

In 1995 the population of China had reached over 1,200 million. This has several immediate consequences for classrooms: in a developing country it means limited resources are available; it means that in primary or middle schools classes of 60 students are common. Also, given China's foreign language policy that all middle school students should study a foreign language (usually English) and that all university students should study English for at least two years, it means that China almost certainly has more learners of English as a foreign language than any other country. Exact figures are hard to come by but estimates are staggering. To Hildebrandt and Liu's (1991) estimation that there are 50 million ten-year-olds learning English in China, or Zhu and Chen's (1991) figure of 57 million school and university students enrolled in English classes, we would need to add Dzau's (1990: 32) reckoning of over 150 million part-time learners: many in university and college evening classes or in classes organised in workplaces, others in private classes or following China's popular English by radio and TV programmes. A more recent yet conservative estimate is that China has around 200 million English users (Zhao and Campbell 1995: 38).

To alleviate population pressures China has had mandatory family planning since the 1970s, whereby only one child is permitted to urban families; rural families may have a second child in some circumstances. There are several educational consequences of this. It is now rare for a child at school to have brothers or sisters and understandably parents want the best for their only child. Consequently, many kindergarten teachers have to cope with spoilt, wilful children who are not used to playing or working with others (Lin 1994). Teachers therefore put great importance on obedience, self-control, conformity to the group and awareness of others. This collective consciousness and recognition of teacher authority has been a significant aspect of Chinese traditional values since Confucius and a strong element in Chinese approaches to learning. Far from being eroded by contemporary trends this is reinforced by effects of the one-child policy.

Similarly, the traditional Chinese diligence in learning has been strongly emphasised by parents who put pressure on their child to strive to learn English and other subjects and get high exam scores. Parents fear that unless they push their child hard, for example, by giving them extra homework or extra English classes, the child will fail to grasp current opportunities. This is critically important in China since many parents of current students were themselves deprived of secondary and university education during the Cultural Revolution (1966–1976) when schools and universities were closed and foreign language study was viewed with suspicion.

During the 1990s it has been widely recognised that China has the world's fastest developing economy. China's economic growth rate has reached 13 per cent. The development of the 'socialist market economy' with many new opportunities for private businesses, the burgeoning of special economic zones and the multiplication of joint ventures with foreign companies have led to the recognition that China needs a large number of educated people speaking English. This societal recognition, together with a general awareness of job opportunities available to those who speak English, has impinged heavily on students' motivations to learn. Zhu and Chen (1991) found that 33.7 per cent of university students said that 'finding a good job' was their chief motive for studying English. In 1993, we asked 244 students from four Chinese universities the open-ended question, 'Why are you learning English?' As one of their three main reasons, 55.7 per cent of the students specifically mentioned that learning English would help them in their future jobs.

China's economic boom has greatly promoted the demand for English but it has led to two paradoxes: one in education in general, the other in the English classroom itself.

The first paradox is that parents all wish to get good teachers for their children, they push their offspring to study hard to pass exams to enter a 'key' middle school and to get through the fierce competition of the National Entrance Exam for a university place, yet hardly any parents would like their children to become teachers.

While the traditional Chinese respect for teachers is still generally held, the economic status of teachers is clearly low. In 1994 the average income of an associate professor, after a substantial rise in salary, was around 400 yuan (¥400) per month ($45), slightly above the average income of workers in Beijing. However, the newspapers were full of success stories of individuals making money in unskilled work, for example, people selling lunch boxes on the street were reported to earn a minimum of ¥4,320 per month ($496) (Chen 1994), while someone selling the scrap parts of tractors was said to make ¥6,000 per month ($689) (Zhang 1994). Many schools have to make money to survive. In 1993 one school in Shanxi hired out classes of its pupils as funeral mourners; another in Beijing sent each pupil home for the summer holiday with five new-born chicks telling them to come back in September with four full-grown hens, or pay a fine (Gracie 1993). These schools are doing more than reflect social and economic forces; they are joining the economy through the children, they are modelling children's perceptions of certain teaching behaviour.

Many teachers are not keen to remain in the classroom. A 1993 survey of 4,000 Beijing teachers found that 96 per cent would leave their posts if given a chance. That year 2,922 teachers in Shanghai switched to other professions (Xi 1994). While we were visiting Chinese universities between 1993 and 1995, worries about the lack of English teachers between the ages of 28 and 40 were commonly expressed. Young scholars are simply unwilling to teach English. This exodus must have a serious effect on the morale of those who remain as teachers.

The second paradox, related to the first, is that while there is strong motivation for students to learn English to get good jobs, the English teachers are among the first to seek such jobs for themselves. Many English teachers either leave teaching altogether or have unofficial part-time jobs as translators, interpreters or business assistants. Through such part-time work they may earn four or five times their teaching salary. Other teachers are forced to teach extra English classes for fee-paying students. The Normal Universities, which specialise in teacher training, are buckling under market forces. They are unable to attract enough students, even after lowering entrance standards and offering scholar-ships (Cai 1994). Prospective teachers entering the Normal Universities often do so only because they failed to reach the more prestigious General Universities. Many teacher trainees work very hard at mastering English in order to become graduate students. Their motive, however, is not to teach English but to avoid teaching it – by studying abroad or getting more lucrative jobs in business (Cai 1994). Others use their knowledge of English to find employment outside teaching. In Anhui province in 1993, for example, in one Normal University only 5 per cent of the graduating students trained to teach middle school English actually got jobs in schools.

The consequence of these social paradoxes for the English classroom is that many students are eager to learn from their English teacher, as a gatekeeper to the language of economic success, and they have respect for the teacher, yet they see the teacher as one who has failed economically and perhaps linguistically: many of the best teachers no longer teach and the best English speakers work in business, not in the classroom.

However, such changes are recent and any long-term effects remain to be seen. In any society, what changes very much more slowly is the culture of learning. In China, children are socialised into a culture of learning in kindergarten and primary school. For language learning this takes firm root when they learn to read and write Chinese and major aspects are later transferred to the foreign language classroom.

In their early years Chinese children are taught to learn through memory, imitation and repetitive practice. Although there is some recent emphasis on the importance of understanding word meanings before memorising written characters, the notion persists that final understanding (enlightenment) will only come after full mastery, when the level of input has reached a high level of quality and quantity. There is also a persistent belief that anyone can achieve success in language learning – whether Chinese or English – by hard work. Again, this hard work is commonly demonstrated by memorisation and practice. The transfer of these aspects of the culture of learning can be clearly observed in the Intensive Reading Course.

The English Intensive Reading Course in China

The Intensive Reading Course is the premier language course carried out at all stages of English learning from school to university. It is a compulsory course using uniform syllabuses, textbooks and final examinations at the school level. There is a corresponding system of teaching and examination at the university level. In most of the 1,000 or so universities in China, four hours per week are allocated to this course during the first two years for all students not majoring in English. (English majors study Intensive Reading for more hours.) Students will be in large classes of between 40 and 100. They learn one text per week from a textbook such as the widely used *College English* (Zhai 1991; Li 1991), a course of four levels which prepares students for the compulsory examinations, Band One through to Band Four. Some students will pass the more advanced Bands Five and Six. A few hours are given to other English courses for speaking, listening comprehension and reading for science and technology, but the Intensive Reading Course is widely regarded as the backbone of the English programme. The significant role of Intensive Reading is underlined by Dzau (1990: 44):

> So important is this course that ELT in China cannot be fully understood without knowing something about the teaching materials and the teaching methods.

Despite its name, the Intensive Reading Course is not designed primarily to improve reading comprehension. Rather, using the text as a base students learn grammar and vocabulary through teacher exposition and practice exercises.

A typical unit in *College English* begins with a two-page text followed by a list of new words, phrases and expressions with the pronunciation given and meaning indicated by English synonyms and Chinese translations. This is followed by explanatory notes on the historical background and idioms. There is then a sequence of multiple-choice comprehension questions, more general discussion points, blank-filling exercises for word building and sentence structure, a cloze passage, and sentences for translation. Finally there is a further reading text with more multiple-choice questions and a writing exercise which usually focuses on a grammar point.

The Intensive Reading Course has the following functions, based on our observations and experience and comments by Wu (1990). The course enables students:

1 to read the text aloud (or recite or paraphrase it) with fairly good pronunciation;
2 to learn hundreds, if not thousands, of new vocabulary items with detailed explanations of meanings and to use these new words in exercises through blank filling, paraphrase, word formation and other methods;
3 to learn and to practise certain grammatical points exemplified in the text;
4 to speak on a limited range of subjects related to the texts;
5 to write generally correct sentences, short compositions and do translations based on the content and language of the texts.

The Intensive Reading Course is highly structured. There is an emphasis on the learning and use of grammar and vocabulary in a heavily teacher-centred approach. This situation is not surprising since traditional approaches to Chinese language learning stressed the learning of Chinese characters and words as a base to develop from sentences to texts to literature. The learning of characters (*Zi*), words/phrases (*Ci*), sentences (*Jiu*), paragraph (*Duan*) and text (*Wen*) is considered a fixed order of learning.

A common sequence starts with students preparing for the new unit themselves before the class, referring to dictionaries for unknown words. If a cassette is available they may listen to a reading of the text and new words. Students often practise by reading aloud, sitting in odd corners of the campus. In class, the teaching begins by the teacher asking students to read aloud. The teacher will check pronunciation and intonation and ask some general comprehension questions. The teacher then explains new words in the text. These are practised in word study exercises involving pronunciation, translation, use of synonyms and paraphrase. Then there are comprehensive explanations of selected grammatical points and their functions in the text. These points are practised by drills, translations, sentence manipulation and blank-filling exercises. Further practice includes paraphrasing, summarising and retelling the content of the text. Occasionally there will be class discussion, debate or role playing, but more often there will not be enough time for such activities. The assessment of whether the text has been understood depends largely on how well students can remember the new words and grammar and how well they are able to use this knowledge to complete exercises and pass regular tests.

Teachers prepare extensively. In the belief that they may be asked grammar or vocabulary questions by students, they go over each text in meticulous detail. Teachers' own copies of the textbook are full of pencilled margin notes which enable them to expound every likely grammar point or word meaning which may arise. This level of preparation turns out to be rather paradoxical since, as will become clear later, the students rarely ask questions. However, the teachers believe that they should have authoritative knowledge of all aspects of the text.

As noted above, the students also prepare extensively. They work hard at understanding the text. They learn the vocabulary. Many memorise the grammatical examples. Some will memorise the whole text. Certainly the students are deeply involved with the language of the text.

The Intensive Reading Course has been the target of much criticism from Western teachers (e.g. Cotton 1990; Maley 1990) and comment by Chinese teachers (e.g. Wu 1990). We have repeatedly heard a number of similar points from teachers in China. These teachers recognise that the Intensive Reading Course dominates the practice of and thinking about English teaching. They have argued that reading is not treated in terms of meaning, form is isolated from function, oral skills and integrated skills are under-developed, and a limited range of fairly formal styles is tackled in texts. More seriously, language as communication is neglected and the excessive focus on teacher-centred activities puts students into a passive role of listening and memorising. Interactive, interpretative and personal aspects of language are ignored; for example, the comprehension questions in the textbooks are predominantly literal and rarely deal with implication or personal understanding of texts.

However, it is not easy to change this situation since the courses are intimately tied to the national system of exams. Effective change is unlikely to be managed unless the exam system changes. Yet this change of itself would be insufficient because the teaching approach has become institutionalised as part of a Chinese culture of learning. Also it needs to be recognised that the Intensive Reading Course is a product of particular social, economic and linguistic circumstances which have strongly influenced the teaching of English in China since the 1950s.

China had been largely isolated from the English-speaking world between the 1950s and 1970s. Teachers had virtually no contact with native speakers or with international textbooks so there was a need for a set of national unified texts. Among other functions, such texts would serve as a model for methodology for teachers, using an adapted grammar-translation method. Crucially, this focused on the teacher's explanation and the learners' internalisation of language through memorisation, fitting a centuries-old Chinese approach to learning. In this approach language ability and mastery of content came through the close study of words and texts learned by heart, illustrated by the proverb, 'Learn 300 Tang poems by heart and one becomes a poet.' The teacher and the text are models: exemplars worthy of imitation, whose words learned now will be cognitively internalised and later understood – perhaps – in a long apprenticeship which will lead to ultimate mastery. For such traditional reasons, and because the Intensive Reading Course has been dominant for over a 30-year period in which many students of several generations have (we should recognise) successfully learned English, these practices are, in Sampson's words, 'not trivial or accidental, but inherent in the fabric of Chinese society' (1984: 30).

This does not mean that such practices should not or cannot be changed. If such changes are made in more communicative directions, as Western (and many Chinese) teachers would advocate, then a prerequisite for effective change is to examine how Western ways of teaching and Chinese ways of learning relate to each other.

Western teachers in China

In 1993 we asked 15 highly experienced Western teachers of English (British, North Americans and Australians) working in Chinese universities about the strong and weak points of Chinese learning styles. There was unanimous agreement that, on the positive side, Chinese students were diligent, persistent, thorough and friendly. They were very good at memorising. They had a strong desire to learn English well. They were a joy to teach.

These teachers had attempted to use a range of communicative methods in the classroom, but they were often disappointed. Major difficulties were attributed to the negative aspects of the students' approaches to learning (as seen by the Western teachers). The teachers agreed that the students paid a lot of attention to grammar, vocabulary and reading, largely as a result of the way in which the Intensive Reading Course was taught. However, this meant that the students were weak at communicating orally and in writing. They were not active in class. They assumed that they were there only to listen. They were unwilling to work in groups and preferred whole-class work or individual work. This was not seen as a problem of co-operation or information sharing but as a result of the students' desire to concentrate on learning tasks without the distraction of talking to their peers. Students paid great attention to grades and exams but not to the processes of learning. They did not seem to be independent or open to alternative ideas.

There is a danger in such interpretations: the students' abilities and ways of learning are being interpreted according to current Western notions of English language teaching. It could be argued that this is a kind of linguistic or cultural imperialism (Phillipson 1992) in which one culture of learning is being imposed on those who naturally follow another, and that the latter way is made to appear inadequate or second class. The fact that it is the native speakers of English who adhere to the first culture of learning strongly reinforces the process of viewing the Chinese culture of learning in terms of deficit. Therefore students are 'weak at communicating', 'shy', or 'passive'. But this is a little one-sided. It does not take into account the Chinese culture of learning, or students' achievements and expectations. For example, it is not unusual for students to memorise extensive lists of English words: we met a dozen or more students who could recite the whole of a good-sized dictionary by heart. Wang (1986), contributing to a book about communicative language teaching, describes his (successful) efforts to memorise 10,000 words as a basis for free production in communication, as if this were a quite normal accomplishment in China. Chinese students' undoubted achievement in acquiring an advanced knowledge of grammar or memorising many English words is seen by Western teachers as being primarily a negative factor: rather quaint, a misguided use of effort and a barrier to communication. The Chinese mastery through memory

– which students say brings confidence and a feeling of success – is commonly characterised by Westerners as 'parrot learning' and a 'burden'. This seems a one-sided judgement predicated on current Western conceptions of the overriding importance of oral interaction in the classroom and learner-centredness. When one considers the place of needs analysis in current communicative approaches, it is ironic that such views often fail to consider what the students bring to the language learning situation – their culture of learning. Unless Western teachers take account of this culture of learning, which includes students' perceptions of their needs and expectations, mismatches are likely.

This kind of possible mismatch of cultures of learning is illustrated in the following exchange which took place towards the end of a semester in a Chinese university when a student was thanking her Western teacher for her classes:

Student: I've really enjoyed these classes, but what did I learn?
Teacher: You spoke every week.
Student: But what did I learn?
Teacher: You learned to speak!
Student: But what can I take home? I have nothing in my book, no notes, no grammar.
Teacher: But you can speak English now.
Student: Will that help me in the exam?

The student left, feeling that she had failed to get help for the crucial exam (which emphasised reading, grammar and vocabulary but had no oral element), while the teacher was left feeling that she had failed to convert the student to a communicative way of thinking or to a process model of learning.

Expectations of good teachers

Two key questions underlying a culture of learning concern students' expectations regarding good teachers and good students. A common way to investigate such questions is to use a questionnaire. However, there are two reasons to be cautious about this: generally subjects can answer only according to what they are asked, and there is a danger that the researcher's own cultural background can determine the type of question, the manner of asking and the choices given to respondents. Our prime interest was in obtaining the subjects' own interpretations of what they expect from good teachers and what they believe about good students, i.e. what are their experiences and cognitive-cultural schemas for 'good' teachers and students? Favouring a more interpretative

Table 1. *Chinese Students' Expectations of a Good Teacher (N=135)*

A good teacher	% of respondents
has deep knowledge	67.0%
is patient	25.0%
is humorous	23.7%
is a good moral example	21.5%
shows friendliness	21.5%
teaches students about life	17.5%
arouses students' interest	17.0%
is warm-hearted and understanding	16.2%
uses effective teaching methods	16.2%
is caring and helpful	14.8%
explains clearly	6.7%

approach, therefore, we initially held interviews with several groups of students. This elicited a number of insightful comments but it was time-consuming and difficult to arrange. Thus we concluded that a practical solution might be to ask students to write responses to simple open-ended questions. So in 1993 we asked 135 university students at Nankai University in Tianjin and at the People's University in Beijing to write answers in English to the open-ended questions: 'What do you expect from a good teacher? What makes a good student?' The replies were scrutinised for common elements and these are examined below. Quotations are given from the students' writing both to exemplify points and to allow their voices to be heard. Our aim is to build up a picture of the students' culture of learning. We begin with the students' expectations of a good teacher.

From Table 1, it is clear that overwhelmingly the most common expectation which Chinese students have of a good teacher is that the teacher should have deep knowledge of his or her subject. This can be compared with the far lower percentages of students who mentioned the pedagogic skills of arousing interest, using effective teaching methods or explaining clearly. In China, students believe that teachers should be 'erudite', 'very learned', 'they should be able to answer all sorts of questions'. 'They should have profound knowledge, which is the most important thing'. 'The teacher is a symbol of knowledge', 'a key to the treasure house of knowledge' (these and the following extracts are from student data, 1993). This is entirely in keeping with the traditional Chinese notion that the central aim of teaching is to provide knowledge for students. It also fits current practices of training teachers in China where the acquisition of subject knowledge represents the core of the curriculum, methodology courses take little more than five per cent of the total programme, and the teaching practice may occupy only four to six weeks in a four-year course (Gumbert 1990; Paine 1990).

A good teacher does not only teach the subject in hand, however. In the students' view, he or she should also teach students about society: 'he should teach us to solve problems in life', 'teach us not only knowledge in books but also the reality of society', 'help me learn more of the world and about life so that I can deal with others more successfully.'

It is also apparent from Table 1 that high among Chinese students' expectations of a good teacher is that the teacher should have a moral character and be an example worthy of imitation: 'I expect the teacher to be a good model for every student'; 'he should have great virtue', 'he sets an example to students as a person with morality.' Again, this matches traditional Confucian values and the Chinese culture of learning does not seem to have changed in this respect. However, this expectation may partly explain the phenomenon of teachers and teacher trainees leaving their profession since the character and example of their teachers are a strong influence on students' career choice. With many of their most talented teachers leaving for other professions it is not surprising if students follow them. This may seem a little far-fetched. As mentioned earlier, teachers in China who leave their profession do so primarily for economic reasons and for similar motives students do not want to become teachers. However, in the collectively-oriented Chinese cultural tradition, students do model both their academic and moral behaviour on teachers whom they respect. When such teachers leave, the example is a very powerful one for their students. Students, acting within a collective framework, assume that the best course is what those in authority – teachers who are models – think is best for them. The teachers' action in leaving therefore strongly reinforces the tendency for students to yield to the same economic pressures.

While students expect the teacher to be strict (i.e. to keep order, collect homework, etc.) and fair (i.e. deal equitably with all students), they also expect the teacher to be a friend, even a parent. 'He should care for his students just as parents do.' 'He should sometimes be strict like a father, sometimes be kind like a mother.' This means being friendly, gentle, showing concern, offering to help students who have personal problems, talking to students socially and giving advice *outside* the classroom. 'The teacher should be available after class, should give a chance for students to ask questions or just talk to the teacher', 'he should talk with students now and then and help them to become good students.' Western teachers are seen as friendly but they do not have the Chinese parental approach: Western teachers 'make me think I have one more friend but not one more father or mother.'

Expectations of good students

Turning now to expectations of what makes a good student, from our conversations with Western teachers in China it seems that their general impression is that Chinese students are hardworking and friendly, but passive. Their students seem to expect the teacher to instruct them from the front of the class while they listen and remember in what is basically a transmission model of learning: knowledge comes from the teacher, is retained by the student and returned in exams or assignments. Western teachers feel that Chinese students do not ask questions and do not have their own opinions. They are reluctant to speak in class. As seen from Table 1 this Western teachers' view is partly supported by Chinese students' own version of their expectations of teachers but Table 2, which lists the major categories of Chinese students' responses to the question 'What makes a good student?' shows that there is more to the picture than the above would indicate.

Table 2 confirms that the Chinese students themselves believe that to be hardworking is the major characteristic of a good student. Students should be diligent in studies, 'they should study heart and soul', 'they must work hard, put study in the first place.'

However there are strong social and moral elements to studying which reflect a collective culture of learning: to respect, obey and co-operate with the teacher; and to develop a good character. As Cheng (1990) points out, Chinese teachers believe that learning is an activity to cultivate the ability of a student. This ability can be improved. This is in contrast to most Western teachers' culture of learning which embraces the ideas that ability is fixed, teachers should meet individual needs, and

Table 2. *Chinese Students' Expectations of a Good Student (N=135)*

A good student	% of respondents
is hard working	43.0%
is sociable, learns from/with others	18.5%
pays attention to the teacher	15.5%
respects and obeys the teacher	15.5%
is active in class	14.8%
co-operates with the teacher	11.8%
studies independently	11.1%
applies knowledge	7.4%
is well-motivated to study	6.6%
develops a good character	6.6%
asks questions	6.6%

students should work at their own level. All Chinese students are encouraged and are believed to be able to achieve the same expected standard as long as they work hard. This conformity and concept of attainability is part of Chinese educational tradition, which emphasises students' socialisation according to social norms and expectations from a very young age. This ideology is reflected in our data. 'Students should get on well with others', 'not only learn from books but also from classmates'. 'Students should not only learn knowledge but also the way of life'. 'Most important is the moral quality, a good student should like to help others.'

This preference for being sociable and learning from others seems at variance with the Western teachers' observation that their Chinese students do not work well in groups, mentioned earlier. The difference lies in the fact that the Western teachers expect group work in class, whereas the Chinese students believe that the best use of class time is for the teacher to explain things. The teacher who does not do so, by setting up group discussion among students, is probably not a good teacher, in their eyes. 'Sociable' for the Chinese refers to a general friendly manner. It is a moral and social characteristic related to collective Chinese traditions of caring for others within the in-group, in this case the class. In fact, 'learning from others' or 'learning with others' takes place outside classroom hours, where the teacher is not present, when those who have understood the teacher help the others. Students who are ready and willing to offer such help are considered sociable. Often they will realise their peers have problems, for example with English grammar, and will spontaneously offer help without waiting to be asked. By the same token, Chinese students with problems in the class expect the teacher to realise this and offer help, whereas the Western teachers will usually assume that any students with problems will ask for help; yet, as our evidence presented later shows, Chinese students rarely ask questions like this in class. The Western and Chinese cultures of learning sometimes weave past each other without linking.

The continuity of the Confucian or transmission model is supported by the data in Table 2, as shown by high percentages of mentions of paying attention to teachers, respecting and obeying them and co-operating with them. 'Passive' learning is shown in some students' comments: 'A good student should listen carefully to the teacher, take notes then review them later and memorise.' The influence of early socialisation into such a pattern is apparent. 'In China when we were children we were told that a good student should learn everything from the teacher. In the class a good student should keep quiet and just listen. As time goes by we've grown up and we have been used to keeping silence in class.'

Nevertheless, this may be changing. It is noticeable in Table 2 that fairly high percentages of students mention that a good student is active and asks questions in class. 'He should not only learn everything from the teacher but create things through this learning.' 'He learns actively, not passively.' 'If there is anything which can't be understood he will raise his hand immediately and discuss it with the teacher.' However, the nature of Chinese students' questions may differ from those of Western students. Chinese students value thoughtful questions which they ask after sound reflection, whereas Western students appear to ask spontaneous questions. The purpose of the Chinese students' questions is to elicit confirmation from the teacher. Sometimes they ask questions if they believe they are not able to solve a problem themselves by using reference books. Some students value the kind of thoughtful question which elicits a systematic account from the teacher, including the origin, philosophical background, related arguments and current conclusions concerning a given topic. To tackle such questions the teacher needs fairly profound knowledge, since likely answers are found in relatively few books. Less thoughtful questions may be laughed at by other students.

Also contrary to Western stereotypes of the 'passive', over-dependent student, Table 2 clearly indicates that a high percentage of Chinese students value independent study. The good student 'should not be dependent on textbooks only'. 'He not only listens to the teacher but also thinks about it himself.' 'He masters what the teacher has taught and knows other things by himself.' The inner mental activity, questioning, reflection and self-effort of a student are as important as the teacher's instruction: 'he should be good at asking questions which he meets in study and in life.' 'A really good student should have his own idea, he can know how to get knowledge with the teacher's help.' 'He should pay attention to what is a good student and find the gap between a good one and himself.' 'He should be willing to learn, not forced by parents or teachers', 'a good student is half made by himself and half made by the teacher.' Some students also value the expression of diversity of opinion. Good students 'have their own opinions', 'like to think about the lesson in their own minds and draw their own conclusions', 'have the courage to bring up opinions different from those of the teacher.' This is, of course, combined with politeness and respect, 'a good student must respect the teacher', but not necessarily with obedience, 'A really good student doesn't always obey the orders of the teacher. He or she should have their own brains.'

Such comments show that these students are not passive – they are active, reflective, independent thinkers but, importantly, such qualities are differently aligned from ways in which Western teachers expect them to be expressed. They are less manifest in the classroom, but, in many students' minds at least, they are already an inherent part of 'being a good student.'

Chinese views of Western teaching

To explore the question of Chinese and Western cultures of learning languages further, we felt that we ought to elicit students' views and reactions to having Western teachers of English. Again, a questionnaire would normally be used to investigate such a question, but, for the reasons given earlier, we favoured a more open-ended approach that would give students more opportunity to voice their interpretations in their own way. In 1994, therefore, we collected 105 university students' essays on the theme 'Western Ways of Teaching and Chinese Ways of Learning'. The students, in the second year of study in English, Economics or Tourism departments, had all had Western teachers: from Britain, the USA, Canada, Australia and Denmark. The essays were written in English. They were requested by Chinese teachers so that students would not simply write what they believed Westerners would like to read.

Quotations from these student essays are given below. They are surprisingly well-written grammatically. Likely reasons for this are that the topic is directly within students' experience, they have been trained to write essays on similar topics, and it is our clear impression that Chinese university students can write fairly well grammatically, if they are given sufficient time – as was the case with these essays.

Among the students' essays there is general agreement that Western teachers in China have different styles and influences from Chinese teachers. The Western teachers are appreciated for the ways in which they encourage learners' oral language and self-expression. They are seen as good models for pronunciation and are regarded as having the 'authority', or even 'superiority', of native speakers 'to teach true English'. This specifically includes their ability to present information about the history, cultures and customs of Western societies.

The Western teachers bring a useful cognitive dimension to the classroom. They stimulate students to think, as they said, in part because 'their ways of thinking are very different from Chinese ways.' 'They look at things from another angle which can benefit my thought.'

While many students recognise the benefit of exposure to this different thinking – arguably a major educational purpose for learning English – some see that it leads to problems in writing classes, perhaps because Western teachers are not aware of, or explicit about, differences in discourse patterns and the organisation of writing:

'Sometimes in our writing class we prepared a lot before the writing and thought it was a good essay but the grade given by a foreign teacher was very low and sometimes I thought my essay was not very well written but I got quite a high mark. This really puzzles us. Maybe there's some differences between our minds and foreign teachers' minds.'

'I write a composition, I organize it carefully and logically but the foreign teacher comments that he can't understand it. Why? We have different ways of thinking. But an essay should be related to your own ideas and ways of thinking.'

'Especially in writing classes I really don't think a Western teacher is better than a Chinese teacher.'

Chinese teachers are said to be more effective at teaching vocabulary. This is important because 'when Chinese students learn a language they think vocabulary is the most important thing.' Western teachers seem patronising. They oversimplify vocabulary and underestimate students' ability. Again, the root cause of the difference lies in different conceptions of knowledge, language and teaching. Where Western language teachers emphasise skills and language use, Chinese teachers give knowledge for learning. 'Western teachers give us simple English, simple stories. I don't think they are worth learning.' 'Sometimes their classes are too easy for us. It is perhaps because they are innocent about how well we grasped English and what kind of knowledge we have already learned.' 'Western teachers seem to think, "Simple is best" but students always think, "I can't use such common words."' 'Western teachers use the most simple words to communicate with Chinese students but Chinese teachers prefer to use difficult ones to show their knowledge and high level of teaching ability.' 'Students have the impression they can get much more knowledge from Chinese teachers than from foreign teachers.' For such reasons some students concluded, 'Western teachers are very welcome for oral classes but not for Intensive Reading.'

The Chinese emphasis on knowledge is linked to accuracy of expression. This leads to many students' belief that Chinese teachers are more effective for teaching grammar. This seems to be due to Western teachers' reluctance to explain grammatical rules and correct students' errors. Where Western teachers stress fluency, Chinese teachers emphasise accuracy. 'Western teachers don't pay much attention to grammar. They don't care about our mistakes.' 'Usually their knowledge of grammar is poorer than that of most Chinese teachers of English.' 'Sometimes Western teachers don't mind students' grammar mistakes but Chinese teachers correct them.' 'Western teachers should point out errors when they appear because students think it has been reviewed by a native speaker and they accept it.'

The lack of questions

Among Western teachers in China there is general agreement that Chinese students ask fewer questions in the classroom than Western students do, although our data have demonstrated that asking questions is definitely part of a Chinese way of learning. To explore Chinese students' views on this aspect of learning, in 1993 we further asked the same group of 135 university students the open-ended question: 'Why don't students ask questions in class?' We should perhaps explain the negative phrasing of this question. In interviews in 1992 and 1993 we found that Chinese students repeatedly indicated that they were very conscious that they did *not* ask questions, although they knew they were expected to do so by Western teachers. This having been established, we wanted to find out possible reasons for the absence of questions. Arguably, had we asked this question in a positive way ('Why do students ask questions?') this might have seemed biased in the Chinese context. When we asked the question negatively as we did ('Why don't students ask questions?'), students could have pointed out that they *did* ask questions if in fact they did so. However, no one replied like this.

The students' responses are classified and shown in Table 3. As can be seen, the most common reason given for not asking questions is that Chinese students are too shy. This response can be linked to other major reasons: other students may laugh, they are afraid of making mistakes.

Table 3. *Why Chinese Students do not Ask Questions in Class (N=135)*

Reasons for no questions	% of respondents
students are too shy	40.7%
other students may laugh	23.7%
prevented by Chinese tradition/habits	19.3%
they do not want to interrupt	17.0%
they ask *after* the lesson	17.0%
they are afraid of making mistakes	14.1%
they do not know enough to ask	12.6%
they are too lazy/bored	9.6%
nobody else asks	8.9%
the teacher does not encourage it	8.2%
students can solve the problem themselves later	8.2%
they have no questions	7.4%

A common factor behind these reasons is 'face', that Chinese students do not want to be singled out in public, they do not want others to laugh at them or at their mistakes because they will lose face in the classroom. 'They are afraid of being ashamed', 'they are afraid of asking foolish questions', 'they fear others' murmurs', 'they pay too much attention to others' opinion of them', 'those who don't ask questions actually have a lot to say but they are too shy to speak in class. They need outside help to have the courage to open their mouths.' 'Students in China are not as extrovert as those in the West. They often prefer to be asked to answer a question rather than initiate one. It's a kind of cultural difference.' 'When all the other students are silent it is impossible to expect one student to ask a question.'

Western students also feel shy, of course, and can lose face, too. However, this aspect of face can be very powerful for Chinese students and extremely common, probably more so than for Westerners. It is linked to the collective nature of Chinese society in that students are expected to avoid standing out or risk shame in front of others whereas many more individually-oriented Western learners feel much more at ease about asking questions in a more individualistic culture, since the realisation and effect of face is different. To elaborate this point, both Western and Chinese cultures have individual and collective tendencies and they seem to be held in tension in all cultures. However, they apply differently in different contexts, and in general Chinese culture emphasises the collective end of the individual-collective continuum. In Chinese society, the individual is expected to contribute to society and meet society's needs. This traditional aspect of culture has continued to be strongly emphasised in China even since 1949, for example until the early 1990s all graduates were assigned to a work unit and place of residence, which could be anywhere in China, with the widely recognised rationale that individuals (especially those with advanced education) must be prepared to serve society. In this collective context, the loss of face of the individual can often cause others to lose face or even the whole group to do so. In China, losing face has a wide social, intellectual and even a moral dimension. It implies selfishness. In the classroom, therefore, a student will try to sense whether the question is in everybody's mind before asking – this will meet the needs of all. In contrast, in Western societies (insofar as one can generalise) society attempts to meet the needs of all individuals, seen for instance in the widely accepted notion of meeting individual needs in education, particularly special needs. It is hard to imagine the Chinese concept of the subordination of the individual to society being put into practice in a Western society, except under extreme circumstances of national emergency or war. With these concepts of 'individual', 'collective', 'face' and 'asking questions' the exact realisations can be complex and always need to be contextual-ised, but it is often the case that the Chinese ways and Western ways of realising them are differently aligned, and often miss each other.

Further, many students do not wish to interrupt the lesson, either because there is not enough time for questions or because they wish to show respect for the teacher or for the collective nature of the class, so they ask their questions individually *after* the lesson. 'No questions can be allowed when the teacher is talking to the class so we should ask during the break. We should not interrupt the teacher's thought. This is a kind of respect for the teacher.' 'I will not ask at once because this may not be a question of my classmates.'

Table 3 shows that a relatively high percentage of students make explicit reference to Chinese traditions or habits regarding teachers' and students' roles. This crucial element in a Chinese culture of learning can be seen as having its origin in the kindergarten in the following comment. 'In China, from kindergarten and primary school children are strictly taught to be obedient and obey orders and rules. They are not taught to develop their own unique personalities and bring out strange questions. They only answer teachers' questions or are silent. Such virtues will be praised by both teachers and parents.' 'It is because of the characteristic long-inherited Chinese ideology: obedience, harmony, congruence with good orthodoxies.' 'Students consider themselves as one-sided receptacles.' 'They don't think of themselves as the kings of the class.' The act of asking questions, of any sort, is seen by some as questioning authority: 'Most Chinese students think that what books and a teacher says is right. They only learn to accept it but not to question it.' 'Chinese students are used to being ready to absorb know-ledge, they are not used to trying to broaden this knowledge through questions.' 'Perhaps this is due to the character of the Chinese.' 'In China, asking questions is not a good habit.' 'This question is about the nature of the Chinese people, it is a question concerning the whole society in China.'

Whereas for many Western students questions have a clear heuristic function ('If you don't ask you won't know') and are often welcomed by teachers as discussion-promoting devices, in Chinese society questions to those in authority are likely to be interpreted as challenges or as showing disrespect to that authority. In a hierarchical culture questioning can therefore have negative connotations, which leads to a strong reluctance to ask. Instead of using questions as an immediate way of finding out, Chinese students tend to use them as a last resort; first they attempt to read more or ask their peers. Only if this fails do they ask the teacher, and then not in front of the class but alone, after the class, when there is less risk of loss of face. This tendency to postpone questions is reinforced by Chinese students' sensitivity to unnecessary questions – they do not want to waste other students' time or sidetrack teacher talk through their own questions. Given these reasons, questioning 'is not a good habit'.

However, some students did indicate that this aspect of the culture of learning is changing: 'It is the tradition that students in China try to listen to the teacher and learn what the teacher says in class by heart so there is no time left for students to ask questions. But the situation is changed for the better now for it is known that asking questions is an efficient learning method.' The Chinese students' explicit awareness of such processes, as shown in these comments, may be a crucial step in this cultural change.

Not wanting to interrupt the lesson is linked to deeper cultural ideas of learning and teaching. A few students reported that they did not want to give problems to the teacher: if the teacher could not answer a question the teacher would lose face – the student who caused such a thing to happen would also lose face. Also the good teacher would predict students' questions and structure a presentation to answer such (unasked) questions, since a teacher is supposed to know much more than students. A Chinese saying explains the relationship between knowledge and teaching, 'Only a person who possesses a bucket of water can easily offer a spoon of water to others.' Such a capacity of knowledge is the guarantee for the success of teaching, in Chinese terms. A student's question will therefore interrupt because the teacher is probably about to give the answer in any case. Understanding this, students who have questions do not ask but wait. If the answer is not forthcoming, the question is not worth asking because the teacher, as the authoritative source of knowledge, has already predicted the good questions. As students said in interviews, 'A Chinese teacher anticipates students' questions. He prepares an explanation with the anticipated questions in mind, so they don't need to ask.' 'A good teacher will predict the students' questions. If you ask a question then you are making the teacher look foolish because he didn't predict that part.' 'If you have a question it is probably not important because a good teacher should explain the important points anyway, so your question is not important.'

Some students also believe they need to know more in order to ask questions, as shown in Table 3. Since they do not yet know what the teacher knows they cannot ask. This cultural concept effectively postpones questions until a high degree of knowledge has been mastered. 'Only through learning can students find questions. If they don't study further, they cannot find any questions.' 'The reason why they don't ask is because they haven't mastered enough knowledge to keep up with the teacher.'

All this is, of course, in stark contrast with most Western teachers' understanding of the importance of questions: students' questions lead to learning and discussion; they show interest and attention; the teacher can diagnose students' learning through their questions. In the foreign language classroom students' questions are vital, not least because asking questions is itself an important linguistic and social skill for communication.

In contrast to Western students' more spontaneous, and sometimes superficial, questions, some Chinese students reflect on the value of the question in advance, which again postpones asking, 'When students want to ask questions they always think too much over it, whether it is worth asking or not.' This reflective element is also shown in Table 3 by the relatively high percentage of independently-minded students who believe they can solve the problems raised through questions by themselves. 'I think I can find out by myself after class.' 'Students can ask other students or use reference books after class.' Once more, such comments run counter to the stereotype of teacher dependency.

Whether the students ask questions remains partly in the teachers' hands. It is affected by how the students perceive the teacher's ability to facilitate the asking and answering of questions. 'The teacher doesn't ask students if they have questions and they don't like to cut in.' 'Although some teachers encourage students to ask questions they do not do well enough. Their way of encouragement is only a kind of routine work.' 'I don't ask questions because I feel I can't obtain the answers I want from teachers.'

Some conclusions

In this chapter we have examined Chinese ways of learning in language classrooms, with specific examples of learning to read Chinese and English. These ways have their roots in Chinese culture and society. They seem to be enduring even in times of rapid social development in China, although some aspects are changing. We focused mainly on the perspectives of the majority of the participants in the language classroom – the students – to give a partial picture of the larger scene. The students' comments give teachers insight into a vital aspect of language teaching – the learners' perspective. However, they are unlikely to be the whole truth, for at least two reasons. First, Chinese students are changing – and their culture of learning will probably change in further respects – in response to social change. It is worth noting also that it is in the nature of education for learners to be changed by what they study and by the process of study. Perhaps we would obtain different perceptions from graduates. Second, for a full account, complementary versions held by teachers, curriculum planners, decision makers, materials writers and setters of examination questions would also need to be researched.

Where a Chinese culture of learning emphasises knowledge of vocabulary and grammar, and the result of learning, Western cultures of learning stress communication skills, language use and the process of learning. Chinese learners look for a sudden final enlightenment after mastering all aspects of the knowledge of a subject through reading, imitating, memorising – perhaps without full understanding in the early stages. Both approaches can achieve high standards. The quotations from Chinese students cited here were written in the target language in the classroom and many of them are testimony to a high level of thoughtfulness and expression in English.

Where Western approaches to language learning currently emphasise student-centred activity and classroom interaction, a Chinese culture of learning may seem to lead to student passivity and teacher-centredness. However, Chinese students abroad are known to be hard working, conscientious in preparing for classes and successful in academic study. From our evidence, it seems that both cultures of learning emphasise activity, but where the West favours verbal activity Chinese culture stresses mental activity. As a Chinese student in a British university said, 'We are active in our minds. We are thinking all the time. Our minds follow the lecturer with questions and challenges. We are just not used to speaking out. But all of us know very well what is going on and we know the answers to the questions those lecturers asked or other students raised.'

Examples of differences in Chinese and Western interpretations of what it means to be active are given in Table 4. The interpretations are not absolute; they illustrate tendencies. For Western teachers, being active has a strong verbal component of talking to the teacher and other students; for Chinese learners, it has a strong reflective element of listening and learning from an authoritative teacher, memorising, and preparing for classes. The danger is that Western teachers think of the latter as being passive.

It may be, of course, that what we have characterised as Chinese occurs in other societies, including Western ones. No society has a monopoly on behaviour. After a questionnaire study into the learning styles of adult migrants to Australia, Willing (1988: 151, 1989: 19–20) found that different learning preferences and styles were represented in similar proportions in all ethnic groups, including Chinese. Our findings clearly indicate, however, that Western teachers and Chinese students do believe that there is a characteristic Chinese way of learning which differs in key areas from that expected by Western teachers. We should

Table 4. *Examples of Contrasting Interpretations of 'active' by Western Teachers and Chinese Students*

Student behaviour	Interpretations	
	Western teachers	Chinese students
asking questions in class	useful, shows students' activity and learning	a device to elicit confirmation after reflection before and during the class; high risk of wasting time, being thought foolish
asking questions after class	shows response, slightly annoying, wastes time, why not ask in class?	less risk to face, avoids interrupting class, receives authoritative answers from the teacher only
volunteering comments in class	good, shows interest and activity	showing off, preventing teacher talk
group discussion in class, listening and responding to each other	useful interaction, language practice, student-centred learning	the teacher should give us knowledge and best skills, fruitless student discussion, wastes time, risks learning errors from peers
helping each other outside class	risk of cheating, not independent	shows sociability, good character and collective responsibility
initiating requests for help; expressing anxiety or lack of understanding	expected part of normal learning process	embarrassment, gives burdens to others; the teacher should be sensitive and willing to offer help
preparing classwork	bonus, pleased	duty, necessary, active learning

note that our methodology and the research context differ from that of Willing's study: the present study is based on interviews and open-ended questions with students and teachers in China, in a foreign language context. Even where there are similarities with other groups, Chinese expectations and behaviour in the language classroom seem to have their roots in a specific culture and social environment, into which Chinese learners have been socialised from an early age.

Some Chinese students concluded that in English classrooms in

China it is better for Western teachers to teach oral English and to deal with relevant social, cultural and historical background studies while Chinese teachers teach Intensive Reading, vocabulary, grammar and writing. However, the vast majority of English teachers in China are Chinese. Relatively few students have the opportunity to be taught by Western teachers, although this opportunity is becoming more widely available.

Cultural synergy – a proposal

Many Chinese language teachers have adopted or wish to adopt more communicatively oriented approaches since they are more modern and seem to lead to improved performance in language skills. It can be argued that this would be to use a Western culture of learning for Chinese learners; the target language would be learned using the target language culture as medium. Others, such as the Chinese teachers of English cited by Burnaby and Sun (1989) have rejected this on the grounds that these approaches are difficult to apply in Chinese contexts.

However, different cultures of learning might be combined in a cultural synergy (Jin 1992; Jin and Cortazzi 1995). This would mean that teachers or students from two or more cultures interact systematically, co-operating for the common purpose of students' language development with an attitude of being willing to learn, understand and appreciate the other's culture without loss of their own cultural status, role or identity. It would attempt to raise conscious awareness of differences in cultures of learning, making them explicit so that teachers and students would articulate their expectations of each other. It would imply that teachers not only teach culture in the language classroom, but that they are prepared to teach about cultures of learning and that they enable students to reflect on their own culture. (Teachers would need to reflect in this way too, of course.) Cultural synergy thus involves developing intercultural competence.

Cultural synergy might be viewed as a cultural extension of accommodation theory, which proposes sociolinguistic explanations for the ways in which speakers adjust their communication actions, converging or diverging, relative to those of their conversational partners (Giles and Smith 1979; Giles, Coupland and Coupland 1991). But accommodation theory has been rarely applied to the language classroom (Zeungler 1991). Cultural synergy would mean mutual convergence of cultures of learning or a one-sided convergence provided that both sides have explicit understanding of each other's culture. It would thus differ from the Acculturation model of second language acquisition (Schumann

1978a, 1978b) by being fundamentally a two-way acculturation in which neither side loses and both benefit.

To give one example of the practical application of this proposal, we have found it useful when working with British university teachers in staff development sessions and with international students on pre-sessional courses in Britain to give brief case studies which involve situations which have occurred in language classrooms and academic contexts which are familiar to one side but not to the other. Both sides then share their understanding of the situation and how they interpret it according to their culture of learning. This exercise is helpful in raising awareness of cross-cultural issues which occur in the classroom because it invites participants to be explicit about their interpretations of real incidents. Such case studies and material to develop role plays may be found in Bristow and Shotnes (1987), Kinnell (1990), Jin (1992), Jin and Cortazzi (1993, 1995) or adapted from the more general intercultural training materials found in Brislin *et al.* (1986).

When we turn to the students' views in the present data, we find that many of the Chinese learners who have experienced a Western culture of learning by having Western teachers believe that they could have the best of both cultures: 'We should absorb some fresh elements from Western ways of teaching to adjust to Chinese ways of learning.' 'Western ways of teaching and studying and Chinese ways of learning belong to different systems and are formed by different cultural backgrounds. Chinese students should learn from Western ways to develop their skills and abilities.' 'Each nation has its own culture so the learning and teaching process is different between different countries. I think foreign teaching methods plus Chinese learning processes may be of some good to the students.'

Western teachers working in China need to move towards the Chinese culture of learning, but do not have to abandon the strengths of their own approach. Chinese students can learn much from Western ways in the language classroom, from Western or Chinese teachers, but to do so they do not have to uproot themselves from their society's culture of learning. If both sides adopt an approach involving cultural synergy, the students will learn English; but there is more: both sides will gain and neither will lose, culturally.

References

Alptekin, C. 1988. Chinese formal schemata in ESL composition. *British Journal of Language Teaching* 26 (2): 112–16.

Brindley, G. 1989. *Assessing Achievement in the Learner Centred Curriculum.* Sydney: NCELTR, Macquarie University.

Brislin, R., C. Cushner, C. Cherrie and M. Yong. 1986. *Intercultural Interactions: A Practical Guide*. Beverly Hills, CA: Sage.

Bristow, R. and S. Shotnes (Eds.) 1987. *Overseas Students – at Home in Britain?* London: UKCOSA.

Burnaby, B. and Y. Sun. 1989. Chinese teachers' views of Western language teaching: Context informs paradigms. *TESOL Quarterly* 23 (2): 219–38.

Byram, M. 1989. *Cultural Studies in Foreign Language Education*. Clevedon, Avon: Multilingual Matters.

Byram, M. and V. Esarte-Sarries. 1991. *Investigating Cultural Studies in Foreign Language Teaching*. Clevedon, Avon: Multilingual Matters.

Cai, H. 1994. The ivory tower confronts the market economy. *China Daily* p. 4, 14 March 1994.

Cazden, C. B., V. P. John and D. Hymes (Eds.) 1972. *Functions of Language in the Classroom*. New York: Teachers College Press.

Chen, L. 1994. Vendors make a quick yuan dealing fast food. *China Daily* p. 6, 29 April 1994.

Cheng, K. M. 1990. The culture of schooling in East Asia. In N. Entwhistle (Ed.) *Handbook of Educational Ideas and Practices*, 163–173. London: Routledge.

Cook, V. 1993. *Linguistics and Second Language Acquisition*. London: Macmillan.

Cotton, I. 1990. Why Intensive Reading hinders the development of both English language teaching and English language learning in China. *Teaching English in China; ELT Newsletter* 20: 49–52. Beijing: British Council.

Dzau, Y. F. (Ed.) 1990. *English in China*. Hong Kong: API Press.

Ellis, R. 1994. *The Study of Second Language Acquisition*. Oxford: Oxford University Press.

Gardner, R. C. 1985. *Social Psychology and Second Language Learning: The Role of Motivation and Attitudes*. London: Edward Arnold.

Giles, H., J. Coupland and N. Coupland (Eds.) 1991. *Contexts of Accommodation*. Cambridge: Cambridge University Press.

Giles, H. and P. Smith 1979. Accommodation Theory: Optimal levels of convergence. In H. Giles and R. StClair (Eds.) *Language and Social Psychology*, 45–65. Oxford: Blackwell.

Gracie, C. 1993. Parental panic at the start of the rat race. *BBC Worldwide* October pp. 28–30.

Gumbert, E. B. (Ed.) 1990. *Teacher Education in International Perspective*. Atlanta: Georgia State University Press.

Gumperz, J. J. and D. Hymes (Ed.) 1972. *Directions in Sociolinguistics: The Ethnography of Communication*. New York: Holt, Rinehart & Winston.

Harrison, B. (Ed.) 1990. *Culture and the Language Classroom*. London: Modern English Publications.

Hildebrandt, H. W. and J. Liu. 1991. Communication through foreign languages: An economic force in Chinese enterprises. *Journal of Asian Pacific Communication* 2 (1): 45–67.

Jin, L. 1992. Academic cultural expectations and second language use: Chinese postgraduate students in the U.K. – a cultural synergy model. University of Leicester: Unpublished Ph.D. thesis.

Jin, L. and M. Cortazzi 1993. Cultural orientation and academic language use. In D. Graddol, L. Thompson and M. Byram (Eds.) *Language and Culture*, 84–97. Clevedon, Avon: Multilingual Matters.

Jin, L. and M. Cortazzi 1995. A cultural synergy model for academic language use. In P. Bruthiaux, T. Boswood and B. Du-Babcock (Eds.) *Explorations in English for Professional Communication*, 41–56. Hong Kong: City University of Hong Kong.

Kinnell, M. (Ed.) 1990. *The Learning Experience of Overseas Students*. Milton Keynes: Open University Press.

Li, Y. 1991. *College English, Intensive Reading* Book 3, 4. Shanghai: Shanghai Foreign Language Education Press.

Lin, S. 1994. Early studying may backfire. *China Daily* p. 5, 7 April 1994.

Maley, A. 1990. XANADU – A miracle of rare device: The teaching of English in China. In Y. F. Dzau (Ed.) *English in China*, 95–105. Hong Kong: API Press.

Matalene, C. 1985. Contrastive rhetoric: An American writing teacher in China, *College English* 47 (8): 789–808.

Moerman, M. 1988. *Talking Culture: Ethnography and Conversation Analysis*. Philadelphia: University of Pennsylvania Press.

Mohan, B. A. and W. A. Y. Lo. 1985. Academic writing and Chinese students: Transfer and development factors. *TESOL Quarterly* 19 (3): 515–34.

Nunan, D. 1988. *The Learner-Centred Curriculum*. Cambridge: Cambridge University Press.

O'Malley, J. M. and A. U. Chamot 1990. *Learning Strategies in Second Language Acquisition*. Cambridge: Cambridge University Press.

Oxford, R. C. 1990. *Language Learning Strategies: What Every Teacher Should Know*. New York: Newbury House.

Paine, L. W. 1990. The teacher as virtuoso: A Chinese model for teaching. *Teachers College Record* 92 (1): 49–81.

Phillips, S. U. 1982. *The Invisible Culture: Communication in Classroom and Community on the Warm Springs Indian Reservation*. New York: Longman.

Phillipson, R. 1992. *Linguistic Imperialism*. Oxford: Oxford University Press.

Richards, J. C. and C. Lockhart 1994. *Reflective Teaching in Second Language Classrooms*. Cambridge: Cambridge University Press.

Rubin, J. and T. Thompson 1994. *How to be a More Successful Language Learner*. Boston, MA: Heinle and Heinle.

Sampson, G. P. 1984. Exporting language teaching methods from Canada to China. *TESL Canada Journal* 1 (1): 19–31.

Saville-Troike, M. 1982. *The Ethnography of Communication: An Introduction*. Oxford: Blackwell.

Schumann, J. 1978a. Social and psychological factors in second language acquisition. In J. Richards (Ed.) *Understanding Second and Foreign Language Learning: Issues and Approaches*. Rowley, MA: Newbury House.

Schumann, J. 1978b. The acculturation model for second language acquisition. In R. C. Gingras (Ed.) *Second Language Acquisition and Foreign Language Teaching*. Arlington, VA: Center for Applied Linguistics.

Scollon, R. 1993. Maxims of stance: channel, relationship, and main topic in discourse. (*Research Report* no. 26.) Hong Kong: Department of English, City Polytechnic of Hong Kong.

Scollon, R. 1994. As a matter of fact: The changing ideology of authorship and responsibility in discourse. *World Englishes* 13 (1): 34-46.

Scollon, R. and S. W. Scollon. 1995. *Intercultural Communication*. Oxford: Blackwell.

Sharwood-Smith, M. 1994. *Second Language Learning: Theoretical Foundations*. London: Longman.

Shih, Y. H. 1986. *Conversational Politeness and Foreign Language Teaching*. Taipei: The Crane Publishing Co.

Stevick, E. H. 1989. *Success with Foreign Languages, Seven Who Achieved it and What Worked for Them*. London: Prentice Hall.

Tarone, E. and G. Yule. 1989. *Focus on the Language Learner*. Oxford: Oxford University Press.

Taylor, G. and T. Chen. 1991. Linguistic, cultural and sub-cultural issues in contrastive discourse analysis: Anglo-American and Chinese scientific texts. *Applied Linguistics* 12 (3): 319–35.

Towell, R. and R. Hawkins. 1994. *Approaches to Second Language Acquisition*. Clevedon, Avon: Multilingual Matters.

Valdes, J. M. (Ed.) 1986. *Culture Bound: Bridging the Cultural Gap in Language Teaching*. Cambridge: Cambridge University Press.

van Lier, L. 1988. *The Classroom and the Language Learner*. London: Longman.

Wang, D. 1986. Optimal language learning based on the comprehension-production distinction. In C. Brumfit (Ed.), *The Practice of Communicative Teaching*, 99–122. Oxford: The British Council/Pergamon.

Wenden, A. and J. Rubin. 1987. *Learner Strategies in Language Learning*. New York: Prentice-Hall.

Willing, K. 1988. *Learning Styles in Adult Migrant Education*. Adelaide: National Curriculum Resource Centre.

Willing, K. 1989. *Teaching How to Learn. Learning Strategies in ESL, A Teacher's Guide*. Sydney: NCELTR, Macquarie University.

Woods, P. (Ed.) 1980a. *Teacher Strategies*. London: Croom Helm.

Woods, P. (Ed.) 1980b. *Pupil Strategies*. London: Croom Helm.

Woods, P. 1990a. *Teacher Skills and Strategies*. Basingstoke: The Falmer Press.

Woods, P. 1990b. *Pupil Skills and Strategies*. Basingstoke: The Falmer Press.

Wu, Z. 1990. Reading with a purpose – a reassessment of the English reading programs adopted in China. In Z. Wang (Ed.) *ELT in China*. Beijing: Foreign Language Teaching and Research Press.

Xi, M. 1994. Only a collective effort can solve the problems in the education system. *China Daily* p. 6, 27 April 1994.

Young, L. W. L. 1994, *Crosstalk and Culture in Sino-American Communication*. Cambridge: Cambridge University Press.

Zeungler, J. 1991. Accommodation in native-nonnative interactions: Going beyond the 'what' to the 'why' in second-language research. In H. Giles, J. Coupland and N. Coupland (Eds.) *Contexts of Accommodation: Developments in Applied Sociolinguistics*, 223–44. Cambridge: Cambridge University Press.

Zhai, X. 1991. *College English, Intensive Reading* Book 1, 2. Shanghai: Shanghai Foreign Language Education Press.

Zhang, T. 1994. Tractor scrappers make it big with their spanners. *China Daily* p. 6, 27 April 1994.

Zhao, Y. and K. P. Campbell. 1995. English in China. *World Englishes* 14(3): 377–90.

Zhu, W. and J. Chen. 1991. Some economic aspects of the language situation in China. *Journal of Asian Pacific Communication* 2 (1): 91–101.

Part 4　Socialisation and the language classroom

In the final chapter of this collection, Dick Allwright adopts an approach which in some ways differs from that taken by the other contributors. Allwright argues that 'the socialisation of their learners into the target language community is [the] prime and ultimate goal' of language teachers and so, with this objective in mind, he concerns himself with 'the forms of pedagogy that seem most current for most learners in most places'. Language teaching which has this socialisation as its aim is contrasted with 'foreign language courses with an exclusively literary or "paper qualificatory" aim.'

Such 'socialisation of their learners into the target language community' does indeed constitute the purpose of the teaching investigated by Ballard in Chapter 8, but such a characterisation cannot be easily applied to the language teaching contexts studied by the other contributors to this volume. Nevertheless, the importance of Allwright's contribution lies in its reminder that the classroom is a social microcosm in itself. What happens in classrooms, he suggests, can be described as the outcome of the conflict between the social and the pedagogic pressures to which all the participants are subject. Allwright recognises that some of the social pressures experienced inside the classroom can be best understood with reference to the broader society from which the participants come and in which the lessons take place. However, he insists that there are also pressures which arise within the classroom itself and that these can best be studied in their own terms.

Allwright's chapter illustrates how the conflict between the social and pedagogic pressures seems typically to be resolved in favour of social rather than pedagogic value systems. To this extent, therefore, there is a parallel with the analysis presented by Chick in Chapter 2, the difference lying in Chick's detailed search outside the classroom for explanations of the social pressures experienced inside the classroom.

Allwright suggests that we may need to think of a range of different forms of socialisation, including three types of 'external' socialisation and two types of 'internal' socialisation. Of course, we must not forget that the external social and internal classroom pressures are inextricably bound up with each other. As Ballard reminded us in Chapter 8:

> In a society that emphasises respect for the past and for the authority of the teacher, the behaviour of both teachers and students will mirror these values. A society that rewards independence and individuality will produce a very different classroom etiquette.

Allwright's conclusion recognises this. He states that 'teachers and learners cannot simply choose between the pedagogic and the social pressures and opt to allow themselves to be influenced by one set of pressures rather than the other.' He accepts that classroom behaviour is not 'a simple binary matter of a set of straightforward either/or decisions.' Instead, Allwright suggests that it is more realistic to think of classroom behaviour as a 'balancing act' or 'tightrope walk ... between competing social and pedagogic demands.' If we make use of this analogy to reassess some of the other contributions to this collection, then we come to realise how difficult it is – in so many classrooms in different parts of the world – for even the most dedicated of teachers to maintain that delicate balance between the social and the pedagogic.

10 Social and pedagogic pressures in the language classroom: The role of socialisation

Dick Allwright

What motivates classroom behaviour?

Put somewhat cynically, and in extremely crude terms, the set of choices facing anyone, teacher or learner, about how to behave in a classroom could be represented by the following set of questions:

1 am I going to take this lesson as a social event, and just try to have fun or at least stay out of trouble (or perhaps even create trouble) even if I learn/teach nothing? *or*
2 am I going to take it as a pedagogic event, and seriously try to teach/ learn something, even if it means getting into trouble and not having much fun? *or*
3 am I going to try to take it as both simultaneously, and try to learn/ teach something while having some fun and without getting into any more trouble than is absolutely unavoidable? In which case, if there turns out to be a conflict between my desire to have fun and/or stay out of trouble and my desire to learn/teach something, which pressure am I going to allow to guide and perhaps to dominate my behaviour?

This chapter analyses the arguments underlying this probably somewhat depressing representation of what might motivate classroom behaviour, principally by discussing the relevance of socialisation as a pedagogic aim, and providing a preliminary schematic analysis of what appears to be involved in the language classroom. This analysis distinguishes importantly between 'internal' and 'external' socialisation – socialisation for life in the classroom itself and socialisation for life in the external world. Language pedagogy is fundamentally more complex, I propose, than other subjects in its relationship to socialisation as a pedagogic aim.

Within language pedagogy it is important to deal with the distinction between 'second' and 'foreign' language pedagogy and its importance to the role of the socialisation process. After that, we need to consider the sorts of hypotheses we might generate from a consideration of the role of socialisation, and the sorts of data we might need in order to investigate them. This chapter will therefore turn from a concern for conceptual analysis to a concern for research method. Can we expect lesson transcripts to prove adequately revealing by themselves, for example, or will more 'introspective' sorts of data prove indispensable?

When we have focused on teacher behaviour and discussed at some length socialisation as a classroom *process*, we can then turn to the interpretation of learner behaviour and use that discussion to introduce a brief reconsideration of the more obvious possibility of interpreting classroom behaviour as the *product* of prior socialisation processes.

Finally, at the very end of the chapter, we will be in a position to discuss, though briefly, the implications for language classroom pedagogy of what we can now say about the apparent complexities of the relationship between social and pedagogic pressures.

The basic argument

In several places (see especially Allwright 1989, 1992) I have argued that there is an inherent conflict between the social and the pedagogic pressures that obtain in the classroom. The argument is applicable to all classrooms, not just language classrooms. My use of the argument appears to be somewhat novel in the context of language pedagogy but it has a considerable history in general educational research (see for example Riesman 1950, and the conflict between 'getting on' and 'getting along'), and is reflected in Breen's distinction between 'survival' and 'achievement' orientations (Breen 1987).[1] I have then used this analysis as a basis for looking again at language classroom discourse, to see if such a putative conflict could help us understand why, on inspection, so much of classroom behaviour, of both teachers and learners, seems so decidedly 'unpedagogic' – why it seems not to serve well the supposed immediate pedagogic purposes of the classroom lesson, because it leaves episodes of interaction discoursally resolved but pedagogically unresolved.

I have suggested then that what lies behind the apparent inadequacies of the pedagogy is probably a tendency to allow social considerations to outweigh the pedagogic ones. I have even referred, although so far with no more than purely anecdotal evidence, to the possibility of a 'conspiracy' between teachers and their learners to give priority to social considerations, to pretend to each other that 'all must be well pedagogically if all is apparently well socially' (see also Chick's argument in Chapter 2).

My argument is based on the contention that pedagogic discourse (regardless of the subject matter, incidentally) must contain at least potential challenges to the topical, discoursal, linguistic and procedural competence of the participants (not forgetting possible challenges to the pedagogic competence of the teacher). These potential challenges arise from the necessary inclusion in the classroom discourse of previously unlearned elements – new topical, discoursal, linguistic, procedural material. Such previously unlearned elements must be there if there is to be anything for the learners to learn, if the event is to be seen by the learners as a lesson rather than simply as a more or less unmarked social occasion (a chance for a conversation with friends). Such new material must itself, almost by definition, pose challenges for learners (especially if the event is to be perceived as a lesson, as noted above), and such challenges must hold the risk of upsetting the social equilibrium in a classroom group, because any difficulty learners may have in coping with the new material is potentially embarrassing to such learners, and any difficulty the teacher may have in helping such learners smoothly over such difficulties is also potentially embarrassing, for the teacher. That may be why, I have suggested, teachers and their learners may prefer even to conspire with each other, covertly, to allow social considerations to outweigh the pedagogic ones. That will be detrimental to the pedagogy, as noted above, but they will do it essentially to avoid causing each other social embarrassment (promoting 'getting along' at the expense of 'getting on').[2]

A basic flaw in the argument?

Though it may still be useful as a starting point, the fundamental argument I have made (that the relationship between social and pedagogic considerations is inherently conflictual) could be importantly flawed in at least one important and interesting respect – in its failure to take explicitly into account the extent to which some part of the teacher's responsibility can be said to be socialisation. To this extent the social considerations (and therefore the concomitant social pressures) can be seen as part of the pedagogy. That is to say, part of the teacher's job, in many if by no means all situations, is perhaps that of helping the classroom group to learn to act in a socially acceptable way, both inside the classroom and outside it. If we accept this, then we can properly say that at least some of the social pressures of classroom life are fundamentally pedagogic in nature, since they arise directly from part of what it is intended that the learners should learn. There might still arise conflicts within such pedagogic considerations, of course, but it would no longer be accurate or helpful to seek to portray them as conflicts simply between general and wholly incompatible social and pedagogic pressures.

It is especially easy to see socialisation as a normal part of the teacher's role in the context of compulsory schooling in state school systems, where the teacher is perhaps legally *in loco parentis*, and may be officially expected by 'society' both to socialise learners into the immediate educational environment, and simultaneously to play a major role in socialising learners into the wider society outside of and subsequent to the compulsory school system itself.

That socialisation role may also be evident, however, in the post- or non-compulsory situation, where teachers will probably accept it as a part of their responsibility to try to establish, if only for their own comfort and safety, at least the minimum of socially acceptable behaviour in the classroom. In such settings they may well also accept it as a major part of their directly pedagogic responsibility at least to try to help the learners form some sort of effective 'learning group' (see Stevick 1976 for the importance of thinking of a class group as a 'learning community', albeit a 'fragile' one).

The special case of language pedagogy

What may be evident in classrooms in general, across all subjects, may of course look very different in any particular subject area. Language as a subject area does indeed raise subject-specific and highly complex possibilities for the analysis, to the extent that language pedagogy may be concerned precisely and explicitly, in its own stated aims, with preparing learners to be able to cope with that part of 'the world outside the classroom' where the language being taught is regularly used. Language teachers may therefore be importantly different from mathematics teachers, for example. Teachers of mathematics in secondary schools may have to concern themselves with what we might call 'internal socialisation', with establishing socially acceptable behaviour patterns in the classroom, and may also concern themselves with what we might call 'subject-oriented' internal socialisation, with trying to help the learners form a learning community within the classroom. At the same time, however, they may well be able (but again see Chick's chapter in this volume) to minimise the extent to which they concern themselves with 'external socialisation', with the everyday world outside the classroom (and for the most part they are probably not centrally concerned, at compulsory schooling levels, with preparing their mathematics learners for the special discourse world inhabited by professional mathematicians). In some settings (more than we might wish, probably, perhaps even a majority) language teachers may approach their subject in much the same way as teachers of mathematics as I have portrayed them, and argue that preparing their learners for a paper qualification in the target language is the predominant need, while other teachers in other settings may adopt a purely literary orientation to their subject and its underlying purpose. For many language teachers around the world, however, preparation for the target language world outside the classroom constitutes a major, if not the major (and only ultimately worthwhile?), underlying purpose for the job. For such language teachers, my exclusive concern for the remainder of this discussion, the socialisation of their learners into the target language community is their prime and ultimate goal.

'Second' and 'foreign' language pedagogy

The situation is further complicated when we note that language teachers themselves distinguish importantly between 'second language' and 'foreign language' pedagogy. In 'foreign language' pedagogy the language teaching takes place somewhere where the language being taught is not a normal part of the regular lives of the learners (for example, teaching French in an English secondary school is an example of 'foreign language' teaching). In 'second language' pedagogy, by contrast, the teaching takes place in the target language community itself (for example, teaching English to non-English speakers newly arrived in England). If we can, as noted above, exclude from consideration the many foreign language courses with an exclusively literary or 'paper qualificatory' aim, then for many teachers involved in both sorts of language pedagogy the ability to cope with the target language community can be seen as the ultimate goal. For both sorts of language pedagogy, also, it can be seen that coping with the target language community is not an exclusively and narrowly linguistic matter. Coping with the target language community can be seen as a problem in culture learning, the most extreme form of socialisation – knowing how to cope not only with your own community in your own society in your own culture, but also with that of some other community in someone else's society in someone else's culture. The advantage for the second language situation is that the target language community is immediately available for study, practice and reality testing. The corresponding disadvantage is that, being immediately available, the problems it poses must also be addressed immediately – they cannot simply be delayed to suit the institutional or other conveniences of the learning situation.

Language pedagogy, then, can be importantly different from other subject area teaching in its relationship to what I am calling here 'external socialisation'. At the same time, the fact that language pedagogy itself is not unitary but importantly divided between second and foreign language situations may lead us to expect each situation to have its own distinctive implications for the issue of socialisation. Nothing has been said so far, however, to challenge the fundamental argument that there is something inherently conflictual in the relationship between the pedagogic and the social pressures in the classroom. What we can now see is simply an infinitely more complex situation for classroom participants to work within, and for us researchers to try to investigate and hope to understand. It may help to try to set out the analysis in schematic form.

A schematic representation of the analysis

It might perhaps clarify the situation a little for the purposes of discussion and for future research if we pursue the distinction made above between 'internal' and 'external' socialisation, and then make a further, if crude, distinction between 'socialisation-oriented' pedagogy and 'subject-oriented' pedagogy, between pedagogy the prime aim of which is to socialise and pedagogy aimed more directly at enhancing learners' command of a school subject. 'Internal' socialisation, as introduced above, would refer to the development of patterns of behaviour appropriate to the classroom as a social setting, while 'external' socialisation would refer to the development of patterns of behaviour appropriate to the world outside and beyond the classroom. Within the notion of 'internal' socialisation there would be a distinction to be made between patterns of behaviour appropriate to the more purely social aspects of the functioning of the classroom group as a *social* group (perhaps covering such notions as general courtesy in interpersonal relationships), and those more directly relevant to the functioning of the classroom group as a *learning* group (perhaps covering such notions as co-operation on learning tasks).

This sort of analysis would bring all social considerations under the heading of pedagogy, leaving to one side for the time being the problem of whether there was anything at all that could be said to be uniquely social rather than pedagogic. Figure 1 is an attempt to represent this pedagogy-centred analysis.

Purely 'Social Matters' – at the far left of the diagram – are left unanalysed at this stage (to be reconsidered in the discussion of 'Socialisation as process and socialisation as product'), but expanded by the subheading of 'Social Survival' to differentiate such concerns from those that could more properly be considered socialisation as a process (a deliberate pedagogic intent to establish socially appropriate behaviour

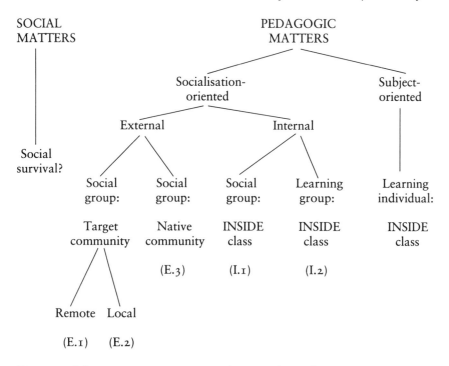

Figure 1: Schematic representation of types of socialisation

patterns in others). Pedagogic Matters themselves are first of all divided between those related to socialisation-oriented pedagogy and those related to subject-oriented pedagogy.

The subject-oriented area is represented as relating directly to the learning individual, rather than to the group (since it is individual performance in relation to particular subject matter areas that will typically be used as the test of the system's efficacy – though this state of affairs is no doubt better seen as a widespread socio-historical phenomenon rather than as a universal logical necessity).

The socialisation-oriented area is further subdivided into external and internal considerations. Furthest away from the subject-oriented area is the potential 'external' aim of enabling learners to cope with (become tolerable, and preferably effective, contributing members of) 'society at large'. This general 'external' aim is subdivided to distinguish between, on the one hand, socialisation aimed at preparing learners for their own native language community and, on the other hand, socialisation for the target language community, which may be either 'remote' or 'local' (permitting different analyses for foreign and second language situations). The internal considerations are themselves subdivided to distinguish between the potential aim, on the one hand, of enabling learners to cope with (and again become tolerable, effective and contributing members of) the social society of the classroom itself, and, on the other hand, the potential aim of enabling learners to cope with (again become tolerable, effective and contributing members of) the classroom society as a 'learning group' rather than as a purely social group.[3]

If the above analysis is at all convincing in itself, then we need to look at the possibility of two types of conflict, not just one. Firstly, there would be what we took as a starting point – the possibility of conflict between any of the types of socialisation described above and the subject-oriented aspects of classroom behaviour. And secondly there would now be the possibility of conflict *among* the five conceptually distinct types of socialisation identified:

E.1 External socialisation type 1:
> for the social situation of the *target* language community where this is *remote* from the learning situation (foreign language pedagogy).
E.2 External socialisation type 2:
> for the social situation of the *target* language community where this is *local* to the learning situation (second language pedagogy).
E.3 External socialisation type 3:
> for the social situation of the *native* language community where this is local to the learning situation.
I.1 Internal socialisation type 1:
> for the *social* group inside the learning situation.
I.2 Internal socialisation type 2:
> for the *learning* group inside the learning situation.

It would surely be wrong, however, to give the impression that the notion of socialisation as a classroom process will by itself offer an adequate framework for the understanding of all instances of 'unpedagogic' behaviour in the language classroom.

One problem is the fact that the analysis which I have presented here so far has been almost exclusively teacher-centred. This is presumably because the term 'socialisation' itself refers to an educational aim, an intention, that it may be much more reasonable to expect of a teacher than of a learner.[4]

Of course, some language learners will be aware of the socialisation aspects of formal education, and some may positively embrace such aims, especially learners who have seen the possible value to themselves of being able to use another language in the rest of their lives. Some may even embrace the aim of trying to form a 'learning community' in the classroom.[5] But many may not recognise such aims, or may even recognise them only to reject them (as noted in the introduction, some may even want to create trouble). We have therefore to include in our analysis the possibility that some learners want, at best, simply that the classroom situation be socially tolerable (the point of the 'social survival' subheading for Social Matters in Figure 1), while other learners, for whatever reason, may actively seek to disrupt the pedagogic business of the classroom, and perhaps also its social equilibrium. Even teachers may, *in extremis*, decide that the best they can hope for in their classrooms is a tolerable social situation, and that no serious pedagogy (whether subject-oriented or properly socialisation-oriented) is possible, or even worth aiming at.

So we return to the original set of choices outlined in the introduction to this chapter, and see that the concept of socialisation as a classroom process complicates the issues very significantly, for all concerned. But we also see again that it does not eliminate the basic (if novel only to our field) insight – that there is still a fundamental choice to be made, or at least a balance to be struck, between social and pedagogic priorities in general, and even within pedagogical concerns, between the socialisation and subject matter aspects of the pedagogy. Unless, of course, we can find ways of conducting classroom lessons which successfully reconcile a social need for harmony with a pedagogic need for challenge, with all its attendant risks to social equilibrium. Such thoughts will be left until the end of this discussion of social and pedagogic pressures (see 'The problem for classroom pedagogy', below). For now it may be more appropriate to consider how the complexities of the analysis so far could be pursued in research on language pedagogy.

Using the analysis in research on language pedagogy

We now have, if the above analytical framework is to serve any useful purpose, a more subtle way of approaching classroom data that contains examples of puzzlingly 'unpedagogic' behaviour. But what sorts of interpretations will we now want to consider, and what sorts of data will permit us to arrive at plausible interpretations that make the fullest possible use of the framework, and, preferably, permit us to develop and refine it further? The sort of data that prompted the original speculations about the relationship between social and pedagogic pressures in the language classroom was basically lesson transcript data – standard orthographic transcripts made from audio recordings of lessons. But how far can we expect such data to take us, now that the analysis is much more complex, and deliberately incorporating considerations external to the classroom itself?[6]

A brief look at one or two samples from transcript data may help at this point. First, a particularly minimal example of an actual classroom event that could be said to be pedagogically puzzling in some way:

Learner: *Look* is *see*, right?
Teacher: Yes.

The learner was apparently querying the meaning relationship between the words *look* and *see*. *Look* was in the textbook sample sentence that the teacher had just read out to exemplify his teaching point – the relationship between *what* and *which*. The teacher's *Yes* terminated the episode dealing with this particular query, and the analyst's problem is simply that this *Yes* is not strictly speaking accurate as a representation of the 'facts of the language', in that it allows the learner concerned, and any others in the class who happen to be paying attention, to infer that the relationship between *look* and *see* is one of complete synonymy. If we consider the possible hypotheses that could be invoked to account for this apparent pedagogic lapse, what additional or alternative sorts of data might we need to make a sensible choice between competing accounts in order to eliminate the least plausible of them?

The most obvious hypothesis to consider first is the purely pedagogic one that the teacher lacked the linguistic competence to deal more 'adequately' with the learner's query. Perhaps the teacher simply did not know that *look* and *see* are not synonymous terms. This is no doubt an unlikely account, given that the teacher was a native speaker of English, and had a high level of training and very considerable experience in the field (the incident is a genuine one recorded many years ago now), but could it be investigated adequately simply by the study of transcript data? We would surely need many more examples of the teacher apparently misleading the learners on this or other issues of meaning relationships before we would be willing to impute to the teacher a lack of linguistic knowledge. However many examples we found, we might still find other ways of explaining their occurrence.

For example, there is a second purely pedagogic account to consider – the possibility that the teacher is subordinating, in this instance, the pedagogic 'good' of dealing thoroughly with a learner's query to the arguably 'greater' pedagogic good of keeping the class more narrowly focused on the teacher's own teaching point by returning as quickly as possible to the *what* and *which* issue that was his main teaching point. Some might perhaps query the wisdom of such a decision on the part of the teacher, but we should at least acknowledge that it would suffice to account for such teacher behaviour, and would render redundant an appeal to a possible gap in the teacher's knowledge of the facts of the language. But how would we establish the plausibility of this second hypothesis? Again, would transcript data suffice? And again, if we found many examples of learners' queries being dealt with more summarily when the teacher was otherwise busy trying to explain a teaching point than when there was no obvious teaching point to claim priority attention, would we be fully justified in lending more credence to this 'greater pedagogic good' account? And what would we be willing to conclude if we were unable to find many such examples in our database?

It seems clear that in our search for the most plausible account transcript evidence would indeed be useful, but it seems equally clear that it would not necessarily be at all conclusive. The difficulty is that still other more or less plausible accounts are also imaginable. It should be acknowledged nevertheless that the 'greater pedagogic good' argument, however difficult to substantiate in particular cases, must remain a prime candidate for the interpretation of otherwise puzzlingly 'unpedagogic' episodes of classroom interaction, at least with respect to teacher behaviour. To dismiss such an interpretation prematurely would be to deny quite unreasonably the potential validity of teachers' own perceptions that they are constantly faced with the choice between 'the immediate and the important'. To be fair to teachers and to their probable professional commitment we should perhaps always look first to the 'greater pedagogic good' hypothesis. So many things are happening all at the same time in the classroom that even noticing them all is a considerable achievement, and yet it seems to be the teacher's job to identify the truly important ones instantly and develop them rather than spend time on the less important ones, however immediately compelling the relatively trivial issues may be. (Notice that we are considering only the teacher's perspective at this point, although, as we shall see later in 'Taking the learners' perspective into account', there may be a parallel phenomenon of priority selection discernible in learner behaviour.)

When we move away from the purely pedagogic accounts (the extreme right-hand side of Figure 1) we have several more possibilities to consider. First, moving from right to left in the diagram, there is the possibility in principle, under the subheading of 'internal socialisation' (in this case I.2), that the teacher's behaviour could be accounted for in terms of an imputed intention to develop in the learners a pattern of behaviour appropriate to the formation and/or maintenance of a 'learning community' in the classroom. On the face of it there is nothing in the transcript episode itself that would lend plausibility to such an account, but then we have to ask whether we would have a reason to expect the appropriate evidence to appear in a transcript in the first place. We may certainly be able to imagine what such evidence would look like – for example it might take the form of the teacher discussing with a group of learners, as they are preparing to undertake a group task, just how they could most usefully use the experience to develop ways of working more effectively together[7], but it is not obvious that we have a right to expect such explicitness to be the norm, given the likelihood of a teacher preference for an indirect approach to such matters. For relevant evidence we might therefore have to look elsewhere than in transcript data.

Looking elsewhere might sensibly take us first to the teacher's lesson plans. These might be expected to be helpful, but again the general intention to promote the development of a 'learning community' in the classroom could most probably be seen by the teacher as an ongoing commitment without any particular planned manifestation, in a written lesson plan, on any particular occasion. That suggests a need to consult the teacher more directly, perhaps by pre-lesson interviews, and/or by asking the teacher to keep a teaching diary or log in which issues would perhaps be raised that might not be expected to find a place in specific lesson plans. We might then also ask for retrospective accounts from the teacher, again in diary or log form. None of this would necessarily give us the right to interpret any particular episode of the lesson in a particular way, of course. If we are determined to try to erect plausible accounts for particular episodes of classroom interaction then we will need some form of prompted recall – working through a videotape of a lesson with the teacher, asking directly for reflections on episodes of interest perhaps. Such a procedure is clearly subject to the possibility of yielding *post hoc* rationalisations rather than fully 'reliable' accounts, but even an extensive picture of a teacher's pattern of *post hoc* rationalisations would give us interesting data to work with and to compare to any other relevant data we may have (from learners, for example).

Immediately we move away from purely pedagogic accounts, then, we find ourselves unable to get very far with transcript data alone, because we are now inevitably dealing with intentions rather than with competence. Interestingly the problem may not be so acute for the form of internal socialisation that deals with generally acceptable classroom behaviour (I.1). Here it may be much more likely that a teacher will explicitly refer to norms of behaviour ('Just one person to speak at a time, please' or 'Not so much noise, please, or we'll disturb the class next door'). But could the teacher's *Yes* to the learner's query about *look* and *see* be construed in such terms? Not from the transcript data alone, presumably, but it is just imaginable that someone would wish to interpret the teacher's very brief *Yes* as an indication to the student that such interruptions to the smooth treatment of the teacher's teaching point will be dealt with as summarily as possible, and will thus be effectively discouraged, precisely as unwelcome interruptions. Notice that it would not be necessary to claim that such an account was by itself sufficient. Much more plausibly we can imagine that a teacher's intentions would be multiple rather than unitary. But how would we go about trying to establish the relative plausibility of this particular account? Again we would need more than transcript data, presumably, and again we would no doubt find ourselves working towards a generally plausible overall picture rather than towards a highly specific and fully credible account of any particular episode.

It would be tedious to pursue the three forms of external socialisation to the same extent as the two forms of internal socialisation that have just been discussed. Enough has probably been said, in any case, to justify the two suggestions already made: first that we must expect to need to go well beyond transcript data into the realms of more subjective, more ethnographic, investigatory techniques, and second that along the way we must expect to lose confidence in the wisdom of hoping to establish credible accounts for particular episodes of classroom discourse, however valuable such episodes may be as initial prompts to fruitful speculation.

Taking the learners' perspective into account

A further point needs to be made here: that the above discussion has focused exclusively on attempting to imagine what might account for the behaviour of the teacher. The learner's behaviour, by implication, was considered unproblematic. Certainly there would have been no particular reason for the learner, on this occasion, to have pursued the query, since there was no obvious reason for the learner to know, or even to suspect, that the teacher's response might be in some way linguistically inadequate, given the clarity and definiteness of the simple *Yes*. On other occasions, however, learner behaviour is itself in need of elucidation. For example, it is difficult so easily to dismiss as unproblematic and unpuzzling the behaviour of learner An (a pseudonym) in the following extract from the same lesson:

An: *Fear* is the same thing as (angry) *angry*?
T: As what?
An: I don't know, *angry*?

T: Angry. Sort of. Yeah, you don't like something. If you don't like something and you don't like it very much, you *hate* it.
Lu: You
T: Hate something. If you don't like it very much. For example, I hate asparagus. OK?
An: I love it.
M: You like everything.
/Students muttering./
T: I hate asparagus.
Lu: What's asparagus?
Si: Asparagus?
T: Asparagus.
Si: I like it.
An: You, I like it too. Yeah.
M: I like it good.
T: Well, anyway, that's the meaning for *hate*. OK?

Before beginning to discuss this particular episode, it will perhaps help to note that the lesson in question was designated as a 'grammar' lesson. It was given – on an intensive English summer course at a tertiary institution in the USA – to a small group of intermediate level students who were taking the course in the hope of gaining entry to academic courses at the same institution in the next academic year. They were all Spanish speakers, from southern and central America. Their teacher for the grammar lessons was a native speaker of English, as already noted, and a very experienced professional who was also course director.

Returning to the episode itself, the original query seems to have become completely transformed, but the learner makes no apparent attempt to resurrect his initial concern for the relationship between *angry* and *fear* (again a lexical issue arising directly from the content of the sample sentences in the textbook). Is the learner simply pedagogically incompetent – unable to recognise the problem and take the appropriate pedagogic action (in this case at least to remind the teacher that his original query has not been adequately addressed)? Alternatively, can we appeal to a learner equivalent of the 'greater pedagogic good' hypothesis? Such a possibility must certainly not be dismissed out of hand. Discussions with learners suggest strongly that they are likely to be well capable of recognising the discoursal dilemma facing both them and their teacher, and of deciding that, in the circumstances, and in the long run, they will profit more, in terms of their own learning, from a 'wait and see' policy rather than from a dogged determination to pursue their pedagogic concerns publicly and immediately 'to the bitter end'.

Of course it is also possible to think of 'social survival' reasons why this particular learner should not have returned to his query at this point in the lesson. It might well have been personally embarrassing both for himself and for his teacher to have called public attention to the teacher's failure to deal adequately with his original query, however sensitively the learner himself handled the situation. But we cannot easily decide whether such social considerations were more influential on this occasion than the alternative and potentially pedagogically very sensible 'wait and see' policy the learner might have been invoking, even if we may have some suspicion, perhaps quite unfairly, that the 'wait and see' interpretation is too obviously 'convenient' and is more likely to be a *post hoc* rationalisation than a 'genuine' account in many cases (just as we might suspect, as noted in the previous section, that a teacher's 'greater pedagogic good' account of his or her own behaviour would be too 'convenient' to be accepted immediately at face value).

To return to the issue of research method, would we expect to be able find enough in transcript data alone, or would we not need to have recourse to alternative types of data? And, again, could we hope to 'explain' a particular episode, or are we going to have to settle for a much more general aim, and for a much more general understanding of learner behaviour?

Moreover, it must now be abundantly clear that, in our investigations of social and pedagogic pressures, we are going to need multiple data sources. And, at best, they will 'throw light' on the overall situation rather than enable us to 'explain' particular incidents. And in any case we are going to have to accept the necessity of interpreting classroom behaviour as springing from highly mixed motives.

Underlying the above discussion is the fundamental point that teachers and learners cannot simply choose between the pedagogic and the social pressures, and opt to allow themselves to be influenced by one set of pressures rather than the other. Classroom behaviour, in spite of how I represented it initially in the introduction, is not a simple binary matter of a set of straightforward either/or decisions. It is perhaps much better represented as some sort of balancing act between opposing forces, a tightrope walk for the most conscientious of teachers and learners, a continually reinvented compromise between competing social and pedagogic demands.

Socialisation as process and socialisation as product

But adopting the learner's perspective should serve to remind us of another aspect of the situation that the analysis so far has not dealt with: the more obvious possibility that we can use the notion of socialisation in at least two ways when we are attempting to interpret classroom behaviour. First, we can think of socialisation as a *process* which we can see happening during lessons (i.e. we are actually looking at people being socialised), and second we can think of classroom behaviour as the *product,* or result, of socialisation processes that have already had their effect (we are looking at learners who behave in this way because they have already been socialised to behave this way). So far, when we considered the classroom situation from the perspective of the teacher, we focused exclusively on the possibility of interpreting the teacher's behaviour as being motivated by the intent to further the process of socialising learners in one or more of the five ways set out in Figure 1. Surely, however, it must be at least equally, if not even more, plausible to attempt to interpret classroom behaviour, both of teacher and of learners, as in large measure the product of their prior socialisation experiences.

If we return to the second sample lesson extract and pursue the possible 'social survival' interpretation introduced in the previous section, we can now more plausibly interpret the learner's behaviour as the result of prior experiences which have perhaps suggested that it is likely to be construed as impolite to remind a teacher of a failure to deal adequately with a query, and it is therefore also likely to be counter-productive, in the sense that embarrassing the teacher is likely to cause even more embarrassment to the person who does it. As Karp and Yoels put it: 'in the college classroom "getting along" means students and teachers avoiding any situation that might be potentially embarrassing to one or the other' (1976: 273). The 'prior experiences' that lead to this sort of behaviour may be very remote in time, and certainly not necessarily traceable in any transcript record of the current course. They may also, especially in the second language classroom, be very remote in geographical origins, and by the same token in cultural origins, given the possibility of the second language classroom group consisting of representatives from a good many parts of the world. In the foreign language pedagogy situation, by contrast, there may be some degree of homogeneity of prior experience among the learning group, but the teacher, if he or she is a native speaker of the target language and an expatriate, may represent a very different culture and thus a potentially very different set of prior socialisation experiences. Notice also that even in the most mono-cultural of settings, with teachers and learners all from the same restricted geographical area (perhaps all from the same village) there are very likely to be major differences in prior socialisation experiences between male and female students, leading to manifestly different patterns of classroom behaviour (by both learners and their teachers, it should perhaps be added). Any comprehensive study of the motivations behind classroom behaviour must at least attempt to address such complexities.

A brief overview

This chapter has used a crude, even simplistic, analysis of classroom socialisation to make the point, ironically, that life in language classrooms is even more complicated than we may have previously thought. In the field of language teaching we have tended to insulate ourselves from general educational research, where such complexities have been taken for granted for some time. This insulation has occurred at least partly because we have had our own tradition of subject-specific research (the whole field of second language acquisition), and have allowed our otherwise very healthy tradition of classroom research to be dominated by a concern for language teaching method, probably because of the connection between the development of systematic classroom observation and language teacher training, which itself has been method-driven. These two research traditions are only slowly giving way to a wider conception of what it would be interesting to try to understand better. This wider conception is well exemplified in the title of a 1995 paper by Peirce – 'Social identity, investment, and language learning' – and by her use of a wide range of investigative procedures including diaries, questionnaires, individual and group interviews and home visits.

In our attempts to reach some general understanding of language classroom behaviour, therefore, we now have a multitude of possibilities to try to take into account. Just from the possibilities discussed in this chapter we can see that language classroom behaviour might be motivated by pedagogic considerations, or by social ones, or most probably by both simultaneously, in a continuously reinvented balancing act between opposing forces. Pedagogic considerations themselves include at least five different types of socialisation, and social considerations may well involve multi-cultural and gender-sensitive dimensions.

Methodologically, in order to investigate such complexity with any hope of success, we are going to need a variety of approaches, using techniques that go far beyond the mere observation and inspection of the behaviour we are hoping eventually to understand better. Also, as we have already seen, we are going to have to look for some sort of overall understanding rather than for definitive explanatory accounts of particular episodes, and we are going to have to accept, in our overall understanding, that mixed motivations are more likely than unitary ones.

Meanwhile, the problem for classroom pedagogy

But, while we are waiting for the outcome of such investigations, can pedagogic procedures be suggested that might actually help teachers and learners avoid the possible 'unpedagogic' consequences of allowing social considerations to outweigh 'purely' pedagogic ones? Perhaps all that can be said at present is what we have learned from extensive discussions with both teachers and learners – that the social pressures which they themselves feel cause them to act in an 'unpedagogic' way are at their most acute when their behaviour is on public display. This is most obviously the case when the teacher is operating with the whole class as the pedagogic unit, so that anything the teacher says, even if it is to respond to a purely individual enquiry (the case for the two examples of classroom data discussed above), is said effectively in front of everybody, and therefore has to be tailored with this fully public dimension in mind.

For some people (learners and teachers alike) it is clear that in such circumstances the teacher's purely pedagogic competence is itself also under strain, because it is indeed seen as much more difficult to explain adequately a linguistic phenomenon in a way that everyone in the class can be expected to comprehend, than it is to frame an adequate explanation for a particular learner (or, we might add, to a small group of learners). Such a challenge to the teacher's pedagogic competence constitutes a further potential source of social embarrassment.

For the learners, also, public performance in front of the whole class is quite clearly a prime potential source of social embarrassment, and it is therefore likely to be avoided even if it means that important questions forming in their minds go unasked. As one Algerian senior secondary school learner put it (originally in French):

> Sometimes I feel like asking the teacher a question, but just realising that perhaps some of the class already understand I hesitate. (From data collected by Cherchalli, 1988)

Another learner in the same study, an altogether less hesitant person apparently, captured the situation somewhat differently, and in so doing provided what might have served as a good alternative title for this chapter:

> Ah, a teacher is a teacher. They're made to make trouble for us!

If teachers are indeed in a position where they must 'make trouble' for their learners, then it looks as if the best advice for the moment is for them to try to minimise the extent to which it is done in public.

Notes

1 In my own, as yet unpublished, work I would now prefer to make a double distinction. The first would be between an 'achievement orientation' ('getting on') and a 'harmony orientation' ('getting along'), much as in other people's work, but where both orientations would be represented as dimensions, with negative and positive poles. This enables us to deal, for example, with people who, on the one hand, are against classroom harmony, wishing actively to disrupt it, or who, on the other hand, are against achievement, for whatever reason (personal or political), wishing actively to work against it, either for themselves personally or for others. The second distinction would then be between both of these and a third orientation, for 'survival' ('getting by'), which would be represented as the neutral point on either or both of the other orientational dimensions. It would therefore be possible to cover the case, rare as it may be, of learners who are positive about achievement but neutral about classroom harmony – who are willing to take the risk of making enemies in order to 'get on', because they merely wish to 'survive', socially speaking.

2 We should not of course forget the possibility that forms of pedagogy (e.g. autonomy projects) may exist which change the nature of the classroom situation very substantially, and perhaps in so doing serve to minimise such problems, even if they do not eliminate them altogether. My concern here, however, is with the forms of pedagogy that seem most current for most learners in most places.

3 A more ideologically oriented formulation (as found elsewhere in this volume) would alternatively see socialisation as the prior educational aim of state school systems, with pedagogy as a subcategory of socialisation.

4 We should not forget that, in a sense, learners could sometimes perhaps be said to socialise their teachers into being the sorts of teachers they themselves want. This does not appear to be normally a conscious, intentional process, but it is one that would repay further study in any comprehensive attempt to understand classroom behaviour.

5 The so-called 'humanistic' approaches differ considerably in the extent to which they concern themselves with this group dimension to the learning process, as no doubt do the more recent attempts to do 'learner training' in the language classroom.

6 For a fuller discussion of the limits of classroom observation see Allwright 1987.

7 For an early and highly imaginative set of group activities that make

such 'learning community' goals explicit see Buckley, Samuda and Bruton 1978.

References

Allwright, D. 1987. Classroom observation: Problems and possibilities. In B. K. Das (Ed.) *Patterns of Classroom Interaction in Southeast Asia*, 88–102. Singapore: SEAMEO RELC.

Allwright, D. 1989. The social motivation of language classroom behaviour. In V. Bickley (Ed.) *Language Teaching and Learning Styles Within and Across Cultures*, 266–79. Hong Kong: Department of Education, Institute of Language in Education.

Allwright, D. 1992. Interaction in the language classroom: Social problems and pedagogic possibilities. In *Language Teaching in Today's World*, Volume 3 of the Proceedings of the 1989 International Symposium on Language Teaching and Learning (Les Etats Généraux des Langues), 32–53. Paris: Hachette.

Breen, M. P. 1987. Learning contributions to task design. In C. N. Candlin and D. Murphy (Eds.) *Language Learning Tasks*, 23–46. (Practical Papers in English Language Education, 7.) Englewood Cliffs, N. J.: Prentice Hall International.

Buckley, P., V. Samuda and A. Bruton. 1978. Sensitizing the learner to group work: A method. *Practical Papers in English Language Education*, Vol. 1. Lancaster: Lancaster University Institute for English Language Education.

Cherchalli, S. 1988. Learners' reactions to their textbook (with special reference to the relation between differential perceptions and differential achievement): A case study of Algerian secondary school learners. Lancaster University, Department of Linguistics: Unpublished Ph.D. thesis.

Karp, D. A. and W. C. Yoels. 1976. The college classroom: Some observations on the meaning of student participation. *Sociology and Social Research* 60 (4): 429–39.

Peirce, B. N. 1995. Social identity, investment, and language learning. *TESOL Quarterly* 29 (1): 9–31.

Riesman, D. 1950. *The Lonely Crowd: A Study of the Changing American Character*. New Haven, Conn.: Yale University Press.

Stevick, E. W. 1976. *Memory, Meaning, and Method*. Rowley, Mass: Newbury House.

Glossary

accommodation

The (usually unconscious) tendency of speakers in a conversation to modify the way they speak towards the way of speaking employed by their conversational partner.

acculturation

The process of adapting to, and learning to function appropriately in, a second or other culture.

autonomy

A perspective which holds that certain social phenomena (such as literacy) are expected to play identical roles regardless of the social context in which they are situated. Contrasted with **ideology**, a perspective which recognises that social phenomena are situated in the social context in which they occur and are thus open to multiple interpretations. A distinction originally proposed by Brian Street.

collectionist perspective

A view of formal education systems characterised by clear demarcations between subject areas; collectionist systems tend also to be highly hierarchical in nature. On the other hand – in a distinction first proposed by Basil Bernstein – an **integrationist** perspective is centrally concerned with the development of skills without being over concerned with subject boundaries; integrationist systems tend also to be more democratic.

context of culture

A term originally proposed by Bronislaw Malinowski and developed by J. R. Firth and Michael Halliday to refer to the non-linguistic macro-level elements in society which constrain the way in which language is used. Contrasted with **context of situation**, the features of micro-level social situations which influence the way in which language is used.

cultural synergy

The mutual learning process in which members of two different cultures try to understand each other's culture without losing their own sense of cultural identity. Both groups gain insights, knowledge and skills from this process.

culture of learning

The cultural aspects of teaching and learning; what people believe about 'normal' or 'good' learning activities and processes, where such beliefs have a cultural origin.

doxa

The beliefs and practices shared by members of society which are so fundamental that they are never available for conscious analysis and debate. This term was introduced by Pierre Bourdieu and contrasts with **orthodoxy** (beliefs and practices which are shared and *consciously* adhered to by most members of society) and with **heterodoxy** (beliefs and practices which are accepted by some sections of society but questioned by others).

ethnography

The investigation of the behaviour of groups of people, paying particular attention to the cultural context in which the groups are located. A **micro-ethnography** examines behaviour in a small social group (such as a classroom), while a **macro-ethnography** looks at behaviour in a much larger organisation (such as an education system).

ethnomethodology

The sociological study of everyday behaviour, concerned primarily with how individuals make sense of their experiences, their social interaction and the people with whom they interact; a procedure developed by Harold Garfinkel. The term also refers to the study of this way of doing sociology.

exchange value

The social value of an educational qualification (e.g. in gaining employment or increased social status), contrasted with the **intrinsic value** of the educational process (in terms of increased knowledge or skills).

function

In structural-functional theory, all the constituent elements of society and the behaviours observable in society have roles or functions. Essentially, these elements and behaviours contribute to the maintenance of an equilibrium and so when one of them is disturbed readjustment will take place elsewhere in the system. Many social structures and behaviours may have both **unintended** functions (those not recognised by members of society) as well as their more transparent **intended** functions.

Gemeinschaft and *Gesellschaft*
A distinction proposed by Ferdinand Tönnies between small social groups characterised by social relationships of mutual support ('community' or *Gemeinschaft*), and large-scale societies characterised by contractual relations between isolated individuals ('society' or *Gesellschaft*).

normative-re-educative approach
An approach which argues that effective change in human behaviour can be brought about only when deep-seated beliefs are altered. Contrasted with **power-coercive** approach (sanctions are required to effect change in behaviour) and **rational-empirical** approach (clear evidence and a logical argument are enough to persuade people to change the way they act).

orthographic transcripts
Transcripts in which speech is represented much as it would be in a playscript, following standard conventions of spelling, for example, rather than trying to represent the actual sounds made by the speakers (e.g. in 'phonetic script').

phenomenology
An approach in sociology which, independent of any ideology, looks at social phenomena 'as they appear'; it is primarily concerned with the way in which 'common-sense' knowledge about society feeds back into the recreation of society itself.

prosodic system
The ways in which pitch, loudness, tempo and rhythm vary in language use.

socialisation
The process whereby people learn and/or are taught to behave and to think like other members of society.

systematic classroom observation
Classroom observation undertaken in such a way that the lesson is recorded and/or analysed in terms of the frequency of occurrence of categories of behaviour that have been previously identified and set out in an observation 'schedule' – or 'system' – of such categories.

tissue rejection

A medical phenomenon in which transplanted organs are sometimes rejected by the host body. An analogy originally proposed by Eric Hoyle and later developed by Adrian Holliday, which suggests that even well-intentioned curriculum innovations may fail to take root in their host institution.

value conflict

A clash between two contrasting sets of beliefs.

Author index

Aaron, J., 30
Adams, P., 11–12
Adendorff, R., 37
Alexander, L. G., 82
Allwright, D., 10–11, 82, 207–8,
  209–28
Alptekin, C., 172
Arthur, L., 110
Atkinson, P., 89
Azer, H., 101
Aziz, A. A., 70

Bailey, K. M., 12
Ballard, B., 7, 9–11, 62, 70, 141–6,
  148–68, 207–8
Barro, A., 12
Bartholomae, D., 133
Bazergan, E., 82
Becher, T., 162
Becker, A. L., 75
Becker, H. S., 165
Beebe, L., 54
Beeby, C. E., 70, 72–3
Bernstein, B., 229
Bickley, V., 11–12
Bloome, D., 133
Bloor, M., 12
Bloor, T., 12
Bolam, D., 102
Bot, M., 21
Bourdieu, P., 141, 230
Bowden, J., 153
Bowers, R., 41–2, 86
Breen, M. P., 107, 210

Brick, J., 82
Brindley, G., 170
Brislin, R., 202
Bristow, R., 202
Brock, M. N., 12
Bruton, A., 228
Buckley, P., 228
Burnaby, B., 201
Byram, M., 172

Cai, H., 180
Campbell, K. P., 178
Candlin, C. N., 8, 82, 107
Cazden, C., 29, 172
Chamot, A. U., 170–1, 173
Chen, J., 178–9
Chen, L., 180
Chen, T., 172
Cheng, K. M., 189
Cherchalli, S., 226
Chick, J. K., 9–11, 17–18, 21–39, 61,
  207, 210, 212
Clanchy, J., 7, 143, 150–2, 160, 162,
  165
Clark, J. J., 40, 50
Claude, M., 22, 24–5, 29, 37
Coleman, H., 1–15, 17, 19, 59–62,
  64–85, 95–6, 102, 137, 141–2,
  145–6
Collier, M., 90, 92, 100
Collins, J., 35–6
Condon, W., 30
Connor, U., 161
Cook, V., 171

Subject index